JEAN-PIERRE CHAUFFOUR

THE POWER OF
FREEDOM

UNITING HUMAN RIGHTS
AND DEVELOPMENT

CATO INSTITUTE
WASHINGTON, D.C.

Library of Congress Cataloging-in-Publication Data

Chauffour, Jean-Pierre.
  The power of freedom : uniting human rights and development /
Jean-Pierre Chauffour.
     p. cm.
  Includes bibliographical references and index.
  ISBN 978-1-933995-24-3 (alk. paper)
  1. Economic development   2. Human rights—History   I. Title.

HD82.C468 2008
338.9--dc22   2008049125

Cover design by Jon Meyers.
Cover painting by Dan Cooney.

Printed in the United States of America.

CATO INSTITUTE
1000 Massachusetts Ave., N.W.
Washington, D.C. 20001
www.cato.org

Dedicated to my children,
Jeanne and Basile,
and my wife,
Brigitte

Contents

Although we have a tendency to make distinctions among fundamental human rights in terms of abstract "categories" such as "civil and political" and "economic, social and cultural," or "first generation," "second generation," etc., this approach lacks intellectual rigour. Such categorizations overshadow what is common to all human rights, and overemphasize irrelevant differences.

Louise Arbour,
UN High Commissioner for Human Rights,
Geneva, January 14, 2005

And yet this apparent victory of the idea and use of human rights coexists with some real skepticism, in critically demanding circles, about the depth and coherence of this approach. The suspicion is that there is something a little simple-minded about the entire conceptual structure that underlies the oratory on human rights.

Amartya Sen,
Nobel Prize–Winning Economist,
Development as Freedom, 1999

Acknowledgments

This work began in 2005 when I was the International Monetary Fund's representative to the World Trade Organization and the United Nations in Geneva. While the book has benefited from the comments and the perspectives of many, the ideas discussed in it originated from my participation in the UN High-Level Task Force on the Implementation of the Right to Development and the lively exchanges with Joe Ingram, Ellen Johnson-Sirleaf, Stephen Marks, Ibrahim Salama, Arjun Sengupta, and other members of the task force. Many people read early drafts of this book. Without implications, I would like to thank Geoff Barnard, Daniel Bradlow, Pierre Dhonte, Klaus Enders, Marion Jansen, Flemming Larsen, Ross Leckow, Ramanand Mundkur, Catherine Patillo, Mark Plant, Margot Salomon, and two anonymous referees for their insightful comments. For fruitful dialogues on key sections of the book, I am especially grateful to Carstens Fink, Michael Keen, Hans Peter Lankes, Simonetta Nardin, and Doris Ross. I am also indebted to Mark Allen, Benedicte Christensen, William Easterly, Anne Krueger, and Saleh Nsouli for their encouragement at various stages of this project. This work also reflects endless discussions with my friends Alain Féler and Sébastien Dessus on the role of government and individuals in economic development. Last but certainly not least, Judith Campbell provided first-class editorial support and my friend Dan Cooney let me borrow one of his great paintings for the book cover.

I thank the Cato Institute and, particularly, Ian Vásquez, director of the Center for Global Liberty and Prosperity, for their trust, support, and continued commitment in the final phase of this project. Ian has been invaluable in getting me to focus my work so as to address the various intended audiences in an intelligible way. He also brought in Cato's excellent publication team to polish the draft. In line with the Jeffersonian philosophy that animates Cato's work, I hope this book will contribute to broadening the parameters of public policy debate to allow more consideration of the liberal principles of limited government, individual liberty, free markets, and peace.

The findings, interpretations, and conclusions expressed in this book belong solely to the author, and nothing contained in it should be interpreted as representing the views of the International Monetary Fund, the World Bank, their executive boards, member governments, or any other entity mentioned herein.

Introduction

Development, freedom, and peace are, perhaps more than ever before, the topics of our time. They have been placed at the top of the global geopolitical agenda and acknowledged on many solemn occasions as the interlinked and mutually reinforcing foundations for collective security and well-being. The evidence is there: without peace, there can be no sustainable development; without development, there can be no lasting peace; and without respect for fundamental freedoms, there can be neither peace nor development. The three pillars of peace and security, human rights, and development have thus been proposed as the foundation of the multilateral architecture to address today's international challenges (United Nations 2005a).

Yet although the nexus between human rights and economic development has long been recognized in principle,[1] actual human rights and development practices have generally advanced independently and on parallel tracks. Complex human rights machinery dealing with international standards in human rights and related monitoring mechanisms has been established alongside—but separately from—no less complex machinery to deal with development policies and poverty reduction strategies. To illustrate the current state of the art in the human rights and development debate, international law professor Philip Alston (2005) uses the metaphor of two ships passing in the night, each with little awareness of the other, and with little, if any, sustained engagement with each other.

The premise of this book is that the lack of any practical recognition of the link between human rights and development lies at the core of two momentous failures of our time: the failure of the development community to keep its promise to the world's poor that extreme poverty and hunger will be eradicated and other Millennium Development Goals (MDGs) achieved by 2015;[2] and the human rights community's failure to deliver on its claim of promoting universal respect for and the observance and protection of all human rights

1

and fundamental freedoms for all.[3] A further premise of this book is that a common factor lies at the heart of these two failures: the incoherent and inconsistent treatment of freedom in both the development and the human rights paradigms. Because development and human rights are not properly understood and attended to in developing countries, domestic policies—even when well-intentioned—often tend to be ineffective if not downright harmful.

Although human spiritual and material achievements have been rooted for time immemorial in human freedom, the current, traditional approach to economic development has tended to pay only lip service to the fundamental role of freedom in development. More often than not, orthodox development strategies resulted—intentionally or not—in self-defeating policies that had the effect of hampering people in exercising their free will to own, work, save, invest, trade, innovate, create, and so on. As New York University economic professor William Easterly (2001, p. xii) put it, while busy promoting new remedies (from foreign aid to investment in education and machines) and engineering new schemes (from giving loans conditional on reforms to debt relief), the development community has too often "peddled formulas that violated the basic principles of economics in practical policy work." The problem was not the failure of economics, but the failure to apply the basic principles of economics in a consistent manner, starting with the key role of freedom as the ultimate incentive for people to lead lives that they value.

In the same vein, while freedom for all without distinction as to race, sex, language, or religion has been the subject of great rhetoric in human rights circles, an entire part of the international human rights edifice conceiving of individual rights as positive claims on other individuals has had the effect of surrogating human rights for a subjective form of social justice, such as the elimination of social disparities and inequalities. As a result, a certain human rights orthodoxy cannot, paradoxically, be reconciled with a free society. Paraphrasing Easterly, the human rights community has also too often peddled formulas with a high moral ground that violated the basic principles of human rights. The problem was not the failure of human rights, but the failure to apply basic human rights principles—starting with the protection of all fundamental freedoms for everyone—in a coherent, consistent, and practical way.

This book will argue that liberty in all its civil and political, as well as economic, social, and cultural dimensions is the only viable

2

way for thinking about development and human rights in an internally consistent and mutually supportive way. It will take the Declaration on the Right to Development as its specific object of examination. The reason for choosing the Declaration on the Right to Development is that it is the main universal normative instrument adopted by the United Nations at the crossroads of the human rights and development paradigms. The right to development was introduced more than 20 years ago as an overarching human right, by virtue of which every human being and all peoples are entitled to participate in, contribute to, and enjoy economic, social, cultural, and political development, in which all human rights and fundamental freedoms can be fully realized. Whether one is mesmerized or dismayed by the aspirations of the Declaration on the Right to Development, it provides fertile ground for reflection on the meaning of a number of basic human rights and development principles.

First, how should one think about the right to development? Is the right to development really a "right" in the same way as the right to life is a "right" not to be deprived of life? Or is the right to development more like the right to happiness—a right for each person to pursue his or her own development and happiness as he or she sees fit? If the latter is true, as will be argued in this book, are there elements of the right to development that nevertheless constitute key empowerments (as opposed to entitlements) to think about development as the respect for, protection of, and promotion of core legal rights? Second, how do these core rights relate to other human rights instruments, such as the International Bill of Human Rights? Third, are these rights reconcilable with the concepts of freedom, liberty, or free will? If so, how then are limits to individual freedom to be dealt with given one's subjection to various determinisms? And if this can be answered, how then can economic development actually be advanced as the promotion of various freedoms? Fourth, are there any concrete applications of a human rights—based approach to development? In particular, to what extent have the MDGs, developing countries' poverty reduction strategies, or the official development assistance of developed countries been permeated by the human rights discourse?

Turning to the economics of the right to development—that is, the linkages between human rights, capital accumulation, and wealth—a no less fundamental set of questions arises. First, what are the characteristics of a macroeconomic paradigm consistent with human rights? In particular, what would the scope of the state be to make it consistent with economic freedom and the protection of civil and political rights? To what extent are these fundamental freedoms and rights important to economic growth? In this relationship, what is cause and what is effect? Second, if freedom is indeed a determinant of economic growth, what then are the key institutional features of a free society? How can the rule of law enable the government to control the governed, yet oblige it to control itself? To what extent should the property rights system define the permissible forms of competition in society? What is the meaning of participation in a democratic system? How can governance be ensured to operate for the common good, particularly in the area of public-sector management? Third, how can a country's set of macroeconomic policies (fiscal policy, monetary and exchange rate policy, trade and competition policy, and so on) be gauged in the light of human rights? For instance, is there a human rights–friendly tax system, public investment program, monetary framework, inflation rate, exchange rate regime, foreign exchange regulation, tariff policy, labor-market regulation, and so on?

In answering these questions, the main purpose of this book is to build a bridge between the human rights and development "communities," to join the dots between the fundamental role of freedom in human rights and the no less fundamental role of freedom in economic development, and to make a logical case for a true human rights approach to economic development. Although the book challenges a number of human rights and economic orthodoxies, it does not offer any paradigm shift or, for that matter, any leap forward in the areas of human rights or development economics. What the book suggests is a shift of attention on how to think about human rights in a development context and development in a human rights context.

To be sure, many human rights specialists will find many points objectionable in the book and will find other aspects incomplete. Likewise, many philosophers, economists, historians, or sociologists will express misgivings about the superficial treatment of their subject matter. Yet the purpose of this book is not to tell the reader everything on such notions as human rights, free will, democracy, good governance, economic growth, happiness, and so on. Neither is it to delve into the arcane nature of macroeconomic policymaking. This book simply aims to see beyond the comfort zones of the development and human rights "communities" and to show how the power of freedom can unite them in their quests for development and human rights. The purist may not approve of this approach. However, any attempt at integration of different fields, and evidence across selected time and studies, is usually unsatisfactory to purists, partly because the weights one places on different aspects are pregnant with biases. As rightly noted by economists Raghuram Rajan and Luigi Zingales (2003, p. x), "We would apologize for these were it not for our firm belief that bias is inevitable in all work, and it is competition between biases that generally drives thought ahead."

This book is divided into two parts and seven chapters. Part I introduces foundations for thinking about human rights in general and the right to development in particular. Chapter 1 presents the Declaration on the Right to Development in its historical context and legal dimension. Chapter 2 discusses the origins of the Declaration on the Right to Development, in particular as it relates to other instruments of international human rights law, such as the UN Charter, the Universal Declaration of Human Rights, and the International Covenants on Human Rights. Chapter 3 lays out the logical (and less logical) concepts for thinking about human rights and elaborates on the notions of positive rights, positive liberty, rights holders, core rights, economic needs, and economic rights. Chapter 4 then reviews the practice (or lack thereof) of the right to development, especially as it relates to the mainstreaming of human rights in developing countries' poverty reduction strategies, the MDGs, and the official development assistance of developed countries.

Against the principles discussed in Part I, Part II develops a broad policy framework for thinking about the economics and institutions of the human right to development. Although the framework can be applied in a wide variety of country circumstances—from the situation of the overly regulated economies of western Europe to that of the often badly regulated economies of many developing countries—it is mainly targeted at the circumstances of low-income countries and stagnant economies. Chapter 5 discusses the key features of an economic paradigm consistent with the right of everyone to pursue his or her own development, including the fundamental role of economic freedom, the importance of civil and political rights, and the scope of the state. Chapter 6 analyzes the main institutional dimensions needed to support such a rights-based paradigm to development, in particular as they relate to the rule of law, property rights, participation, and governance. Finally, Chapter 7 examines the set of macroeconomic policies—from fiscal policy to monetary and exchange rate policy, competition and trade policy, and other macro-related structural policies—that are consistent with the economic paradigm and institutions of a free society.

Before we start, a note on method. Among the issues that recur throughout this book is the question of the tension between normativeness and utilitarianism in addressing human rights and development challenges. A utilitarian solution to a problem would conclude that a policy is good if the good outweighs the bad, or if there are more winners than losers. The fact that someone's rights may be abused along the way is irrelevant as long as the result is a positive-sum game. Because utilitarianism is an ends-justifies-the-means philosophy, widespread violations of individual rights could be consistent with this philosophy. In a normative approach, the end does not justify the means. If rights have been violated, the policy is automatically inappropriate, even if the result would be a net positive-sum game. Achieving a critical comprehension of development as freedom requires keeping these two sets of perspectives in mind. Development is neither a normative-free nor a utilitarian-free process but requires the reconciliation of these two whenever possible. This is also what this book has strived for.

Part I: The Human "Right" to Development

The basic premise of the human right to development is to consider human rights and development as essentially cosubstantial notions: the fundamental capability of peoples to free themselves from various wants and unfreedoms (to borrow a term from Sen [1999]). In this conception, poverty can no longer be defined undimensionally as lack of adequate income, as had been traditionally assumed in development policies. For some (OHCHR 2004, p. 7), inadequate income even ceases to be a dimension of poverty at all, because "income is not a capability and hence not an aspect of well-being in itself, although it may contribute to the achievement of capabilities." Development can only be pursued in a human rights way, and human rights must be integrated into sustainable human development.

The shift in emphasis toward a rights-based foundation of development should imply that development is no longer simply a matter of development policies but of legal entitlements.[1] Realizing the human right to development is therefore conceptually different from conventional policies and programs for development, whether seen as increasing the growth of gross domestic product, supplying basic needs, or improving the index of human development (Sengupta 2000). Underpinning this approach is the fact that, in the last 60 years, traditional development policies have not delivered as promised, and the perception that governments and international agencies have failed too many peoples in too many parts of the world.[2] As a result, a new approach to economic development based on human rights has gradually emerged as an alternative framework for lifting people out of poverty.

The "rights" paradigm to development encompasses various approaches through which human rights thinking is applied to development.[3] Although all approaches are meant to be "people centered" and assume that poverty constitutes a denial or nonfulfillment of human rights,[4] they tend to differ as to the scope of the

7

rights involved. For instance, while the concept of the right to development and human rights–based approaches to development overlap, the latter is a narrower concept. A rights-based approach would focus on the rights perceived as essential to development and thus would not consider the nonfulfillment of any kind of human rights as constituting poverty.[5] OHCHR (2004, p. 301) illustrates this point in observing that "if a tyrant denies his political opponent the right to speak freely, that by itself would not make the latter poor in any plausible sense."[6] In contrast, the right to development would encompass the overall development process, including planning, participation, allocation of resources, and priorities in international development cooperation. It captures former UN Secretary-General Kofi Annan's point: "Even if he can vote to choose his rulers, a young man with AIDS who cannot read or write and lives on the brink of starvation is not truly free. Equally, even if she earns enough to live, a woman who lives in the shadow of daily violence and has no say in how her country is run is not truly free" (Annan 2005, p. 6).

For the purpose of this book, the analysis will focus on the broad concept of the right to development as adopted by the United Nations in the Declaration on the Right to Development. It will argue that, although the declaration has achieved a high degree of international consensus on its purposes, the human right to development is a flawed concept that has been politically skewed since its inception and, thus, proved to be largely impractical. It will further argue that, while the right to development is unlikely to ever deliver on its promises, other human rights instruments, such as those dealing with economic freedom and civil and political liberties, provide a consistent subset of rights that can indeed realistically form the foundation for a rights-based approach to development.

The four chapters in this first part provide a logical foundation for thinking about the human right to development. Chapter 1 presents the content of the right to development as adopted by the UN in the Declaration on the Right to Development. Chapter 2 provides background information on the origins of the right to development in relation to other instruments of international human rights law. Readers familiar with the genesis of the right to development and other human rights instruments could skip Chapter 2 and move directly to Chapter 3, which is more central to the thesis of this book. Chapter 3 discusses the theoretical conceptions and misconceptions underlying the right to development. Chapter 4 examines the actual practice of the right to development and the mainstreaming of human rights in various instruments of the international development architecture.

1. Content

The right to development has been introduced as a holistic approach that considers development itself a human right to be respected, protected, and fulfilled by states and the broader international community. Given its overall ambition and elusiveness, the right to development has aroused heated debate and controversial interpretation as to its actual meaning and scope, in particular whether its nature should be regarded as individual or collective. Its content has also been colored by the historical and philosophical context surrounding its inception at the time of the cold war and the decolonization movement. While its legal status has remained ambiguous, the Declaration on the Right to Development is primarily a statement of policy intentions that cannot claim legal enforceability.

Definition

The right to development is defined in the United Nations' Declaration on the Right to Development. The declaration was adopted in 1986 and consists of a short preamble and 10 articles (Box 1 and Appendix).[1] The declaration aims at establishing the basis of a new human right with potentially far-reaching implications for the development of every human being and all peoples, and its thrust is captured in its first article, which states, "The right to development is an inalienable human right by virtue of which every human person and all peoples are entitled to participate in, contribute to, and enjoy economic, social, cultural and political development, in which all human rights and fundamental freedoms can be fully realized" (Article 1.1).

The overall philosophy of the declaration is to consider the human person as the "central subject of development" (Article 2.1)—that is, an active participant in the right to development and also a beneficiary of it. It calls on states to "formulate appropriate national development policies that aim at the constant improvement of the well-being of the entire population and of all individuals"

Box 1. The 10 Articles of the Right to Development

Article 1

1. The right to development is an inalienable human right by virtue of which every human person and all peoples are entitled to participate in, contribute to, and enjoy economic, social, cultural and political development, in which all human rights and fundamental freedoms can be fully realized.
2. The human right to development also implies the full realization of the right of peoples to self-determination, which includes, subject to the relevant provisions of both International Covenants on Human Rights, the exercise of their inalienable right to full sovereignty over all their natural wealth and resources.

Article 2

1. The human person is the central subject of development and should be the active participant and beneficiary of the right to development.
2. All human beings have a responsibility for development, individually and collectively, taking into account the need for full respect for their human rights and fundamental freedoms as well as their duties to the community, which alone can ensure the free and complete fulfillment of the human being, and they should therefore promote and protect an appropriate political, social and economic order for development.
3. States have the right and the duty to formulate appropriate national development policies that aim at the constant improvement of the well-being of the entire population and of all individuals, on the basis of their active, free and meaningful participation in development and in the fair distribution of the benefits resulting there from.

(continued on next page)

(continued)

Article 3

1. States have the primary responsibility for the creation of national and international conditions favourable to the realization of the right to development.
2. The realization of the right to development requires full respect for the principles of international law concerning friendly relations and co-operation among States in accordance with the Charter of the United Nations.
3. States have the duty to co-operate with each other in ensuring development and eliminating obstacles to development. States should realize their rights and fulfill their duties in such a manner as to promote a new international economic order based on sovereign equality, interdependence, mutual interest and co-operation among all States, as well as to encourage the observance and realization of human rights.

Article 4

1. States have the duty to take steps, individually and collectively, to formulate international development policies with a view to facilitating the full realization of the right to development.
2. Sustained action is required to promote more rapid development of developing countries. As a complement to the efforts of developing countries, effective international co-operation is essential in providing these countries with appropriate means and facilities to foster their comprehensive development.

Article 5

States shall take resolute steps to eliminate the massive and flagrant violations of the human rights of peoples and human beings affected by situations such as those resulting from apartheid, all forms of racism and racial discrimination, colonialism, foreign domination and occupation, aggression, foreign interference and threats against national sovereignty, national unity and territorial integrity, threats of war and refusal to recognize the fundamental right of peoples to self-determination.

(continued on next page)

(continued)

Article 6

1. All States should co-operate with a view to promoting, encouraging and strengthening universal respect for and observance of all human rights and fundamental freedoms for all without any distinction as to race, sex, language or religion.
2. All human rights and fundamental freedoms are indivisible and interdependent; equal attention and urgent consideration should be given to the implementation, promotion and protection of civil, political, economic, social and cultural rights.
3. States should take steps to eliminate obstacles to development resulting from failure to observe civil and political rights, as well as economic, social and cultural rights.

Article 7

All States should promote the establishment, maintenance and strengthening of international peace and security and, to that end, should do their utmost to achieve general and complete disarmament under effective international control, as well as to ensure that the resources released by effective disarmament measures are used for comprehensive development, in particular that of the developing countries.

Article 8

1. States should undertake, at the national level, all necessary measures for the realization of the right to development and shall ensure, inter alia, equality of opportunity for all in their access to basic resources, education, health services, food, housing, employment and the fair distribution of income. Effective measures should be undertaken to ensure that women have an active role in the development process. Appropriate economic and social reforms should be carried out with a view to eradicating all social injustices.

(continued on next page)

(continued)

2. States should encourage popular participation in all spheres as an important factor in development and in the full realization of all human rights.

Article 9

1. All the aspects of the right to development set forth in the present Declaration are indivisible and interdependent and each of them should be considered in the context of the whole.
2. Nothing in the present Declaration shall be construed as being contrary to the purposes and principles of the United Nations, or as implying that any State, group or person has a right to engage in any activity or to perform any act aimed at the violation of the rights set forth in the Universal Declaration of Human Rights and in the International Covenants on Human Rights.

Article 10

Steps should be taken to ensure the full exercise and progressive enhancement of the right to development, including the formulation, adoption and implementation of policy, legislative and other measures at the national and international levels.

(Article 2.3). In particular, states operating "nationally and internationally" have "the primary responsibility for the creation of national and international conditions favorable to the realization of the right to development" (Article 3.1).

At the national level, the declaration calls on states to undertake "all necessary measures for the realization of the right to development" and to "ensure, inter alia, equality of opportunity for all in their access to basic resources, education, health services, food, housing, employment and the fair distribution of income" (Article 8.1). States are required to take steps "to eliminate obstacles to development resulting from failure to observe civil and political rights, as well as economic, social and cultural rights" (Article 6.3).

In particular, "effective measures should be undertaken to ensure that women have an active role in the development process" (Article 8.1). More generally, "appropriate economic and social reforms should be carried out with a view to eradicating all social injustices" (Article 8.1).

At the international level, the declaration calls on states "to co-operate with each other in ensuring development and eliminating obstacles to development" (Article 3.3). As a complement to the efforts of developing countries, the declaration emphasizes that "effective international co-operation is essential in providing these countries with appropriate means and facilities to foster their comprehensive development" (Article 4.2).

According to Arjun Sengupta (2000), the UN Independent Expert on the Right to Development for the Human Rights Commission,[2] the Declaration on the Right to Development is a call for a new economic and social order based on equity and justice. It implies that "the have-nots of the international economy have a right to share equally in the decision making privileges as well as in the distribution of the benefits just as the rich developed countries." The right to development is thus an approach to development that "elevates the process of its realization to the exercise of a human right." In his analysis of the declaration, Sengupta highlights four main propositions. First, the right to development is an inalienable human right. It belongs to individual humans and cannot be bargained away. Second, the right to development is a right to a particular process of development in which all human rights and fundamental freedoms can be fully realized. Third, the process itself must reflect a human rights approach, implying the free, effective, and full participation of all the individuals concerned in the decision-making and implementation process. Fourth, the right to development confers an unequivocal obligation on duty bearers: individuals in the community, states at the national level, and states at the international level. Moreover, international agencies have the obligation to cooperate with the states to facilitate the realization of the process of development.

Perhaps the most salient feature of the right to development as an alternative paradigm for development is the proposition that the process itself, through which the full array of socioeconomic-cultural rights as well as civil-political rights is realized, must reflect a human rights approach and satisfy the principles of participation, nondiscrimination, transparency, and accountability. These principles seek to guarantee high levels of empowerment and ownership, including the identification of specific duties and duty bearers in the development process. In this way, it is expected that development would shift from the realm of charity to that of obligation, making it easier to monitor progress in all areas of human development (rather than just selected economic sectors). Development objectives, indicators, and plans can thus be based on the standards of international human rights instruments rather than on imported foreign models, prescriptive solutions, partisan approaches, or arbitrary policies (OHCHR 2004).[3] It is also thought that a human rights analysis would be more thorough and effective than traditional poverty analyses based purely on income and economic indicators, as it would help to reveal additional problems facing the poor, such as the phenomena of powerlessness and social exclusion. Finally, the proponents of the right to development consider their approach to be a more authoritative basis for advocacy and for claims on domestic and international resources, including their allocation.[4]

Interpretation

Given its ambitious objectives, its degree of generalities, and its overall vagueness and open-endedness, the Declaration on the Right to Development has been the subject of enormous controversial interpretation. Its content, nature, and status have been contested by scholars and development practitioners, as well as by some human rights specialists. The intergovernmental process aimed at reaching a political consensus on its meaning and practical interpretation is highly politicized. As noted by human rights professor Stephen Marks (2003b), "It is obvious to anyone who observes the meetings of the various working groups on the right to development and the Commission on Human Rights that the political discourse is characterized by posturing of predictable positions rather than practical dialogue on the implementation of the right to development." Perhaps the right to development's most controversial elements are its legal implications and identification of the duty bearers, primarily the issue of whether it legally obliges developed countries and international organizations to provide development assistance to developing countries.[5]

One interpretation of the Declaration on the Right to Development is to consider the right to development as a holistic or "umbrella" human right. In this interpretation, the right to development would be more than the sum of its constituents (i.e., civil, political, economic, social, and cultural rights) by incorporating the interactions, complementarities, and causal relations among them. Economics professor Siddiq Osmani (2003) notes that besides being a specific human right, the right to development is also a "framework right" for the achievement of all human rights. Although the mainstreaming of human rights generally contributes to the mainstreaming of the right to development specifically, it is not a substitute for it, as "the right to development is not merely a sum of all human rights." For instance, the nutritional benefits to be gained from the right to food depends not only on food intake but also on the overall health of the people, which, in turn, depends on the amount of education received, in particular the mother's ability to ensure better health for her children. Arjun Sengupta (2000, p. 6) provides another illustration when he notes that, when viewed from the perspective of the right to development, the right to adequate housing should not be seen simply as the right for all people, irrespective of means, to live "somewhere" in security, peace, and dignity (with adequate privacy, space, lighting, ventilation, and basic infrastructure and in proximity to work and facilities—all provided at reasonable cost), but to be free to choose where that "somewhere" is, by participating in the decisionmaking process. From the same perspective, the state or any other authority "cannot decide arbitrarily where an individual should live just because the supplies of such housing are made available."

The holistic interpretation not only relates to the right holder but also to the duty bearer(s). Since states operating nationally and internationally have the primary responsibility for creating the conditions favorable to realizing the right to development, they also hold responsibilities and obligations in the sense that it is humanity as a whole—and an increasingly interdependent humanity—that has conferred rights on each other. Osmani (2003, p. 125) goes as far as to say: "As soon as the overall resource constraint facing the poor countries is recognized as a binding constraint on the expeditious realization of the whole array of human rights, the international community can no longer shirk its responsibility by urging a mere reallocation of resources. International cooperation in the fields of trade, capital flows, technology transfer, and anything else that might have a bearing on the growth potential of poor countries then becomes an unavoidable human rights obligation for the international community." In this interpretation, individuals as participants in and beneficiaries of the right to development are not only entitled to have claims against their own states to ensure that the obligations entailed by the right to development are met, but also to have claims against third states and against the international community.

An opposing interpretation is to consider the right to development as essentially the collective right of each individual to pursue his or her own development. This interpretation would reject the holistic approach as a flawed and unreal metaphysical phenomenon, thereby echoing an old line of argument.[6] It is best illustrated by the position repeatedly taken by the United States and some other countries at the UN Commission on Human Rights.[7] In their interpretation, the term "right to development" means that "each individual should enjoy the right to develop his or her intellectual or other capabilities to the maximum extent possible through the exercise of the full range of civil and political rights." Because each person has inherent human rights to life, liberty, and an adequate standard of living (as set down in the Universal Declaration of Human Rights), these rights, taken together, can be seen as "a blueprint for human development."[8] In contrast, the notion of "a nation's right to development" is meaningless, since nations do not have "human rights." Human rights are the rights of individuals, and it is the responsibility of states to see that those rights are respected, protected, and fulfilled. In the context of development, it means that "states have the responsibility to provide their citizens with the political and civil rights, and economic and social freedoms that are essential to each individual's full development." When states fail in that responsibility, they fail their own citizens, and cripple their own hopes for development.

Context

The contradictory interpretations of the Declaration on the Right to Development clearly show the existence of a divide that is best understood by taking into account the contextual ideological, political, and intellectual environment prevailing at the time the declaration was being drafted. Although a number of scholars have presented the right to development as the pioneering political reconciliation of the international community in the field of human rights,[9] it seems more compelling to argue that the declaration reflects the geopolitical environment of its time. It was elaborated during the cold war against the background of the decolonization movement and draws on the mainstream intellectual ideas of that time and is best understood with a "zero-sum" conception of man, nature, and wealth.[10]

The Declaration on the Right to Development could be viewed as the last avatar of the cold war, given that it was adopted just three years before the fall of the Berlin wall and the collapse of the Soviet Union. In many ways, the declaration and its various references reflect the ideological divide of post–World War II, notably the split that had occurred between Western democracies and socialist countries and the resulting formulation of two separate international human rights covenants: one on civil and political rights (supported by the West); the other on economic, social, and cultural rights (supported by socialist countries).[11] So, while the declaration states that "the creation of conditions favourable to the development of peoples and individuals is the primary responsibility of their States," it also affirms that "the human person is the central subject of development."

Overall, the declaration leans toward government interventionism, disregards the role of markets, and glosses over the role of the individual in the development process. It calls on the state to carry out "appropriate economic and social reforms" with a view to "eradicating all social injustices." Although the declaration does not define the exact nature of the state interventions, it does point to an understanding of "social justice" to be realized through public institutions and authorities. In doing so, the declaration brushes aside the fact that "social justice" and the common good could alternatively be realized through the distinctive virtue of free individuals associating freely and cooperating within a free society. Liberal scholars have elaborated on the concept of social justice and the common good based on the concrete intelligence of individuals in their free associations and cooperation to conclude that if "social justice" were to mean anything, it would not mean enlarging the state; rather, it would involve enlarging civil society (e.g., Hayek 1960; Nozick 1974).

For instance, Nobel Prize laureate Friedrich Hayek considered government-sponsored social justice to be an arid, abstract ideal enforced by an all-powerful state that encourages dependency and submissiveness.

Because of its original quid pro quo, the declaration is silent on the type of economic system required to foster development and maximize the creation and distribution of wealth in a sustainable manner. There is no reference to the superiority of market-based economic systems, systems where competition is free and undistorted and property rights protected in the creation of goods, services, jobs, and other favorable economic conditions. More generally, there is no recognition that the market system is about more than economics, that it is inherently social as it brings companies and other voluntary associations into existence; that it nourishes virtues such as honesty, hard work, productivity, and thrift; and that arguably it enriches the social and moral lives of the participants and gives them a sense of meaning and purpose. In contrast, in most UN discourses a market-based economy is seen as having a built-in anti–human rights one and many illustrate violations of human rights by attributing them to the behavior of the private sector, in particular the transnational corporations (Sfeir-Younis 2003). In short, the declaration fails to recognize that the market is a mechanism that coordinates not only dispersed economic information and knowledge but also diverse human purposes, none of which, in the last resort, is economic (Hayek 1944).[12]

The declaration and its various references are equally silent on the individual capabilities required "to make the human being the main participant and beneficiary of development." Although it affirms that "the human person is the central subject of development," the human person appears more as the central "object" of the right to development rather than its central "subject."[13] In particular, there is no mention of the importance of individual freedom and the key individual capabilities needed for any sustainable economic development strategy, such as fostering personal initiative and enterprise, creativity, inventiveness, experimentation, self-reliance, voluntary participation, cooperative effort, social initiative, generosity, and so on. Neither does the declaration recognize that the basic reason countries remain poor is that states typically fail to deliver key public goods (e.g., security, contract enforcement, and public infrastructure) while foreclosing economic opportunity, thus preventing the people from fully demonstrating their capabilities and fulfilling their potential.

Apart from the cold war, the Declaration on the Right to Development was also formulated against the backdrop of the decolonization and emancipation movements of the 1960s and 1970s.[14] It echoes the call of the Non-Aligned Movement (NAM) for the creation of a more just international economic order in the spirit of the 1955 Bandung Conference, which aimed at promoting Afro-Asian economic and cultural cooperation and opposing colonialism or neocolonialism by the United States, the Soviet Union, or any other "imperialistic" nation.[15] In particular, the declaration proclaims that "states should realize their rights and fulfill their duties in such a manner as to promote a new international economic order." It aims at providing a legal framework under which international assistance is due to developing countries, not just because of international solidarity and human rights principles, but also in redress for an unjust international economic order, including compensation for past colonization. Aspects of the 2001 Durban Declaration on Racism, Racial Discrimination, Xenophobia and Related Intolerance resonate with this latter point: "NAM countries declared development to be a human right and used United Nations mechanisms to try to influence international economic relations and the international human rights system (Piron 2002, p. 9)."[16] For instance, during the 2004 Commission on Human Rights, the NAM representative emphasized that the right to development was "clearly defined in international instruments, with little scope for reinterpretation, and it was not about the mainstreaming of human rights into development" but about "development partnerships to realize economic growth and sustainable development for all." The NAM held the view that "effective international cooperation and review and reform of the rules governing global economic, financial and monetary systems were critical for the realization of the right and for the elimination of obstacles to development" (United Nations Economic and Social Council 2004a).

Legal Nature

As far as international human rights norms are concerned, the legal status of the Declaration on the Right to Development is ambiguous. As with other similar solidarity rights that are more inspirational than justiciable in character,[17] the declaration is not a UN treaty, nor are commitments to its provisions legally binding. Like all UN declarations and resolutions, the Declaration on the Right to Development is essentially a statement of policy intentions that have no legal enforceability. As such, it should be distinguished from conventions and treaties that are subject to signature and ratification and that, once in force, are legally binding on the states that have ratified them.[18] The United States has been particularly adamant about the ex–Commission on Human Rights' having no jurisdiction over matters of trade, international lending and financial policy, the activities of transnational corporations, and other aspects of globalization.

This being said, UN declarations—especially when they enunciate principles of great and solemn importance—can nevertheless create high expectations about authority and control. For instance, because of the Declaration on the Right to Development's status of "overall umbrella right" (primus inter pares), some legal scholars take the view that it belongs to the body of "soft law"—that is, the no man's land between "hard" law (e.g., treaty law, customary international law) and nonlaw.[19] These "soft" laws include legal principles, norms, and standards adopted at international diplomatic conferences or resolutions of international organizations that are intended to serve as guidelines to states in their conduct, but which lack the status of law.[20] Soft laws tend to give rise to "soft" obligations that are cast as best endeavors to achieve a particular result rather than as an obligation to actually achieve the result.

2. Origins

The connection between human rights and development has fig-
ured prominently in United Nations deliberations for more than
half a century, with the right to development being proposed in the
early 1970s as a full-fledged human right belonging to peoples and
individuals.[1] Although the Western origins of the concept of human
rights can be traced back to ancient Greece and Rome (Box 1), the
modern origins of the right to development can be found in the
provisions of the Charter of the United Nations (1945) and in what
is collectively known as the International Bill of Human Rights,
comprising the Universal Declaration of Human Rights (1948), the
International Covenant on Economic, Social and Cultural Rights
(1966), and the International Covenant on Civil and Political Rights
with its two Optional Protocols (1966, 1989).[2] Outside the United
Nations, the concept of internationally recognized human rights
was embodied in a number of plurilateral agreements such as the
Helsinki Accords (1975), the Inter-American and European human
rights systems (1950, 1969), and the African Charter on Human and
Peoples' Rights (1981).

United Nations Charter

The Declaration on the Right to Development resonates closely
with the Charter of the United Nations (1945), in particular one of
its three main purposes to "achieve international cooperation in
solving international problems of an economic, social, cultural, or
humanitarian character, and in promoting and encouraging respect
for human rights and for fundamental freedoms for all without
distinction as to race, sex, language, or religion."[3] With a view to
creating "conditions of stability and well-being," the charter calls
on the United Nations to promote "higher standards of living, full
employment, and conditions of economic and social progress and
development." To this end, the charter explicitly reaffirms in its
preamble a "faith in fundamental human rights, in the dignity and

25

Box 1. A (Very) Brief Western History of Human Rights[a]

Most scholars trace the origins of the concept of human rights back to ancient Greece and Rome under the terminology of natural laws. However, it was not until after the Middle Ages that natural laws became associated with the concept of rights.[b] The modern conception of natural rights was elaborated by the philosophers of the 17th century (Hobbes, Descartes, Leibniz, Spinoza, Bacon, and Locke) and the 18th century (Montesquieu, Voltaire, and Rousseau). Most notably, John Locke argued that certain rights pertain self-evidently to individuals as human beings (because these rights existed in the "state of nature" before humankind entered civil society) and that chief among them were the rights to life, liberty, and property; that upon entering civil society, humankind only surrendered to the state— pursuant to a "social contract"—the right to enforce these natural rights rather than the rights themselves; and that the state's failure to secure these rights gave rise to a right to responsible, popular revolution. These and other writings formed the seeds of the revolutionary movements in the United States and France, leading to the U.S. Declaration of Independence (1776), the Declaration of the Rights of Man and of the Citizen (1789), and the Constitution of the United States of America (1789). Since then, although still controversial in many quarters, the idea of human rights has endured. Nineteenth-century German idealism and parallel expressions of rising European nationalism influenced some (e.g., the Marxists) to consider rights, no matter what their derivation, as belonging first and foremost to communities or whole societies and nations, albeit without entirely rejecting the notion of individual rights. However, the atrocities committed by the Nazi, communist, and other dictatorial regimes in the 20th century eventually created a universal consciousness that some actions were absolutely wrong and that no matter what the circumstances, human beings were entitled to simple respect and basic rights. By the second half of the 20th century, the idea of human rights had truly come into its own.

---

[a] This box draws on Weston (2002).
[b] Even then, these natural rights were quite removed from the modern concept of human rights, as they recognized, for instance, the legitimacy of slavery and serfdom.

worth of the human person, in the equal rights of men and women and of nations large and small" and "to employ international machinery for the promotion of the economic and social advancement of all peoples."[4]

Yet even as the 1945 UN Charter reaffirms a "faith" in fundamental human rights, it remains vague, if not silent, on the exact role of the UN in "encouraging and promoting respect for human rights" and on the relationship between human rights and economic development. It is worth noting that a proposal to ensure the protection as well as the promotion of human rights was roundly rejected at the San Francisco Conference where the charter was drafted. In a clear reference to the principles of state sovereignty and noninterference, the charter states that "nothing contained in the present Charter shall authorize the United Nations to intervene in matters which are essentially within the domestic jurisdiction of any state" except upon a Security Council finding of a "threat to the peace, breach of the peace, or act of aggression." Accordingly, the obligations embodied in the charter are subject to limits. Some authorities have argued that, in becoming parties to the charter, states accept no more than a nebulous promotional obligation toward human rights and that, in any event, the UN has no standing to insist on human rights safeguards in member states. However, others insist that as the charter's human rights provisions are part of a legally binding treaty, some element of legal obligation is clearly involved; that the "pledge" made by states upon becoming party to the charter consequently represents more than a moral statement; and that the domestic jurisdiction clause does not apply, because human rights can no longer be considered a matter "essentially within the domestic jurisdiction" of states.[5]

Universal Declaration of Human Rights

In contrast to the UN Charter, which only expresses a "faith in fundamental human rights," the Universal Declaration of Human Rights (1948)[6] elaborates on what constitutes human rights with a view to establishing a "common standard of achievement for all peoples and all nations . . . to promote respect for fundamental human rights and freedoms and by progressive measures, national and international, to secure their universal and effective recognition and observance." The catalog of rights set out in the Universal

27

Declaration draws from the political and civil rights of national constitutions and legal systems. In the spirit of the Virginia Declaration of Rights (1776) and the French Declaration of the Rights of Man and of the Citizen (1789),[7] the Universal Declaration enumerates a number of core political and civil rights essential to human freedom and liberty,[8] including the right to property.[9]

The novelty of the Universal Declaration of Human Rights (beyond being the first major international instrument in the human rights sphere) lies in the introduction of a number of economic, social, and cultural rights. The Universal Declaration states that "everyone, as a member of society, has the right to social security and is entitled to realization, through national effort and international cooperation and in accordance with the organization and resources of each State, of the economic, social and cultural rights indispensable for his dignity and the free development of his personality." It goes on to elaborate that everyone has the right to education;[10] the right "to work, to free choice of employment, to just and favourable conditions of work and to protection against unemployment"; "to equal pay for equal work"; "to rest and leisure, including reasonable limitation of working hours and periodic holidays with pay"; and "to just and favourable remuneration ensuring for himself and his family an existence worthy of human dignity, and supplemented, if necessary, by other means of social protection." In addition, everyone has the right to "a standard of living adequate for the health and well-being of himself and of his family, including food, clothing, housing and medical care and necessary social services, and the right to security in the event of unemployment, sickness, disability, widowhood, old age or other lack of livelihood in circumstances beyond his control." Although not yet bearing the name, the right to development was born, including some notion of obligation.[11]

International Covenants on Human Rights

The commitments of the Universal Declaration of Human Rights were complemented about two decades later by two international covenants detailing in more substantive and enforceable terms the more general commitments of the Universal Declaration.[12] As previously noted, it was decided for political and ideological reasons that two separate covenants be drawn up, each devoted to a different "aspect" of human rights, with distinctive institutional implications.[13] The International Covenant on Civil and Political Rights incorporates almost all the civil and political rights proclaimed in the Universal Declaration—with the notable exceptions of the right to own property and the right to asylum. The ICCPR also designates several rights that are not listed in the Universal Declaration, among them the right of all peoples to self-determination and the right of ethnic, religious, and linguistic minorities to enjoy their own culture, to profess and practice their own religion, and to use their own language.[14] Similarly, the International Covenant on Economic, Social and Cultural Rights elaborates on most of the economic, social, and cultural rights set forth in the Universal Declaration. However, unlike its companion agreement, the ICESCR was not intended for immediate implementation, the state parties having agreed only "to take steps, individually and through international assistance and cooperation" toward "achieving progressively the full realization of the rights recognized in the . . . Covenant," and then subject to "the maximum of [their] available resources."[15] The state parties undertook to report to the UN Economic and Social Council on the measures adopted and on the progress achieved in the realization of the enumerated rights.

Plurilateral Human Rights Charters

Apart from the UN system, the Declaration on the Right to Development can also trace parts of its origins to a number of plurilateral or regional human rights charters. Following proposals by the Soviet Union and other East European states to create an all-European Conference on Security and Cooperation in Europe,[16] the Helsinki Accords (1975) provided an agreed-on set of standards for bringing security to the European continent.[17] The accords went beyond traditional military guarantees of stability by incorporating economic development, concerns for the environment, cultural affairs, and human rights into a comprehensive concept of security. In doing so, it established the principle that human rights and fundamental freedoms, including the freedom of thought, conscience, religion, or belief for all without distinction as to race, sex, language, or religion, are a central and legitimate concern of international relations and an important element of European security. The accords aimed at promoting and encouraging the effective exercise of civil, political, economic, social, cultural, and other rights and freedoms derived from the inherent dignity and free and full development of the human person.[18]

A number of human rights charters have been established for the promotion and protection of human rights at the regional level, notably in Europe, the Americas, and Africa.[19] It is generally agreed that the European Convention for the Protection of Human Rights and Fundamental Freedoms (1950) and its additional protocols represent the most advanced and successful regional experiment to date in the field of human rights (Weston 2002). The substantive provisions of the convention focus on the promotion, protection, and enforcement of civil and political rights, including through the European Court of Human Rights.[20] In some European countries, the provisions of the convention are deemed part of domestic constitutional or statutory law. The core structure of the American Convention on Human Rights (1969) is similar to the European one, but is even more focused on the promotion and protection of civil and political rights and makes greater reference to the relationship between individual rights and individual duties, reflecting the U.S. Declaration of Independence.[21] Like it's American and early European counterparts, the African Charter on Human and Peoples' Rights (1981) provides for a human rights commission, which has both promotional and protective functions. However, in contrast to the European and American procedures, the African Charter provides for economic, social, and cultural rights, including the rights of groups (e.g., family, society, the state, the international African community), and embraces two "solidarity" rights: the right to economic, social, and cultural development; and the right to national and international peace and security. Also, the African Human Rights Court as envisioned in the document has yet to be established.

3. Concept

Although it would be far beyond the scope of this book to do justice to the philosophical debate on the concept of human rights, it is still useful to present some basic conceptual frameworks and to address a number of theoretical questions to grasp the notion of human rights that underpins the Declaration on the Right to Development. Building on the earlier discussion on the definition and origins of the right to development, this chapter aims at questioning the internal consistency of the human rights principles: Are there certain "core" rights that all human beings have, or should have, simply by virtue of being human? How do these human rights relate to the underlying concepts of freedom, liberty, and free will? Can human rights conflict, and if so, how to reason for the recognition of some rights but not others? Rights to what? Against whom? Is there a defensible theory of core human rights that identifies a set of human rights that would be more germane from a development perspective? Is attachment to such a core agenda of human rights realistic or falsely utopian, given the nature of man? What is the concept of economic rights that is most relevant for the purpose of economic development?

Positive Rights vs. Negative Rights

The distinction between positive and negative rights is controversial and at the core of differing interpretations about human rights, not least the right to development.[1] Negative rights conceive of human rights in terms of liberties and "freedoms from."[2] They derive primarily from 17th- and 18th-century reformist theories (i.e., those associated with the English civil war and the American and French Revolutions). Imbued with the political philosophy of liberal individualism and the related economic and social doctrine of laissez-faire, they are fundamentally civil and political in nature and opposed to government intervention in the quest for human dignity.[3]

In contrast, positive rights see human rights more in terms of claims, entitlements, and "rights to." They originated primarily in the 19th-century socialist tradition and were taken up by the revolutionary struggles and welfare movements of the early 20th century. As a counterpoint to "negative" civil and political rights, they tend to favor state intervention for the purposes of providing economic, social, and cultural rights and ensuring the equitable distribution of the values or capabilities involved.[4]

While the Declaration on the Right to Development draws on both the negative and the positive rights incorporated in the International Bill of Human Rights, it enlarges the concept of positive rights to one of collective rights, meaning rights requiring positive action not just by the nation state, but also the concerted efforts of all nations. The right to development has thus been presented as a human right of the third generation, in reference to the analytical framework provided by the Czech jurist Karel Vasak (1977) with regard to three generations of human rights inspired by the French Revolution motto *Liberté, Egalité, Fraternité*. Liberty would correspond to the negative civil and political rights aimed at protecting the individual from excesses of the state; equality, to the positive rights representing the economic, social, and cultural rights that the state is required to provide to the people under its jurisdiction; and fraternity, the third generation of rights, to the more collective, less individualistic rights, such as the right to development. As noted earlier, these third-generation rights resulted mainly from the emergence of Third World nationalism and its demand for a global redistribution of power, wealth, and other important values or capabilities, but also from the nation-state's impotence or inefficiency in trying to deal single-handedly with multilateral issues, such as the preservation of the environment.[5]

A number of scholars view the differences between negative and positive rights as one of degree rather than nature,[6] whereas others point to the fundamental inconsistency of the human rights discourse, with the enforcement of negative and positive rights being intellectually at odds.[7] As far as the latter is concerned, since positive rights can only be guaranteed to any one person by potentially abridging the negative rights of others, positive rights (which include most economic, social, and cultural rights) are not genuine human rights because they impose positive duties on individuals. For instance, if one person's property is confiscated compulsorily (generally by means of taxation) to fulfill another's (positive) right to housing, this political compulsion contravenes the first person's (negative) right to private property. In the same vein, one's (positive) right to food, education, or health can conflict with one's (negative) right to associate freely and only enter into voluntary supplying contracts.[8]

According to a traditional liberal view, negative rights (i.e., rights that impose only negative duties on individuals and states) constitute the only true and consistent set of human rights—or, in other words, core human rights. Hayek (1976) elaborated on the traditional distinction between negative and positive rights to conclude that positive rights were fundamentally incompatible with a free society, in which individuals determined their position according to their own goals and means. For him, fundamental principles of justice and ethics require an "end-independent" approach that focuses on procedures and rules rather than consequences, outcomes, and results. Accordingly, whereas negative rights can be characterized by general and abstract rules that consistently apply to everyone on an equal basis without exception, positive rights cannot. In that sense, the right to development, in its current incarnation with regard to collective rights and positive economic rights, disqualifies itself from being considered an "inalienable human right." It is not just a charming delusion, but a threat to human rights, and a particularly insidious threat because, as noted by professor Donnelly (1985, p. 508), "it plays upon our fondest hopes and best desires, and diverts attention from more productive ways of linking human rights and development."

Acknowledging the intellectual challenge posed by the promotion of both negative and positive rights in international human rights law, a number of scholars have tried to reconcile views by emphasizing the continuum between both sets of rights. First, positive rights have been defended on the grounds that the protection of negative rights also entails positive actions by the state that could be as costly as the realization of a number of positive rights.[9] Second, positive rights have been promoted on the basis that all human rights involve a mix of negative and positive duties and entitlements. However, these theories do not withstand close scrutiny and usually appear just as incoherent as the actual practice of positive rights.[10]

It is a fact that the protection of certain negative rights cannot be ensured without positive actions by the state. To guarantee that rights holders actually enjoy the object of their negative rights (i.e., freedom) to a reasonable level of security and predictability, the state must take certain positive steps.[11] The right to life, liberty, and security; the right to a fair and public trial; and the right to asylum from persecution, and to free elections, for example, need to be secured primarily by state taxation. The right to hold private property has to be supervised and upheld by tax-funded courts, police, and fire departments if it is to be at all meaningful (Holmes and Sunstein 2000). However, this line of argument fails to recognize that the fundamental distinction between positive and negative rights is about the essence of those rights and not, as has often been claimed, about the economic costs of implementing them. Hayek (1960) has elaborated on the good reasons for guaranteeing basic human rights, even if they are costly. Indeed, promoting and protecting negative rights that underpin economic freedom and civil and political liberties require a government that is streamlined, yet strong and effective (see the discussion on the scope of the state in chapter 5).

What is constant in this negative conception of human rights is the notion of liberty, a shield that safeguards the individual—alone and in association with others—against other individuals and the abuse of political authority. This is the essence. Negative rights are directly endowed upon individuals. They are not claims or entitlements. While responsible for securing, guaranteeing, and ensuring these rights, the state should refrain from interfering with them. In contrast, positive rights *do* necessitate state intervention, because they subsume demands more for material than for intangible goods according to some criterion of distributive justice.[12] These resource-intensive rights are fundamentally open-ended claims to social redistribution and equality. Furthermore, although they involve state interference and coercion in the form of national policies and programs, the fact that there are no duty bearers who can eventually be held responsible for assuming the corresponding obligations means that positive rights are not full rights. It is the responsibility that renders finite the notion of rights (Dworkin 1977; Henkin 1990). Proclaiming "freedom from want" as a positive right does not provide society, government, or the courts with the resources to satisfy those wants. Declaring an obligation irrespective of feasibility helps no one (Weede 2008).

Furthermore, critics who regard the distinction between negative and positive rights as artificial tend to blur their fundamental conceptual differences and reinterpret human rights. For instance, the (positive) right to basic subsistence becomes the (negative) right not to be deprived of basic subsistence, for example, the freedom from hunger, disease, and illiteracy (Shue 1996). The (positive) right to food is presented as the (negative) right of the starving person not to be interfered with in taking the surplus food of others (Sterba 1998). At the global level, the (positive) right to basic necessities is reinterpreted as a (negative) right not to collaborate in an unjust global economic order (Pogge 2005b).[13] If taken to extremes, the sophism could go as far as to claim that the (negative) right to life (i.e., protection against any arbitrary deprivation of life) is nothing but the (positive) right to be free from death (i.e., the right to means of survival for every individual and for all peoples at all times).[14] This line of arguments generally confuses one particular sphere of morality—rights—with moral righteousness in general. This distinction—between rights and righteousness, having a right and being right, entitlement and obligation—is of great conceptual importance. As pointed out by professor Donnelly (1985, p. 490), "not all moral 'oughts' are grounded in or give rise to rights: one does not have a right to everything that it is or would be right for one to do or possess; we do not have rights, in the strict and strong sense of titles and claims, to everything that is right."

These criticisms tend to gloss over the fact that *freedom* and *entitlement* are different; in a fundamental sense, they are exact opposites. Indeed, a number of regimes that have striven historically to achieve development through the enforcement of positive rights (such as the communist, national socialist, and other authoritarian regimes of the 20th century) have typically been guilty of gross human rights violations, starting with the right to life.[15] A human right to education, health care, housing, and so on is meaningful only if it is about the individual's freedom to produce, obtain, and pursue education, health care, housing and so on. It cannot qualify as a human right if it means an entitlement whereby someone should provide another with education, health care, housing, or anything else on a subjective list of positive claims. In the same vein, the right to freedom of expression simply means that one can express oneself freely without fear or favor. Although this may involve the state's regulating the public space and channels of communication within which the right can be freely exercised without interference from others (positive action), it does not entitle anyone to a loudspeaker, a free printing press or radio, or any other positive means to exercise this right.

A final point about positive rights is that, contrary to negative rights, they do not relate to the intrinsic, irreducible yet unlimited human capabilities that constitute a human being, such as the capability to live, think, exchange, move, and so on. Negative rights are by definition orthogonal rights. They constitute a set of independent and uncorrelated rights that cannot be reduced to a more fundamental common constitutive element. In contrast, positive rights are nonorthogonal rights. They reflect a subjective set of limited societal objectives that are highly dependent and correlated, and have income as their common constitutive element. Since Amartya Sen (1981), the Nobel laureate economist, made the point, we know that the right to food is not about food supply, but about income. People starve when they do not have money to buy food—an obvious point perhaps, except that most commentators and policymakers have been (and sometimes continue to be) convinced that the problem is caused by food security reasons and a diminishing food supply.[16] Similarly, the rights to housing, health, education, and so on are not so much about shortfalls in housing, health care, or education, as they are about shortfalls in income.

The point is that, from a development perspective (as opposed to a humanitarian perspective), the realization of the various economic, social, and cultural rights can be whittled down to respect for a subset of more fundamental negative rights, whose interplay will bring about the resources needed to fulfill the desired societal objectives. Given that only assets (starting with the individual himself) can generate income, a human rights approach to development should first and foremost focus on the protection of fundamental liberties, including the right to property. The confusion is best illustrated by the United Nations' pursuit of the right to housing while only obliquely recognizing the right to property. The right to hold, protect, and secure assets, to freely invest those assets, and to derive income from them would go a long way toward satisfying the panoply of economic, social, and cultural "rights."

Although it may be anathema from the perspective of human rights law to consider one set of rights (negative rights) as being inconsistent with another (positive rights), it is the only logical option for reconciling the development and human rights approaches to economic growth and poverty reduction in a mutually supportive and internally consistent manner as it relates to the respective role of the states and individual rights in the development process (Chauffour 2005, 2006).

Positive Liberty vs. Negative Liberty

Before accepting the proposition that genuine human rights are essentially about the protection of individual liberties, one needs to understand what exactly is meant by liberty and its underlying concept of free will. At what point does one become ultimately responsible for a choice, taking into account all endogenous and exogenous factors influencing the decision? Are the poor and the unemployed free? Is the smoker free? What about the prostitute or the member of a sect? Or individuals suffering from dementia, schizophrenia, or clinical depression? While it is true that free will can simply be defined as the ability to do, or not do, something, freedom of will is supposedly subject to various determinants, including environmental, social, physical, psychological, biological, and theological.[17] Philosophers have debated this question for over two millennia, and just about every major thinker has had something to say about it.

For the purposes of this book, we will try to understand the notion of individual freedom, in the sense of absence of obstacles, barriers, or constraints on one's capacity for freedom. A basic starting point for a theoretical discussion of the meaning and value of freedom is political philosopher Isaiah Berlin's essay "Two Concepts of Liberty" (2002, p. 169). In Berlin's words, negative liberty involves an answer to the question "what is the area within which the subject—a person or group of persons—is, or should be, left to do or be what he is able to do or be, without interference by other persons?" whereas positive liberty involves answering "what, or who, is the source of control or interference that can determine someone to do, or be, this rather than that."[18] On the one hand, a smoker can be seen as being free to smoke (negative liberty) but, on the other, of being unfree to stop smoking and to realize his or her will (positive liberty). At the same time, the poor can be seen as free to exercise their capabilities, no matter how limited, yet also unfree to achieve their full potential due to their impoverished circumstances and the constraints of their environment. As American philosopher John Rawls (1971, p. 104) pointed out, most people inherit even their virtues so that a person's character and capacity to cultivate his or her talents (for instance through entrepreneurial efforts) depend in good part on "fortunate family and social circumstances for which he can claim no credit." As we will see, much of this discussion relates to one's conception of man and human nature.

While free will is subject to various determinants, Isaiah Berlin differentiates between the two concepts of liberty by declaring one internal to the agent (the "divided self") and the other external (e.g., natural or social). The higher self is the rational, reflecting self, the self that is capable of moral action and of taking responsibility for what it does. This is the true self, since it is what distinguishes us from other animals. The lower self, on the other hand, is the self of the passions, of impulsive desires and irrational impulses.

Positive liberty concentrates on the divided self—the fact that one's higher, rational self is in control and that one is neither a slave to one's passions nor to one's merely empirical self. To enjoy this positive liberty fully, help is often needed to realize this "higher self." The next step consists in pointing out that some individuals are more rational than others, and therefore in a better position to know what is in their own and others' rational interests. This then allows them to say that by forcing less rational beings to do the rational thing, thereby realizing their true selves, they are in fact helping to liberate them from their merely empirical desires.[19] In this light, governments could shape the economy toward some higher conception of human purpose and possibilities rather than subjecting it to the amoral, alienating forces of the market. Berlin and other defenders of freedom came to the view that the positive concept of liberty brings with it the risk of authoritarianism.[20]

In contrast, the concept of negative freedom concentrates on the external sphere in which individuals interact. It would seem to provide a better guarantee against the dangers of paternalism and authoritarianism. In that sense, to promote negative freedom is to promote the existence of a sphere of action within which the individual is sovereign, and within which he can pursue his own projects subject only to the constraint that he respect the spheres of others. For theorists who conceive of constraints on freedom in this way, this would mean that one is only unfree to the extent that other people prevent one from doing certain things. If one is incapacitated by natural factors (e.g., by a genetic handicap, a virus, or certain climatic conditions), one may be rendered unable to do certain things, but one is not, for that reason, rendered unfree to do them. But what about the existence of adverse social factors that incapacitate individuals, for instance, because of obstacles created by impersonal economic forces? Do economic constraints such as recession, poverty, or unemployment merely incapacitate people, or do they also render them unfree? A clear answer can be provided by using an even more restrictive view of what counts as a constraint on freedom to say that only a subset of those obstacles created by others— obstacles created intentionally—counts as a restriction of freedom.[21] In this case, impersonal economic forces, brought about unintentionally as they are, do not restrict people's freedom, even though they undoubtedly render many people incapable of doing many things.[22]

Negative freedom would thus suggest that people are responsible for the harm caused by their positive acts, but not for the harm caused by their omission. While an in-depth discussion of the notion of *intentionality* in the doctrine of acts and omissions (i.e., unintentional act vs. intentional omission) would be beyond the scope of this book, negative freedom could simply be understood as the relatively narrow sphere of strict human responsibility within a broader sphere of human benevolence, charity, and compassion.[23]

Although the dichotomy of positive and negative liberty has been considered specious by a number of political philosophers,[24] it still offers a broad analytical and operational framework in which to think about economic development as the removal of various types of unfreedoms (i.e., civil, political, economic, social, and cultural). The philosophical divide that opposed Voltaire and Rousseau continues to oppose the market-oriented libertarians and the egalitarians. For the former, freedom is the absence of coercion, where to be coerced is to be subject to the arbitrary will of another. For the latter, constraints on freedom are much wider and include not only intentionally imposed obstacles, but also unintended obstacles for which someone may nevertheless be held responsible.[25] However, the near impossibility of defining this "someone"—the duty bearer—has limited the operationalization of such a concept of freedom, including in the context of the right to development.

Rights Holders vs. Duty Bearers

Against this philosophical background, the body of legal opinion has also been divided since the inception of both the International Bill of Human Rights and the Declaration on the Right to Development about whether positive rights should be seen merely as vague and aspirational objectives rather than true, justiciable, individual legal rights. In conceptual terms, the distinction goes back to the foundations of the human rights doctrine. Are human rights legal rights, moral rights, or both? While legal rights are rights that enjoy the recognition and protection of the law,[26] moral rights are not rights in the strict sense but rather moral claims that tend to be universal.[27]

Proponents of the right to development have tended to oscillate between the legalistic and the moralistic approaches to human rights. In Arjun Sengupta's view (1999), human rights should not be confused with legal rights. Human rights precede law and thus are derived not from law but from the concept of human dignity. When a positive right cannot be made legally enforceable, for instance by means of appropriate legislation, it still remains a "moral standard," a moral obligation on potential duty holders "to help to deliver the right."

In contrast, Louise Arbour (2005), UN high commissioner for human rights, considers that "the possibility for people themselves to claim their rights through legal and quasi-legal processes is essential so that human rights have a meaning." In practice, some sectoral attempts have been made at clarifying the relationship between rights holders and duty bearers in a pragmatic policy-oriented way.[28] However, although this approach might be viable and helpful at some microeconomic level, it is less likely to be the case at the level of macroeconomic policymaking. As noted by Philip Alston (2004, p. 43), "The identification of the immediate, underlying and structural causes of the non-realization of human rights is fraught with difficulty, since most problems are subject to diverse and heavily contested causal explanations." In many instances, this reflects the fact that positive rights are impossible to define and therefore unjusticiable, the duty bearer(s) remains unidentified, and the enforcement mechanism is nonexistent or poor.[29] Even in Amartya Sen's "capability approach" (2000), in which positive obligations are mainly limited to relieving poverty, hunger, and starvation, the issue of who in particular is responsible for fulfilling a right and how far one is obligated to go in fulfilling a right is left open.

Not only is the absence of duty bearer in the enforcement of positive rights problematic, but the confusion it entertains threatens the entire human rights edifice. The coexistence of justiciable and nonjusticiable human rights has the effect of legitimizing a notion of relativism in human rights matters, thereby diluting the concept of human rights and placing all human rights, including fundamental freedoms, at the mercy of changing policy decisions. Positive rights are prone to being violated because of their conflict with negative rights, the absence of a legally responsible duty bearer, lack of resources, the need to make tradeoffs between competing objectives, external shocks, or other factors outside the state's control. The gap between formally granted rights and their actual implementation is particularly striking in the area of economic, social, and cultural rights, including the right to development. The lack of enforcement of these mainly nonjusticiable rights tends to have the vicious effect of legitimizing the notion that human rights are somehow relative or optional, that they can be temporarily violated for good reason, thereby weakening and defeating the very concept of human rights as a whole, in particular as they refer to fundamental civil and political liberties.

Furthermore, if a country can carry on with the nonrealization of a number of economic, social, and cultural rights, what does that mean for the value of other rights that are claimed to be interrelated and interdependent? There is already growing concern about the disconnect between de jure and de facto rights.[30] Gross violations of civil and political human rights are noticeably widespread, even in countries that are party to international human rights treaties. There is concern that the ratification of international human rights treaties has no discernible effect on a government's pattern of abuse.[31] As noted by then UN Secretary-General Kofi Annan (2005, p. 64), states have sought the membership of the Commission on Human Rights "not to strengthen human rights but to protect themselves against criticism or to criticize others."[32]

Interestingly, it has become increasingly clear to the proponents of a human rights–based approach to development that identifying the obligations of the duty bearers of various economic, social, and cultural rights is an extremely delicate matter, involving the identification of complex causal relations. As Philip Alston (2004, p. 43–44) puts it, sorting out the role of the various players "will rarely be a routine accounting matter which can be done with ease in the context of complex development strategies" and to assume that decisions on such complicated matters of development programming could be informed by the recommendations of international human rights bodies and mechanisms reflects a "good deal of optimism."[33] There is, however, more room for optimism if one accepts the proposition that, in the final analysis and regardless of the complexity of the causal relations, core rights related to economic freedom and civil and political liberties hold the key to economic development, including the realization of various economic, social, and cultural *goals*.

Core Rights vs. Indivisible Rights

Despite the different nature of human rights and the issuance of discernible sets of human rights instruments, the UN has long considered the different categories of human rights as "interrelated, interdependent, and indivisible,"[34] and that the realization of the right to development would help promote the enjoyment of all human rights and fundamental freedoms.[35] This interrelationship of human rights, which can be traced back to President Franklin Delano Roosevelt's "Four Freedoms" speech (1941),[36] has since been accepted as human rights orthodoxy.[37] Yet beyond the rhetoric, the notion that each right remains indispensable to the whole without any hierarchical categorization raises a number of logical issues, especially when a subset of those rights (i.e., the economic, social, and cultural rights) is subject to progressive realization.[38] As a starting point, if all rights are interrelated, interdependent, and indivisible, it is difficult to understand conceptually how some could be realized progressively, without imperiling the whole. Furthermore, with a number of human rights being defined as positive, one would need to be sure that all possible positive rights had been identified before declaring them interrelated, interdependent, and indivisible. It is not clear, however, how this could be achieved and the list drawn up, especially when opinions vary as to what such a list should include.

Indeed, the rhetorical consensus that all human rights form an indivisible whole suffers greatly from the fact that even some core negative rights are largely absent from UN human rights instruments. Economic freedom is a largely forgotten human right; the

Universal Declaration scarcely dwells on it. The right to property, while not completely omitted from UN discourse, has remained peripheral to the main debate, including that on the right to development.[39] The Declaration on the Right to Development only refers to the right of peoples to self-determination, including the right to full sovereignty over all natural wealth and resources, but does not recognize the individual right to property, notwithstanding the fact that the freedom to hold and legally acquire property, together with the freedom from government expropriation of property (e.g., by confiscatory taxation or inflation), is a major constitutive element of development.[40] Other rights, such as the rights to engage in economic activity, to produce, to earn a living, or to trade, are omitted altogether, although they constitute the basic tools that all people—and most notably the poor—can use to engage in economic activity and to improve their economic condition.

Another key negative right missing in international human rights law is the freedom of people to move across international boundaries, including for economic reasons. While the UN has a long tradition of dealing with refugees, asylum seekers, and other migration flows caused by military conflicts, civil wars, political turmoil, and ethnic and religious repression,[41] it does not deal with the more massive migration motivated by economic and other personal factors.[42] In UN instruments, people's rights are usually expressed in terms of the situation of wage earners or migrant workers, such as in the Convention on the Protection of the Rights of All Migrant Workers and Members of Their Families, which entered into force in 2003. Although the convention aims only at fostering respect for migrants' human rights—not at creating a right to migration—no Western migrant-receiving country has ratified the convention, even though the majority of migrants live in Europe and North America.[43]

However, notwithstanding the fact that international migration has become a highly politically sensitive issue in many countries,[44] one can reasonably argue that the right to migrate and to remit one's earnings to the home country belongs to the set of fundamental freedoms that all individuals should be able to enjoy as human beings. Although race, class, religion, and sex have retreated as rationales for discrimination, it remains socially acceptable for geographical accidents of birth to be held against people for their entire lives. Limits on immigration are necessary for all sorts of political and practical reasons (not the least the need to gradually deal with the large stock of would-be migrants created by decades of government restrictiveness), but these limits should be seen for what they are: intolerable, and therefore hopefully temporary, curbs on the freedom of people to pursue happiness wherever they might find it.

Furthermore, from a utilitarian point of view, migration can offer many opportunities—to the migrants themselves; to the recipient countries that gain a cheaper, often younger workforce; and to the country of origin, notably in the form of remittance payments or the migrants' return home with added human capital (see the discussion on economic freedom in chapter 5). The evidence is unequivocal. Money sent back home by immigrants far outweighs development aid both in volume and in reaching the intended beneficiaries.[45] Although the provisions of the various UN human rights instruments in this area may have represented common ground for agreement among UN members at a certain point in time, they now appear somewhat removed from the realities of today's global economy.

Some dissonant voices have come to recognize that if every possible (positive) element of human rights is deemed essential or necessary, then nothing will be treated as though it were truly important. Alston (2004, p. 47) observes that while "many human rights specialists are carefully trained to avoid any form of selectivity in the name of the indivisibility and interdependence of all rights, it is a misunderstanding of the consequences of this principle to suggest that setting priorities is unacceptable." Law professor James Nickel (2004) has doubts about indivisibility and its relevance to developing countries, given the daunting list of positive rights and the limited resources available to realize them. It would seem that the only practicable way of proceeding would be to recognize that, from a development perspective (as opposed to a humanitarian perspective), some human rights are more fundamental than others and that those fundamental rights correspond to the protection of all civil, political, economic, social, and cultural *freedoms*.

Economic Rights vs. Economic Needs

When economic human rights tend to become more aspirational than legal, they also tend to confuse rights, needs, and wants. It is often proclaimed, for instance, that individuals have the human right to fulfill their basic needs or necessities and that "extreme poverty is a violation of human dignity and frequently represents a violation of human rights" (Bengoa 2005, p. 17). While this may well be the case in most instances, the point is that poverty as such is not a violation of human rights. Robinson Crusoe may enjoy all possible freedoms on his island, yet remain poor. In a world of relative scarcity, there can be only relative fulfillment of competitive needs. The scarce resources that are spent to advance one particular end are, by definition, an opportunity forgone for advancing another. Resources used to fulfill the "right" to food could also have been used to fulfill the "right" to education, health, or housing; or the needs of one disadvantaged population group favored over another. In fact, the concept of human "needs" as it is often used (e.g., housing needs, education needs, and other social needs) has little meaning, as it implies a sense of charity and represents the recipients as passive beneficiaries (i.e., the object of development), whereas rights ought to convey a sense of empowerment.

The human ability to make tradeoffs and substitutions among various wants, desires, or demands in the face of limited and competing human capacities to fulfill them goes to the essence of what is the nature of man. As observed by business school scholars Michael Jensen and William Meckling (1994, p. 2), much policy disagreement among philosophers, scientists, policymakers, and citizens arises from substantial, though usually implicit, differences in the way we think about human nature—"about the strength, frailties, intelligence, ignorance, honesty, selfishness, generosity, and altruism of individuals." Human nature is not just about the selfish desire for money, notwithstanding the fact that self-interest serves to promote the overall general welfare of the public (A. Smith 1776, p. 14)[46] and perhaps even the very concept of human rights (Finnis 1980).[47]

As noted by Nobel Prize–winning economist Ronald Coase (1976), Adam Smith would not have thought it sensible to treat man as a rational utility maximizer. He thinks of man as he actually is: dominated, it is true, by self-love but not without some concern for others, able to reason but not necessarily in such a way as to reach the right conclusion, seeing the outcomes of his actions but through a veil of self-delusion. Coase (1976, p. 116) concludes that "if one is willing to accept Adam Smith's view of man as containing, if not the whole truth, at least a large part of it, realization that his thought has a much broader foundation than is commonly assumed makes

45

his argument for economic freedom more powerful and his conclusions more persuasive."

In Jensen and Meckling's analysis of the nature of man,[48] human beings care about almost everything from knowledge, independence, and the plight of others to peer approval, the arts, the weather, and so on. The fact that every individual cares and is always willing to make tradeoffs and substitutions constitutes the first universal characteristic of the essence of human nature. The second is that individual wants are unlimited, be they material or nonmaterial wants, such as "solitude, companionship, honesty, respect, love, fame, and immortality" (p. 4). The third characteristic is that individuals are maximizers. They act so as to enjoy the highest level of value possible given their constraints and limits, be it on their wealth, knowledge, time, or simply physical laws. The fourth characteristic is that individuals are resourceful. Not only are they capable of learning about new opportunities, they also engage in resourceful, creative activities that expand their opportunities in various ways. The authors conclude that the challenge for our society, and for all organizations in it, whether profit-making or nonprofit enterprises or government agencies, is to establish rules of the game that tap and direct human energy in ways that increase rather than reduce the effective use of scarce resources.

A rights-based approach to development that places the human being as the "central subject" of development ought to recognize and build on the few key characteristics of human nature that are generally perceived to be universal. Short of changing the nature of man, such an approach needs to recognize that human beings are animated by unlimited altruistic and selfish motives that are being pursued resourcefully and to the maximum possible. If one agrees with the idea that human nature is such as to allow most people, regardless of capabilities and circumstances, to organize and promote their lives, act creatively and productively, and advance themselves through ingenuity and entrepreneurial savvy, one can then draw important lessons in the field of political economy to understanding and remedying poverty (Machan 2006a). Development policies that promote and secure the (negative) individual right to liberty and freedom would then provide the most appropriate environment to unleash the potential of each human being to be master of his or her own life and destiny.

In contrast, development policies that view human nature and the conditions of social life as rendering most people victims of their circumstances—that is, mostly passive entities who must be moved via positive state actions in order to thrive and escape the poverty trap—are not only unlikely to address the fundamental causes of poverty (at best its immediate consequences) but may even inadvertently perpetuate the very conditions of poverty they seek to address in the first place (see discussion on development assistance in chapter 4). These two conceptions of human nature have historically led to the two alternative political economy philosophies of classical liberalism and welfare state egalitarianism, embodied in our contemporary era by Robert Nozick (1974) and John Rawls (1971), respectively. While human beings can certainly be seen as both succumbing to their harsh circumstances and being capable of overcoming such circumstances if the environment allows them, development policies (as opposed to humanitarian policies) ought to focus on the latter in order to address the root of poverty.

Economic Rights vs. Economic Rights

Somewhat ironically, the content of most economic, social, and cultural rights discussed in UN debates bears little relation to the actual process of economic development.[49] The Declaration on the Right to Development deals mainly with the proximate factors, not the ultimate explanations of economic development. As we have seen, most economic, social, and cultural rights constitute positive, nonjusticiable claims to free human beings progressively from want. Although these claims can be realized progressively through economic development, they are essentially an output of the development process rather than an input. In addition, their sustainability depends on the level and quality of development in each society.[50] Economic development is not mainly about claims, whether claims of citizens on the state or claims of developing countries on their more developed counterparts; it is primarily about empowerment and freedom.

A look at the economic, social, and cultural rights that would be relevant from an economic development perspective—as opposed to a humanitarian assistance perspective—would lead one to highlight a completely different set of economic rights from the economic, social, and cultural rights usually discussed in UN debates. In the same way that civil and political rights are about civil and political liberties, economic, social, and cultural rights ought to focus first and foremost on the protection of economic, social, and cultural *freedom*. The key ingredients of economic freedom would include personal choice, voluntary exchange (both domestically and internationally), the freedom to compete, and protection of persons and property.[51] Institutions and policies that are consistent with economic freedom would thus provide an infrastructure for voluntary and free exchange (i.e., a market economy); a legal structure; a law enforcement system that would not only put contracts into effect in an evenhanded manner but also protect the property rights of owners, including from governmental expropriation (e.g., through excessive taxation and inflation); and a monetary arrangement that would facilitate access to sound money. This would allow individuals to be free to operate a business, invest earnings, and earn a living. None of these considerations is given attention in UN debates on the right to development.

Last, but not least, as noted earlier, the Declaration on the Right to Development is agnostic about the kind of economic system best able to promote development. In the same way that the declaration glosses over economic freedom as a central constitutive element of both human rights and development, it does not acknowledge that the realization of the right to development depends on the extent to which a market economy is in place—that is, the degree to which it entails the possibility of entering into voluntary contracts within the framework of a stable and predictable rule of law.[52] Such a framework should uphold contracts and protect private property, with a limited degree of interventionism in the form of government ownership, regulations, and taxation. Emphasis on economic freedom would also require that institutions and policies refrain from many activities, particularly those interfering with personal choice, voluntary exchange, and the freedom to enter and compete in labor and product markets. In particular, economic freedom is reduced when taxes, government expenditures, and regulations are substituted for personal choice, voluntary exchange, and market coordination.

4. Practice

For the past 20 years, the right to development has essentially remained a controversial intellectual construct with little concrete application. Although the source of much rhetoric in numerous United Nations summits,[1] it has failed to translate into any jurisprudence at the supranational, national, or regional level. As argued earlier, the reason for this has much to do with its conceptual shortcomings, including the original inconsistency in the pursuit of both negative and positive rights for development purposes. However, while a number of human rights experts have begun to downplay the paradigm shift to be expected from the right to development,[2] elements of a rights-based approach to development have started to permeate the international community's development objectives, including the Millennium Development Goals, the poverty reduction strategies of developing countries, and the official development assistance (ODA) policies of developed countries. Although the practice of the right to development as sponsored by the UN is likely to remain elusive, a genuine paradigm shift based on the promotion of economic freedom, civil rights, and political liberties has begun to emerge as a practical, alternative development strategy to lift people out of poverty.

Right to Development in the UN

Since the adoption of the Declaration on the Right to Development in 1986, the common message of all UN summits and conferences could be summed up as a call for greater recognition of human rights in development. The objective of "making the right to development a reality for everyone and to freeing the entire human race from want" has been reaffirmed in a number of world summits and conferences. In particular, the World Conference on Human Rights held in Vienna in 1993 is often considered an important milestone in putting human rights center stage in the quest for sustainable development.[3] However, the numerous UN summits and conferences of the last decade have usually paid only lip service to the right to development, giving it a mention in the declaration, but neglecting it in the plan of action (Box 1).

UN members have been equally unsuccessful in advancing the work on the right to development through UN resolutions, especially as the resolutions have had a tendency to sound hollow and to antagonize the UN and the Bretton Woods institutions. In particular, the international community has failed to develop jurisprudence of any significance on many of the principal economic rights contained in the Covenant on Economic, Social and Cultural Rights and the Declaration on the Right to Development.[4] In the context of the 50th anniversary of the Universal Declaration of Human Rights, the General Assembly issued a resolution on the right to development to express concern that "more than ten years after the adoption of the Declaration on the Right to Development, and while noting that new challenges and opportunities for development have emerged in an increasingly globalized world, obstacles to the realization of the right to development still persist at both the national and the international levels, that new obstacles to the rights stated therein have emerged and that the progress made in removing these obstacles remains precarious." Its main concern was that the Declaration on the Right to Development was "insufficiently disseminated and should be taken into account, as appropriate, in bilateral and multilateral cooperation programmes, national development strategies and policies and activities of international organizations." Since 1998, annual follow-up resolutions have largely been variations around these themes (Box 2).

Attempts were also made in various UN General Comments to specify the content of a number of economic, social, and cultural rights that underpin the right to development with the objective of assisting state parties in the further promotion and implementation of these rights.[5] Since 1988, General Comments have been issued on the various provisions of the International Covenant on Economic, Social and Cultural Rights, including on the nature of state parties' obligations; the right to adequate housing; the right to adequate food; the right to education; the right to the highest attainable standard of health; and the right to water. However, while the purpose of these General Comments is to clarify the exact scope of a given right, the elaboration often raises more questions than it provides answers,

Box 1. Selected UN Declarations on the Right to Development

In 1986, the UN General Assembly adopted the Declaration on the Right to Development (see Appendix). Its first article states that "the right to development is an inalienable human right by virtue of which every human person and all peoples are entitled to participate in, contribute to, and enjoy economic, social, cultural and political development, in which all human rights and fundamental freedoms can be fully realized."

In 1992, the UN Conference on Environment and Development in Rio de Janeiro proclaimed that "human beings are at the center of concerns for sustainable development" and that "the right to development must be fulfilled so as to equitably meet developmental and environmental needs of present and future generations."

In 1993, the Vienna Declaration reaffirmed that "the right to development as established in the Declaration on the Right to Development is a universal and inalienable right and an integral part of fundamental human rights" and provided a comprehensive program of action. The declaration explicitly called on the international community to support "the strengthening and promoting of democracy," noting that "democracy, development and respect for human rights and fundamental freedoms are interdependent and mutually reinforcing." However, the interpretation that the right to development imposes obligations on third countries and international organizations was not shared by all UN members.

In 1995, the World Summit for Social Development in Copenhagen reaffirmed the link between human rights and development and established "a new consensus on placing people at the centre of sustainable development, eradicating poverty, promoting full and productive employment, and fostering social integration in order to achieve stable, safe and just societies for all."

(continued on next page)

(continued)

In 2000, the UN Millennium Declaration confirmed that no efforts would be spared "to promote democracy and strengthen the rule of law, as well as respect for all internationally recognized human rights and fundamental freedoms, including the right to development." It reiterated the commitment "to making the right to development a reality for everyone and to freeing the entire human race from want" but did not mention the right to development in the various follow-up reports by the UN secretary-general on the Millennium Development Goals.

In 2001, the World Conference against Racism, Racial Discrimination, Xenophobia and Related Intolerance held in Durban affirmed "the solemn commitment of all States to promote universal respect for, and observance and protection of, all human rights, economic, social, cultural, civil and political, including the right to development, as a fundamental factor in the prevention and elimination of racism, racial discrimination, xenophobia and related intolerance."

In 2002, the World Summit on Sustainable Development held in Johannesburg made no mention of the right to development nor, for that matter, of the expression "human rights." It only made reference to the commitment to "building a humane, equitable and caring global society, cognizant of the need for human dignity for all." There is a reference to the right to development in the Plan of Implementation, although again only in very general terms.

In 2002, the Monterrey Consensus emphasized: "Good governance, sound economic policies, solid democratic institutions responsive to the needs of the people and improved infrastructure are the basis for sustained economic growth, poverty eradication and employment creation. Freedom, peace and security, domestic stability, respect for human rights, including the right to development, and the rule of law, gender equality, market-oriented policies, and an overall commitment to just and

(continued on next page)

(continued)

democratic societies are also essential and mutually reinforcing." However, with the exception of South Africa and the United States, delegations did not mention human rights or the right to development during the summit, preferring instead to focus on the need to open markets to products originating from developing countries and on the various possible means of increasing development assistance (e.g., official development assistance, allocation of special drawing rights, debt cancellation, and possible new sources of funding, such as international taxation). South Africa recalled the commitment made at the Millennium Summit "to making the right to development a reality for everyone and to freeing the entire human race from want." The United States emphasized that "developed nations have a duty not only to share [their] wealth, but also to encourage sources that produce wealth: economic freedom, political liberty, the rule of law and human rights." It further noted that "liberty and law and opportunity are the conditions for development, and they are the common hopes of mankind" and called for "development from the bottom up, helping citizens find the tools and training and technologies to seize the opportunities of the global economy."

In 2005, the World Summit in the context of the 60th session of the General Assembly stressed that "democracy, development, and respect for all human rights and fundamental freedoms were interdependent and mutually reinforcing" and "decided to further strengthen the UN human rights machinery and to establish a UN Human Rights Council with the aim of ensuring effective enjoyment by all of all human rights, including the right to development."

therefore underlining the inherent difficulty in delineating the scope of positive rights. In general, they imply considerable state responsibility and action and neglect important aspects of the issue under consideration (Box 3).

In sum, while the right to development has been acknowledged rhetorically as a priority in various international declarations for

---

Box 2. Highlights of UN Resolutions on the Right to Development

In 1999, the General Assembly underlined that "the full realization of the right to development must be addressed within a global context through a constructive, dialogue-based approach, with objectivity, respect for national sovereignty and territorial integrity, impartiality, non-selectivity and transparency as the guiding principles, taking into account the political, historical, social, religious and cultural characteristics of each country" (United Nations 2000).

In 2001, to increase general consensus on the full implementation of the right to development, the General Assembly welcomed the Independent Expert's proposal for a "development compact" between developing countries and the international community—donor countries and international financial institutions.[a] The resolution also emphasized the need "to address and remedy the national and international dimensions of corruption" and urged states to take all necessary measures to establish a firm legal structure for eradicating corruption. It also emphasized the importance of the role of civil society, free and independent media, national institutions, the private sector, and other relevant institutions in the realization of the right to development. Interestingly, it affirmed the importance of equal rights and opportunities for women and men, including property rights for women and their access to bank loans, mortgages, and other forms of financial credit, taking into account the best practices of microcredit in different parts of the world (United Nations 2002).

In 2003, the General Assembly called on the UN agencies, funds, and programs, as well as the specialized agencies, "to mainstream the right to development in their operational programmes and objectives," and stressed "the need for the international financial and multilateral trading systems to mainstream the right to development in their policies and objectives" (United Nations 2004).

(continued on next page)

(continued)

In 2004, the General Assembly emphasized "the important link between the international economic, commercial and financial spheres and the realization of the right to development" and stressed, in this regard, "the need for good governance and broadening the base of decision-making at the international level on issues of development concern and to fill organizational gaps, as well as strengthen the UN system and other multilateral institutions." In keeping with the quest for a new international order, the 2004 resolution also includes the first reference to the "historical injustices that have undeniably contributed to the poverty, underdevelopment, marginalization, social exclusion, economic disparity, instability and insecurity that affect many people in different parts of the world, in particular in developing countries" (United Nations 2005).

[a] Under the development compact, developing countries would undertake to fulfill their national human rights obligations, while the international community would provide resources and share costs, focusing on (a) trade and access to markets, (b) debt adjustment for the poorest countries, (c) transfer of resources and technology, (d) protection of migrants and labor standards, and (e) restructuring of the international financial system.

more than two decades, the numerous resolutions of the General Assembly and the Commission on Human Rights as well as the General Comments have largely failed to translate its provisions into any concrete application in the social and economic realities of developing countries.[6] Similarly, there is no evidence of any rhetorical reference to the right to development arising in national foreign policy positions having an effect on development policies and practices. The right to development is neither mentioned as an explicit dimension of the poverty reduction strategies nor generally referred to in the national constitutions of developing countries. When the underlying economic, social, and cultural rights are mentioned, such as in the South African Constitution's bill of rights (1996), they tend to suffer from the same practical lack of relevance.[7] Incidentally, a similar conclusion can be reached regarding the relevance of positive rights enshrined in the constitution of many developed countries.[8]

Box 3. General Comments: The Example of the Right to Water

The General Comment on the Right to Water of 2002 requires state action beyond the provision of water for drinking purposes.[a] It involves extending water for environmental hygiene and health generally, as well as for growing food. It also involves accessibility, affordability, and nondiscriminatory access to water; protection against contamination by harmful substances and pathogenic microbes; and the monitoring and combating of aquatic ecosystems that serve as a habitat for disease. While the General Comment elaborates on the state parties' obligations, as well as the obligations of actors other than states, it leaves open a number of difficult economic issues as to the sustainable intertemporal management of water resources. As Salman and McInerney-Lankford (2004) observe, while the General Comment highlights repeatedly the issue of affordability of water, it is unclear what affordability means and how it can be reconciled with the water resource experts' call for cost recovery and full water pricing, or with the private sector's role in the management of water resources. Furthermore, the General Comment is silent on the duties or obligations of users in managing water resources, such as the duty to conserve water, use it in a sustainable manner, or protect and pay for it.

---

[a] While the right to water is not explicitly provided for by the covenant, the General Comment on the Right to Water recognizes the human right to water "through derivation and inferences" from a number of related economic rights and "through an analysis of the centrality and necessity of water" to other rights under the International Bill of Human Rights and other international legal instruments (e.g., the right of everyone to an adequate standard of living for himself and his family, including adequate food, clothing, and housing, and to continuous improvement of living conditions).

The right to development's lack of practical significance is compounded by the fact that the economic success stories of the last 60 years, especially the emergence of newly industrialized countries, have all occurred without any explicit or implicit reference to the right to development and its underlying economic, social, and cultural rights. Most of the constitutional frameworks and policy practices underlying these successful experiences emphasize the rights and duties of peoples almost exclusively in terms of basic economic freedom, as well as civil and political rights (i.e., negative rights), such as the right to life, liberty, and security.

At the regional level, the right to development is seldom a reference in regional North-South or South-South cooperation agreements. For instance, human rights do not feature among the objectives and principles of the New Partnership for Africa's Development,[9] although some of them resonate with those of the right to development.[10] When development cooperation agreements include human rights, such as in the European Union partnership agreement with the African, Caribbean, and Pacific countries, they usually focus on the promotion of basic civil and political rights rather than economic, social, and cultural rights, or the right to development.[11] The right to development is also absent from the existing instruments of multilateral cooperation, even for the agencies that have the most explicit mandates on human rights (e.g., the International Labour Organization; United Nations Educational, Scientific and Cultural Organization; and United Nations Children's Fund).[12] Other agencies, such as the World Bank and the International Monetary Fund, have no explicit mandate on human rights, although many of the same fundamental human rights principles of equity, nondiscrimination, participation, transparency, and accountability may be found throughout the development programs and policies supported by these institutions.

Human Rights, MDGs, and the PRSP Process

The Millennium Declaration (United Nations 2000) overlaps on many points with the international human rights standards. Both share a common commitment to promoting human rights, democracy, and good governance and for "making the right to development a reality for everyone." In particular, the Millennium Development Goals provide building blocks for human development, with each goal echoing a key human right—the right to food, education, health, and a decent standard of living—as enumerated in a number of human rights treaty bodies (Box 4).[13] Goal 8, with its focus on international cooperation, is in keeping with the international responsibilities contained in the Declaration on the Right to Development.[14] This has led observers to emphasize the consistency, commonality, and complementarity of the human rights and MDG frameworks (e.g., Jahan 2002). Within the United Nations, both frameworks are presented as overlapping, mutually reinforcing, and complementary: the implementation of the Millennium Declaration and the MDGs is expected to contribute to the progressive realization of economic, social, and cultural rights, and vice versa.[15]

Similarly, many of the principles underlying the poverty reduction strategy paper (PRSP) approach ring true with the Millennium Declaration and the international human rights framework.[16] For instance, the PRSP emphasis on civil society participation mirrors the right of individuals to take part in the conduct of public affairs, as well as the related rights of association, assembly, and expression. The insistence that PRSPs be country-driven corresponds with the right of peoples to self-determination. Transparency of government processes is consistent with the right to information. The introduction of social safety nets echoes the right to a reasonable standard of living, food, housing, health protection, education, and so forth. A similar congruence can be found between the PRSP approach and the key features of a rights-based approach to poverty reduction (i.e., empowerment and participation; nondiscrimination and equity; accountability and transparency; and rule of law and good governance).[17]

However, notwithstanding the synergies between human rights and the MDGs/PRSPs, the two frameworks have remained intrinsically different and largely independent, evolving in parallel and reporting to separate constituencies. As Alston (2004, p. 7) puts it, "Neither the human rights nor development communities have unreservedly embraced a marriage between the two approaches" and "it would be a mistake to take this love-in too far, either at the conceptual or empirical level."

On the MDGs, human rights experts tend to emphasize that the MDGs and related targets have no fixed normative content and are essentially about objectives in the form of time-bound, narrowly defined quantitative indicators with development aspirations limited to a few areas of human development. Indeed, although the

Box 4. MDGs and Human Rights Standards

Millennium Development Goal	*Key Related Human Rights Standards*
Goal 1: Eradicate extreme poverty and hunger	Universal Declaration of Human Rights Article 25(1); ICESCR Article 11
Goal 2: Achieve universal primary education	Universal Declaration of Human Rights Article 25(1); ICESCR Articles 13 and 14; CRC Article 28(1)(a); CEDAW Article 10; CERD Article 5(e)(v)
Goal 3: Promote gender equality and empower women	Universal Declaration of Human Rights Article 2; CEDAW Article 2; ICESCR Article 3; CRC Article 2
Goal 4: Reduce child mortality	Universal Declaration of Human Rights Article 25; CRC Articles 6 and 24(2)(a); ICESCR Article 12(2)(a)
Goal 5: Improve maternal health	Universal Declaration of Human Rights Article 25; CEDAW Articles 10(h), 11(f), 12, and 14(b); ICESCR Article 12; CRC Article 24(2)(d); CERD Article 5(e)(iv)
Goal 6: Combat HIV/AIDS, malaria, and other diseases	Universal Declaration of Human Rights Article 25; ICESCR Article 12; CRC Article 24; CEDAW Article 12; CERD Article 5(e)(iv)
Goal 7: Ensure environmental sustainability	Universal Declaration of Human Rights Article 25(1); ICESCR Articles 11(1) and 12; CEDAW Article 14(2)(h); CRC Article 24; CERD Article 5(e)(iii)

(continued on next page)

(continued)

Goal 8: Develop a global partnership for development	Charter Articles 1(3), 55, and 56; Universal Declaration of Human Rights Articles 22 and 28; CRC Articles 4, 24(4), and 28(3); ICESCR Articles 2(1), 11(1), 15(4), 22, and 23

SOURCE: United Nations 2004.

NOTE: CEDAW = International Convention on the Elimination of All Forms of Discrimination Against Women; CERD = International Convention on the Elimination of All Forms of Racial Discrimination; CRC = Convention on the Rights of the Child; ICCPR = International Covenant on Civil and Political Rights; ICESCR = International Covenant on Economic, Social and Cultural Rights.

MDGs are intended to improve people's lives by expanding their choices, freedom, and dignity, they do not explicitly contain the civil and political rights dimensions that are crucial for human development (other than the principle of nondiscrimination). In particular, they do not mention expanding the right of people to participate in the decisions that affect their lives. As noted by Alston (2005), there is a lot to be said for terms such as governance, equity, participation, and dignity, but unless rooted in identified standards, their meaning is conveniently open-ended, contingent, and too often subjective. Human rights critics of the MDG framework (e.g., Robinson 2003; Alston 2004) point out that the MDG process is yet another top-down, one-size-fits-all approach; it does not focus on peoples' rights; it is selective and prone to accepting half measures; it could reach its goals more easily by improving only the situation of those who are already better off, hence complying with the letter but not the spirit of the Millennium Declaration; and it could be used by governments and donors to detract attention from the real human rights issues. Pogge (2003) goes so far as to implicitly characterize the MDGs as a crime against humanity, since the MDG approach amounts to accepting that half of today's poor will continue to live on less than one dollar a day by 2015. In contrast, human rights–based approaches lean toward emphasizing that governments should be held fully accountable to the standards reflected in their international human rights obligations.

On the PRSP process, human rights experts formulate similar concerns that PRSPs are not anchored in rights; they look at poverty in too narrow an economic sense, and the approach remains top-down, with the international financial institutions (IFIs) playing a leading role. Far from being a change from the old structural adjustment framework, PRSPs are perceived as being the same thing, only with another name. In particular, the framework continues to be inspired by the so-called Washington consensus, the "neoliberal," economic growth–driven model of development (Williamson 1990). Key macroeconomic and structural issues in PRSPs are viewed as being not open to criticism by developing states and peoples. Participation by civil society is perceived to be either inadequate or not qualitative, and national ownership as more theoretical than real, especially when democratically elected parliaments are not consulted.[18] This uneasiness on the part of the human rights community has also been justified by a sense of disempowerment in relation to the IFIs, in particular the sentiment that there is no development context in which it is considered appropriate, productive, or politically acceptable to mention human rights considerations. For instance, Peter Uvin (2004, p. 47), professor of international humanitarian studies, expressed his surprise "at the amount of skepticism, if not outright hostility, that still prevails in much of the development community toward human rights."

Furthermore, the monitoring arrangements of the MDG and PRSPs are perceived to be lacking in several respects from a human rights perspective, including adequate opportunities for civil society inputs in the process; sufficiently clear, comprehensive, and integrated sets of standards; and the ability to mobilize both public and private support in the event that inadequate progress is being made. At the national level, mention of human rights is generally absent from national MDG reports, reinforcing the view of those who see the MDGs as a human rights–free zone. At the multilateral level, the IMF–World Bank annual *Global Monitoring Report* makes only passing or indirect references to human rights (with the notable exception of property rights). For instance, referring to the 2004 report, Alston (2005) observes that, while a human rights dimension would appear to be both obvious and unavoidable in relation to each of the four priority areas identified in the report to achieve the MDGs (i.e., investment climate, governance, infrastructure, and social-spending targeting), the report succeeds in either ignoring that dimension or addressing it clandestinely.

Conversely, none of the treaty bodies within the United Nations appears to make any significant use of any part of the MDG or PRSP apparatus. As far as the Commission on Human Rights is concerned, and particularly the work of the special rapporteurs whose mandates are of the most obvious and direct relevance to the MDGs (i.e., the rights to development, food, health, and housing), the MDGs have not been taken on board in any sustained way (Alston 2004). They have not significantly influenced the analytical frameworks used by the rapporteurs; they do not feature in any applied sense in their recommendations; and there is no sense that the MDG initiative can contribute significantly to the human rights enterprise.

Overall, despite the obvious synergies and commonalities between the human rights and development frameworks, neither has yet taken the necessary steps to capitalize on the potential for a complementary approach. As Uvin (2004, p. 192) put it, much remains to be done to develop "a language, a framework, a methodology for conversations between economic thinking and rights thinking." This lack of communication may again reflect the ongoing quid pro quo on the essence of economic development, in particular the respective role of negative and positive human rights in these two frameworks. From a development perspective, presenting the MDGs in terms that highlight their status as universally recognized economic, social, and cultural rights will do little to help bring about the resources needed for their actual realization. From a human rights perspective, the commitments made in the Millennium Declaration for promoting human rights, democracy, and governance are just as important, if not more so, than the MDGs, which are often seen as superfluous and distracting.

This being said, there are versions of the MDG strategy that are potentially very human rights–friendly (Alston 2004).[19] Indeed, the proposition in this book is that such a coherent version should focus on the respect for fundamental economic freedoms and civil and political rights as the appropriate legal framework within which the MDGs and PRSPs can be promoted and fulfilled from a human rights perspective. Incidentally, all the actions listed by Alston (2005) to bring an authentic human rights perspective to the issue of governance in the MDGs and PRSPs are of a civil and political rights nature. They include the elimination of laws and practices designed to exclude or marginalize certain ethnic, linguistic, religious, or other minority groups in their efforts to compete in the marketplace on an equal footing; the removal of discriminatory laws and practices that keep women from owning land; measures to ensure freedom of association and freedom of speech; the provision of judicial or other remedies in response to cases of discrimination; efforts to ensure the free flow of information, including a free press, access to economic statistics, and alternative sources of information; and ways of ensuring free and fair elections.

Human Rights and ODA

Like the other aspects of the human right to development, the relation between official development assistance and human rights has been highly controversial. From a legal standpoint, experts have long been discussing whether the commitment made by the international community (i.e., donor countries and official multilateral agencies) in a number of human rights instruments, including the Declaration on the Right to Development, to cooperate in ensuring development and eliminating obstacles to development, has risen to the level of an international obligation under the norms of customary international law. Some have advocated that the responsibility for achieving the right to development or for meeting the MDGs, in particular Goal 8 on developing a global partnership for development,[20] be internationalized so that the international community is responsible for providing resources or other forms of assistance to meet the declared objectives. Others have emphasized that no UN body, nor any group of governments, has accepted the proposition that a government is obliged to provide specific assistance to any other country. Moreover, the persistent rejection of such a claim by developed countries, and the failure of even the most generous donors to locate their assistance within the context of such an obligation, would present a major obstacle to any analysis seeking to demonstrate that such an obligation has already become part of customary law (Alston 2004).[21]

From an economic perspective, the issue of whether the international community has been able to formulate aid policies that foster economic development, including the realization of a number of economic, social, and cultural goals, is also mired in controversy. At an empirical level, it is generally admitted that the literature offers only weak (and not uncontested) support for aid as a means of boosting growth. While economists Burnside and Dollar (2000) provide empirical support for the intuitive idea that aid would be more effective if it were more systematically conditioned on good fiscal, monetary, and trade policies, Easterly et al. (2003) offer new doubts on the basis of new data. Looking at the component of aid that is most likely to stimulate growth in the short run (i.e., budget and balance-of-payments support; investment in infrastructure; and aid for productive sectors, such as agriculture and industry), Clemens et al. (2004) find a relatively strong positive, causal short-term relationship between aid and economic growth, albeit with diminishing returns. They also find some evidence that the short-term effect on growth is somewhat larger in countries with stronger institutions or longer life expectancies (better health). However, looking at the long-run effects of aid on growth, they find no discernible effects, thereby supporting earlier empirical findings (e.g., Hansen and Tarp 2001; Easterly 2003), as well as the more casual observation that despite decades of institution building, low-income countries are still characterized by the low level of capacity in public institutions.[22] In a recent, de novo examination of the aid-growth relationship, International Monetary Fund economists Rajan and Subramanian (2005a) find that, after correcting for the bias that aid typically goes to poorer countries or to countries with poor performance, there is little robust evidence of a positive (or negative) relationship between aid flows into a country and its economic growth. Perhaps more surprisingly, they find no evidence that aid works better in a better policy environment or geographical environment, or that certain forms of aid work better than others.

Although there are examples of successful aid programs,[23] the growing sentiment among many development practitioners with concrete field experience is that a half century of development aid has largely failed to achieve its declared objective. In particular, whether with or without good intentions, aid appears to have been of least benefit to the poorest countries, where the need is greatest.[24] The history of aid would thus seem to be another history of unintended consequences of policy actions (Merton 1936).[25] At one extreme, aid has been given for political reasons to incompetent dictators with wrong-headed economic policies and a record of human rights abuses. In milder versions, aid has contributed to maintaining corrupt, clientelistic regimes that had no incentive to promote state capacity for development. As noted by professor Van de Walle (2005, p. 35), "Because low capacity facilitates rent-seeking and clientelistic politics, the governments in the stagnant low-income states are typically extremely ambivalent about strengthening their own capacity." In these instances, aid has had the perverse effect of undermining civil society, including private-sector development, delaying political and institutional reforms, and even maintaining regimes that might have fallen without external support. This is all the more true for Africa, the poorest continent on earth and the one that should have benefited the most from external assistance. However, as recently pointed out by the Senate of Canada (2007, p. ix): "Forty years of foreign aid has done little to propel Africa from economic stagnation or to improve the quality of life on the continent. Development assistance has been a holding pattern for Africa at best, and a direct facilitator of poor governance and economic mismanagement at worst."

Another unintended consequence of aid has been the emergence of a culture of dependency, whereby large volumes of aid and various donor practices have undermined local ownership of the development process and the generation of institutional capacity (Azam, Devarajan, and O'Connell 1999). Other reasons why aid has proved to be so disappointing have to do with the kind of public choice and moral issues facing the aid industry itself. Aid agencies, aid officials, and recipient governments face incentives to continue increasing aid flows independently of how well those funds are used.[26] Because the aid industry is in the politically correct, self-proclaimed business of "doing good," aid—however responsibly administered—has often been unaccountable in terms of results.[27] Furthermore, aid advocates, including those critical of the way aid has been delivered in the past, often appear to be subject to Moore's paradox.[28] They know that aid is not the answer to economic development, but they do not believe it. For instance, despite his lucid and well-argued assessment of the often-disastrous past effects of aid on the world's stagnant low-income states, Van de Walle (2005, p. 34) still believes that "these countries will not develop without foreign aid."

Looking forward, advocates of a sharp increase in foreign aid suggest that the motivations for foreign aid have changed dramatically in the recent past, so that aid allocation is more likely to be rational today. Stern, Dethier, and Rogers (2005) emphasize that aid effectiveness increased in the 1990s. Development aid is thought to have helped create a positive investment climate by financing infrastructure, helping to improve governance, and supporting reform of macroeconomic policies, at least in countries with relatively good policies and institutions (World Bank 1998). The argument goes that current aid volumes need to be more than doubled if the MDGs are to be reached (Sachs 2005). The 2005 UN Millennium Project claims, for instance, that only a comprehensive, well-focused aid push will enable poor countries to overcome the multiple bottlenecks ensnaring them in a vicious cycle of poverty.[29] Notwithstanding a few harsh critics,[30] this view has received broad rhetorical support, not only within the UN system[31] but also from an unlikely compassionate alliance of rock stars, faith-based institutions, politicians, and grass-roots activists. Among others, former Prime Minister Blair's Commission for Africa has called for a doubling of aid levels over the next three to five years and for 100 percent debt cancellation as soon as possible for poor countries in sub-Saharan Africa. There have been recurring calls for a "Marshall Plan" for Africa.[32]

Notwithstanding these calls for more aid, there is a growing awareness among economists that a major rethink of the relationship between donors and recipient governments is needed—beyond the recycling of old ideas—to ensure that more aid will bring about a structural transformation of the recipient countries.[33] One of the new ideas in the aid industry is to enhance aid effectiveness through greater "selectivity," that is, the notion that aid should be allocated to countries that can do the most good with it because of sound policies and institutions.[34] The Paris Declaration on Aid Effectiveness (2005) provides the most recent plurilateral blueprint for enhancing aid effectiveness through the promotion of a number of partnership commitments, including to strengthen ownership, alignment, harmonization, results, and accountability of aid policies.[35]

However, applying the principle of selectivity for enhancing aid effectiveness is fraught with difficulties. First, a rigorously applied selectivity strategy is unlikely to target countries with the greatest need for poverty alleviation.[36] This refers to the classical dilemma that countries with good policies do not really need aid. In other words, aid would seem largely superfluous when countries get their acts together, while it is wasted (if not downright harmful) when they do not.[37] Either way, doubling aid money is not the answer.

Some would argue that a world without development aid is likely to be a world in which private selectivity and conditionality would have more credibility and thus lead to real conditionality and real reform (Vasquez 1998). Second, while entailing a scaling-up of aid inflows in a few selected countries, a rigorously applied selectivity strategy is unlikely to lead to higher overall volumes of aid. This refers to another dilemma (often downplayed by the donor community) that it is contradictory to promote needs-based and selectivity approaches at the same time (Van de Walle 2005). If all the donors (rightly) decide to follow the same selectivity criteria (i.e., alignment and harmonization principles) and concentrate on the few "good" countries, these countries would have a major problem absorbing that amount of concentrated aid. In particular, a significant scaling-up of aid could bring about a new set of (unintended) macroeconomic policy challenges in the countries selected (Gupta, Powell, and Yang 2005; Heller 2005). Key among them would be the upward pressure on the exchange rate caused by large aid inflows and the related adverse effect on the competitiveness of the economy (the so-called Dutch disease).[38] Also, large inflows of aid can easily complicate governance and the management of fiscal and monetary policy, especially in view of the weaknesses in the institutional environment in many poor developing countries. For Razeen Sally (2005, p. 5), "only the utterly naive or willfully disingenuous can aver that good governance will result from aid that accounts for up to two-thirds of government spending and 20–30 percent of national income (as is proposed in the Sachs Report)."

From a human rights perspective, not only does development aid rarely address human rights issues directly, but its politics and psychology are often paternalistic and corrupting. This is, for instance, emotionally captured by Bryan Mukandi, a medical doctor now established in Ireland, when he writes, "In most cases, there is something very paternalistic about aid, especially with respect to Africa. It is often viewed as bailing out a people incapable of sorting out their own issues. Not only does this lead to a perception of Africans as being in some way inferior, it also does something much worse. It often leaves us Africans with the very same idea, that we are not capable of ourselves running our nations and that we are in some way inferior to other races. . . . Much of the justification for colonization was that Africans couldn't rule themselves. It is as though that argument persists.''[39]

As noted, aid has propped up large, arbitrary, and corrupt governments while crowding out markets and individual economic freedom. Large aid flows tend to relieve social pressures that might otherwise lead to demand for greater accountability; lead to greater patronage spending, which in turn dampens pressures for democratization; prevent independent social groups—precisely those most inclined to demand political rights—from forming; and more generally, distort the notion of what development is all about in society. Unlike trade, which encourages poor countries to boost production and develop new ideas,[40] aid has often gone to leaders who run their countries into poverty instead of developing them, with additional resources going to those who can display the least development (Norberg 2003). The problem is that aid sets up the wrong incentives. For instance, giving aid on the basis of a country's financing gap can create perverse incentives for the recipient.[41] The larger the financing gap, the larger the aid, and the lower the savings of the recipient. This can create an incentive for the recipient to neglect marshaling its own resources for development (Easterly 2001). In recognition that aid can do more harm than good, the Organisation for Economic Co-operation and Development observed that donors' actions may affect human rights outcome in developing countries in negative ways. They can inadvertently reinforce societal divisions, worsen corruption, exacerbate violent conflict, and damage fragile political coalition (OECD 2007).

At a more conceptual level, the relation between human rights, aid, and development is at the center of one's conception of development. Is development essentially a matter of *entitlement* and search for equality of results (i.e., the right of peoples to receive the external assistance they need for their development),[42] or is development a matter of *empowerment* and promotion of equal opportunities (i.e., the right of each individual to pursue his or her own development)? Although the UN's current effort to double worldwide aid flows can be seen as part of a pattern to reinvent foreign aid largely along the same old lines,[43] many bilateral donors and multilateral development agencies have started to reformulate their relationships with recipient governments in focusing primarily on increasing the effectiveness of aid, including via a more appropriate framework for empowering people through the promotion and protection of economic freedom and civil and political rights institutions (Box 5).[44]

Box 5. Human Rights in Selected Bilateral Development Cooperation

At the 2002 Monterrey Conference, the **United States** called for greater aid selectivity and announced the establishment of a new aid mechanism, the Millennium Challenge Account, devoted to projects in nations that "govern justly, invest in their people and encourage economic freedom." Noting that "pouring money into a failed status quo does little to help the poor, and can actually delay the progress of reform," countries selected to receive assistance under the MCA should demonstrate commitments to (a) governing justly and democratically (i.e., promoting political pluralism, equality, and the rule of law; respecting human and civil rights, including the rights of people with disabilities; protecting private property rights; encouraging transparency and accountability of government; and combating corruption); (b) investing in their citizens, particularly women and children (i.e., promoting broad-based primary education and strengthening and building capacity to provide quality public health and reduce child mortality); and (c) encouraging economic freedom (i.e., encouraging citizens and firms to participate in global trade and international capital markets; promoting private-sector growth and the sustainable management of natural resources; strengthening market forces in the economy; and respecting workers' rights, including the right to form labor unions). Although the United States has remained opposed to the overall approach of the right to development as promoted in the United Nations, the underlying MCA principles resonate closely with the overarching objective of placing the human being as the central subject of development.[a]

In 2005, **Canada** announced a major overhaul of its development assistance (CIDA) aimed at strengthening the effect and effectiveness of its development cooperation through greater focus in fewer sectors (good governance; health, with a focus

(continued on next page)

(continued)

on HIV/AIDS; basic education; private-sector development; environmental sustainability; and gender equality) and countries.[b] In particular, the focus on good governance will be built around five main pillars: (a) democratization (to support democratic institutions and practices, including electoral and legislative systems, and citizen engagement, particularly by women) and the role of civil society in the political process; (b) human rights (to support the promotion and implementation of human rights, including the rights of women and of children, particularly those affected by conflict, gender-based violence, and natural disasters); (c) the rule of law (to support legal and/or judicial reform with a focus on institutions, including strengthening the judiciary, the bar, and legal-aid systems); (d) public-sector institution and capacity building (to support the building up of core institutions and technical and managerial competencies, including oversight, accountability, and anti-corruption measures); and (e) conflict prevention, peace building, and security-sector reform, including integrating conflict indicators and early warning systems; demobilization of former combatants; truth and reconciliation commissions, small-arms collection programs; and policing, transparency, and oversight of security organs.

In 2005, the **European Commission** adopted a new development policy that put poverty eradication and long-term development at its core. To achieve this objective, the commission introduced a single framework of principles for the 25 European Union members based on the complementary aims of promoting good governance (including the capacity of states to ensure respect for the rights and freedoms of their citizens and democratization) and respect for human rights (including civil and political rights; economic, social, and cultural rights; children's rights; equality between men and women; sexual and reproductive rights; and the rights of minorities and

(continued on next page)

(continued)

indigenous populations). Such a shift in emphasis in favor of good governance and human rights was already visible in the focus and content of a number of national development assistance policies in the EU. For instance, Sweden (Sida) introduced a new aid policy for global development centered on fundamental values, such as democracy and good governance, respect for human rights, and equality between women and men, and based on two perspectives—the rights perspective and the perspective of the poor. Similarly, the aid policies of Denmark (DANIDA), Norway (NORAD), Switzerland (SDC), and the United Kingdom (DFID), to cite a few, also emphasize the importance of freedom, democracy, and human rights, including equal rights and opportunities for women and men in all areas of society, as main goals of their bilateral development cooperation.[c]

---

[a] As noted by Marks (2003b, p. 137), "Paradoxically, the United States opposes or is reluctant to recognize development as an international human right, and yet the current administration has proposed to nearly double its development spending under a program that is strikingly similar to the international right to development model."

[b] Canada will reorient its overall bilateral programming in a core group of developing countries that "have demonstrated they can use aid effectively." Criteria for assessing the ability of countries to use aid effectively will include the quality of economic management, structural policies, policies for social inclusion and equity, and public-sector management and institutions. It will also be based on the World Bank's Country Policy and Institutional Assessment, which assesses a country's policies and institutional framework to support poverty reduction, sustainable growth, and effective use of development assistance.

[c] Piron (2004) cites examples of bilateral policy statements adopted in the late 1990s and early 2000s by a number of EU members. They include *Realising Human Rights for Poor People* (London: DFID, 2000); *Handbook in Human Rights Assessment: State Obligations, Awareness and Empowerment* (Oslo: NORAD, 2001); *Justice and Peace: Sida's Programme for Peace, Democracy and Human Rights* (Stockholm: Sida, 1997); *Country Strategy Development: Guide for Country Analysis from a Democratic Governance and Human Rights Perspective* (Stockholm: Sida, 2003); *Promoting Human Rights in Development Cooperation* (Geneva: SDC, 1997); and *Creating the Prospect of Living a Life of Dignity: Principles Guiding the SDC in Its Commitment to Fighting Poverty* (Geneva: SDC, 2004).

Part II. The Economics and Institutions of the Human Right to Development

The macroeconomics of the right to development is about the linkages between human rights, capital accumulation, and wealth creation. In line with Armatya Sen (1999), if human rights are to be the primary end and the principal means of development, as he views the expansion of freedom in this light, they ought to be concerned with the removal of substantial unfreedoms that leave people with little choice and opportunity for exercising their reasoned agency.

In this second part, it will be argued that the advancement of a free society provides the economic paradigm, institutional framework, and policy agenda for considering human rights and development in a consistent manner. The argument is that a rights-based approach, grounded in economic freedom and civil and political rights, offers the core conditions for a successful and sustainable development enterprise—individual or collective. This does not simply mean small, technical add-ons or improved discourse on human rights, but is more about the effective mainstreaming of economic freedom and civil and political rights in development strategies and macroeconomic policies. It aims at challenging Uvin's view (2002, p. 7) that there is less to the emerging human rights approach in the development regime than meets the eye and that much of it is about the quest for the moral high ground: "draping oneself in the mantle of human rights to cover the fat belly of the development community while avoiding challenging the status quo too much, cross-examining oneself, or questioning the international system."

From an economic standpoint, the proposition is that the extent to which human interaction in society is formed around the concept of *freedom* constitutes the ultimate determinant of development, the ultimate cause of why economic agents actually accumulate, create, and invent. Although a general theory of economic growth continues to elude the economist profession,[1] the idea that differences in societies' institutional arrangements are the fundamental cause of differences in economic performance has gained enormous momentum in recent years. Since the seminal work of Nobel Prize winner Douglass North, it has become clear that, while factor accumulation, innovation, and technological progress explain the mechanics of economic growth, they are not the causes of growth, they *are* growth (North and Thomas 1973). To pinpoint the ultimate determinants of growth, one needs to push the question back one step further and ask why human accumulation and innovation advance at different rates in different countries or groups of countries. Although the growing consensus is that the answer has to do with differences in institutions, some have tried to push the issue back even further to ask why institutions differ across countries in the first place. For instance, economists Daron Acemoglu and James Robinson (2004), from MIT and Harvard University, suggest that political institutions and the distribution of resources are the fundamental determinants of institutions and therefore of growth.[2] Pushing the issue back even more, the proposition in this book is that the extent to which human interaction in society is shaped by freedom determines the norms, value, and nature of institutions and constitutes the ultimate determinant of growth.

Applying this proposal to macroeconomic policymaking suggests that stabilizing and adjusting economies "by the book" are unlikely to address the ultimate factors of economic development but only its proximate manifestations. To address the more ultimate factors, policymaking needs to focus on the establishment of institutions and implementation of policies consistent with a free society.

The three chapters in this part develop a broad policy-oriented framework for thinking about the macroeconomics of the human right to development. Chapter 5 presents the key features of a macroeconomic paradigm consistent with human rights. Chapter 6 analyzes the main institutional dimensions needed to support such a rights-based paradigm, and Chapter 7 examines the set of macroeconomic policies that are consistent with the economic paradigm and institutions of a free society.

5. Economic Paradigm

Development as freedom is a powerful economic paradigm.[1] It elevates the process of development to the exercise of the human right to freedom. By themselves, the pieces of the paradigm are straightforward: first, it emphasizes the key role played by economic freedom in achieving sustainable development; second, it takes into account all the other dimensions of individual freedom (i.e., social, cultural, civil, and political) as also being part of the economic arena and mutually supporting economic freedom; and third, it limits the role of the state to that of an effective guardian, enforcer, and promoter of individual freedom in all its dimensions. In contrast to the right to development as defined and elaborated within the United Nations system in terms of claims on nation-states and on the broader international community, the proposed macroeconomic paradigm aims at placing the human being in charge of his own development in a unified and coherent system of thought.

Economic Freedom

Economic freedom is in itself part and parcel of the basic liberties that people have reason to value. As Sen (1999, p. 6) puts it, "The freedom to exchange words, or goods, or gifts does not need defensive justification in terms of their favorable but distant effects; they are part of the way human beings in society live and interact with each other (unless stopped by regulation or fiat)." To this, one could add the no less basic—yet grossly violated—liberty that all human beings should have to move freely both within and across national boundaries.[2] Economic freedom in all its dimensions, therefore, has an intrinsic value irrespective of its effect on economic growth and development, and this value is not limited to egotism and selfishness. Indeed, freedom has been defined as "a state in which each can use his knowledge for his purposes" (Hayek 1973, pp. 55–56). As noted by professor of history Jerry Muller (2002, p. 367), Hayek thought that Adam Smith's definition of freedom (1776) as a situation in which "every man, so long as he does not violate the laws of justice, is left perfectly free to pursue his own interests in his own way" inadvertently suggests "a connection of the argument for individual freedom with egotism and selfishness," while "interests" should be understood in the broader sense of "purpose" as covering egotistical or altruistic, idealistic, or materialistic goals.

Yet even since Adam Smith, it has been recognized that economic freedom could simultaneously serve a broader utilitarian motive. Economic freedom and free markets give spontaneous satisfaction to people's demands and constitute the main engine for technological progress and economic growth (Easton and Walker 1997).[3] In turn, sustained, vigorous economic growth creates the conditions for achieving various human development goals, including economic, social, and cultural.[4] Benjamin Friedman (2005, p. 4) argues that economic growth gives benefits far beyond the material: it brings "greater opportunity, tolerance of diversity, social mobility, commitment to fairness and dedication to democracy." And conversely, when there is economic stagnation or decline, the citizen's "moral character" tends to decline accordingly, there being less tolerance, less openness, and less generosity to the poor and the disadvantaged. Although clearly at variance with the human rights orthodoxy about the meaning of economic rights, economic freedom is the recognition that being forced not to behave according to one's preferences is utility reducing and costly. The main dimensions of economic freedom include the freedom to hold and legally acquire property; the freedom to engage in voluntary transactions, inside or outside a nation's borders; the freedom from government control of the terms on which individuals transact; the freedom from government expropriation of property (e.g., by confiscatory taxation or unanticipated inflation); and the freedom to move freely within and across international boundaries.

That economic freedom is an important factor contributing to economic growth and development is probable on purely theoretical grounds. As Berggren (2003) surveyed, there are several reasons why institutions and policies guaranteeing economic freedom conceivably have the capacity to provide growth-enhancing incentives: they promote a high return on productive efforts through low taxation, an independent legal system, and the protection of private property; they enable talent to be allocated where it generates the highest value; they foster a dynamic, experimentally organized economy in which not only a large amount of business trial and error can take place, but also competition among different players, because regulations and government enterprises are few; they facilitate predictable and rational decisionmaking by means of a low and stable inflation rate; and they promote the flow of goods, capital, labor, and services to where preference satisfaction and returns are the highest.

In particular, the freedom to move across national boundaries has the capacity to provide superior development outcomes and "win-win-win" results for the migrants themselves as well as for both sending and recipient countries.[5] From the perspective of the migrant worker,[6] the most important development effect of migration is its direct effect on income and welfare as the migrant moves to areas where his or her work is more valued. In a corrupt environment, it allows one to realize his or her potential abroad without indulging in local corruption. Significant indirect effects also accrue to consumers in recipient countries, through lower prices, and to remittance recipients in the sending country (Ratha 2005). In particular, economists Caglar Ozden and Maurice Schiff (2006) show that the surge in international remittances in recent years has reduced the level, depth, and severity of poverty in recipient countries; increased investment in human capital (education and health) and other productive activities, including housing construction; reduced child labor and raised the level of child education; and increased entrepreneurship. Migration for the individual migrant also goes beyond economics. As pointed out by Indian economist Dilip Ratha (2008), having someone who is doing well abroad brings confidence to the family: "They can hold their heads high." Overall, like most other economic flows, migration operates as an equilibrating mechanism allowing for greater wage and income equality between sending and receiving regions.

Although the composite, multidimensional concept of economic freedom does not lend itself to easy measurement and quantitative analysis, differences in how countries deal with economic freedom are a fundamental cause of cross-country differences in economic prosperity. A number of research institutions (e.g., the Fraser Institute, Freedom House, and the Heritage Foundation) have tried to systematically identify, quantify, and weigh various components of economic freedom, including measurement of the freedom to hold and exchange property, the freedom to participate in the market economy, the freedom to operate a business, the freedom to invest earnings, the freedom to exchange freely domestically and internationally, the freedom to earn a living, and the freedom from governmental expropriation (including through excessive taxation and inflation).[7] In their survey of the issue, Hanke and Walters (1997) found that, although varying in emphasis and approach, the three most common indexes of economic freedom[8] have significant power to explain variation in per capita national income.[9] Not surprisingly, all three indicators are also highly correlated and produce country rankings that have much in common.[10] In the same vein, Blume and Voigt (2005), looking at an even broader set of human rights data, note that income per capita and the human development index are highly correlated among all four categories of human rights they focus on (basic human rights, property rights, civil rights, and emancipatory rights).[11]

In quantitative terms, using the Economic Freedom of the World index reported by the Fraser Institute from 1980 to 2000,[12] Gwartney and Lawson (2004) found that, controlling for initial conditions,[13] the average annual growth rate of real gross domestic product per capita of countries with an EFW rating in the first tier was 3.4 percent, compared with 0.4 percent for countries whose rating was in the third tier. When developed countries are omitted from the analysis, the differential growth rates between the persistently free and the persistently unfree developing economies are even greater. The persistently free least developed countries grew at an annual rate of 5.2 percent during the two decades, compared with 0.6 percent for the least free group. The 10 most free economies out of those with low incomes in 1980 grew more than four times the average of the other countries. Countries with more economic freedom also tend to achieve far better social outcomes.[14] They have substantially higher per capita incomes, including for the poorest 10 percent of the population;[15] they have longer life expectancy, higher adult literacy, lower infant mortality, lower incidence of child labor, better access to improved (treated) water sources, and greater overall "human development" achievement as measured by the UN. Economic freedom is also associated with smaller shadow economies and lower perceptions of corruption (as measured by Transparency International), as fewer regulations, taxes, and tariffs reduce the opportunities for corruption available to public officials.

The key lessons drawn by Gwartney and Lawson (2003) from their analysis of cross-country differences in income levels and the long-run growth process are that (a) the maintenance of institutions and policies consistent with economic freedom over a lengthy period of time is a major determinant of current cross-country differences in per capita GDP;[16] (b) an institutional and policy environment consistent with economic freedom is a key determinant to investment, including foreign direct investment; and (c) economic freedom not only exerts an effect on the level of investment, but also influences growth by improving investment productivity.

Indeed, the unprecedented period of economic growth and development that the world has witnessed in the postwar period would seem directly related to the worldwide increase in economic freedom. According to the EFW index, there was considerably more economic freedom in the world in 2005 than in 1980,[17] reflecting the fact that, during the last two decades, many countries have adopted more market-oriented policies, followed a more stable monetary policy, cut marginal tax rates, reduced tariffs, liberalized controls on exchange rates and interest rates, and eliminated restrictions on current and capital transactions (Cole 2003). Chief among them, the transformation of China and India into dynamic private-sector-led economies and their integration into the global economy have been among the most dramatic economic developments of recent decades. While China was still characterized in 1978 by a deep distrust of the market system, egalitarianism and reliance on collective efforts, and a policy of extreme self-reliance bordering on autarky (Bell, Khor, and Kochhar 1993), more than two decades of market-oriented reform have brought visible economic success, including the lifting of hundreds of millions of people out of poverty.[18] Of course, one has to admit that fundamental freedom rights are by no means secure in China. Nevertheless, the step from Mao's to Deng's rule was a qualitative leap toward liberty (Weede 2008).[19] Similarly, much of India's economic strength in the last 15 years can be ascribed to a broad range of market-oriented reforms undertaken following the 1991 crisis and aimed at liberalizing and deregulating the economy both domestically and externally (Bhagwati 1993; Luce 2006). In short and to quote Economics professor Jagdish Bhagwati (1999, p. 4): "It is not difficult to assert that economic freedom is likely to have a favorable effect on economic prosperity, for the simple reason that the last fifty years of international experience more or less confirm the fact that wherever governments used markets more and engaged in more open policies in foreign trade and investment, indeed in more economic freedom of different kinds, their countries have tended to prosper. By contrast, those countries that turned inward and had extensive regulations of all kinds on domestic economic decision-making in production, investment and innovation are the countries that have really not done too well."

Notwithstanding the strong theoretical underpinnings and empirical evidence of the virtue of economic freedom,[20] a number of economists have questioned the causal relationship between economic freedom and economic growth, suggesting that it may have more to do with the tendency of rapidly growing economies to liberalize economically and politically than economic freedom per se causing growth. Haan and Siermann (1998) find that the positive effect of economic freedom on economic growth is not robust, but depends on the indicator of economic freedom used. Haan and Sturm (2000) conclude that while greater economic freedom will lead a country more rapidly to a steady state of economic growth, the level of this steady state of growth itself is unaffected by the degree of economic freedom. In a further analysis, Haan, Leertouwer, and Sturm (2002) maintain that the various, largely ad hoc indexes of economic freedom are not robustly related to economic growth.

Skeptics notwithstanding, most economic scholars tend to support the notion of an overall positive causal relationship between economic freedom and economic growth.[21] Robert Barro (1997) from Harvard University provides empirical evidence supporting the idea that free markets and maintenance of property rights foster economic growth. Gwartney and Lawson (2004) found that increases in economic freedom, as measured by the EFW index, led to more growth in the future (changes in economic freedom during the 1980s were associated with higher rates of economic growth during the 1990s), but higher growth rates did not improve future EFW index ratings. However, they note that the EFW does not suggest that countries moving from the least free EFW quintile to the most free will rapidly achieve a GDP per capita similar to those countries in the most free grouping. Instead, the relationship between current economic freedom ratings and GDP per capita indicates that institutional change typically occurs *gradually*. In other words, economic freedom is key to economic development but is no quick fix. In a more rigorous empirical testing of the causal relationships among economic freedom, democracy, and growth,[22] both Farr, Lord, and Wolfenbarger (1998) and Vega-Gordillo and Alvarez-Arce (2003) found that economic freedom fosters economic growth but that there is no statistically significant causality running from growth to economic freedom. This conclusion is corroborated by a number of econometric studies surveyed by Berggren (2003). In particular, although the results show that increased economic freedom exerts a positive influence on the development of economic wealth, there is no evidence of any study showing that economic freedom hampers growth or is associated with lower GDP per capita.

As to the relevance of the normative concept of economic freedom for economic policy formulation, it is worth noting that the various indicators and subindicators for measuring economic freedom used by the Fraser Institute, Freedom House, and the Heritage Foundation directly relate to instruments of government policymaking—from the legal structure and security of property rights to the size of government expenditure, taxes, and enterprises; the access to sound money; the freedom to trade internationally; and the regulation of credit, labor, and business.[23] As noted by Hanke and Walters (1997), these indicators make no attempt to gauge the effect of a country's natural, physical, or human resources on economic development; instead, the indicators reflect institutions that can be changed (though perhaps not easily or cheaply) by political means. In turn, the lack of institutions and policies consistent with economic freedom goes a long way toward explaining why the income levels of some developing countries do not converge toward the higher income of their more developed partners—the so-called convergence puzzle—in spite of diminishing returns on factor allocation and diffusion of technologies. According to Gwartney and Lawson (2004), once the quality of institutions, as measured by the EFW index, is held to be constant across countries, the expected trend toward income convergence emerges. The establishment of institutions and promotion of policies consistent with economic freedom would thus appear paramount for unleashing the forces at play in economic development and economic convergence.

Civil Rights and Political Liberties

From a human rights perspective, economic freedom is only one dimension—though one of paramount importance—of individual freedom. Other dimensions, such as those related to civil rights and political liberties, are equally fundamental. To paraphrase some UN terminology, economic freedom, civil rights, and political liberties would indeed seem indivisible, interdependent, and interrelated. All three dimensions of freedom essentially aim at freeing human beings from various types of state and nonstate violence and unfreedoms.[24]

From a utilitarian perspective though, the issue becomes one of the relationship between civil and political rights and economic growth. A country may be liberal in a political sense—that is, be highly democratic with protection of all major civil rights and political liberties—yet adopt policies that conflict with economic freedom. Conversely, a country may promote economic freedom while not respecting or guaranteeing civil and political rights.[25] Although there is plenty of anecdotal evidence to support all manner of combinations at any given point in history (from the dictatorial communist regimes that were able to achieve substantial social and scientific achievements to the political regimes that underpinned the East Asian economic miracle in the 1980s and the current Chinese experience), the fact remains that no model has proved sustainable without respecting economic freedom cum civil and political freedoms, or at least not without major amendments.[26] China's economic miracle cannot be divorced from the fact that, compared with 25 years ago, the Chinese increasingly have the freedom to decide where they want to work, in many cases where they want to live, and whether they want to start a business or hire personnel, and that a semblance of democracy is taking root at the local, village level. In that sense, Francis Fukuyama's insight (1992) that countries will converge, at times painfully, toward the liberal market-economy democratic model would seem to remain valid.

A number of theoretical arguments have been advanced to make the case that civil and political freedom and economic freedom are mutually reinforcing.[27] Civil and political freedom is expected to facilitate the functioning of the market economy by developing a more predictable and stable institutional framework for engaging in productive transactions, including better protection of property rights (M. Friedman 1962). This has a positive influence on economic growth through higher savings and investment rates, and lower rents associated with corruption, government controls, and the non-respect of the rule of law. Democracy is also usually associated with greater gender equality, higher levels of female education, lower reproduction, and infant mortality, all factors contributing to fostering economic growth. Amartya Sen (1999) is of the view that securing economic rights will not achieve the expected economic benefits in case of violation of civil and political rights. When the state does not refrain from physically harming its citizens (from arbitrary imprisonment to politically motivated killings), the resulting climate of fear and anxiety is unlikely to be conducive to investment and growth. Dani Rodrik (2000) from Harvard University conjectures that democratic countries would favor higher-quality growth, that is, a more predictable long-term growth rate, greater short-term stability, better resilience to adverse shocks, and a more equitable distribution of wealth.

However, other scholars have questioned the economic effects of civil and political rights, highlighting in particular the possible growth-hindering aspects of democracy.[28] In particular, majority suffrage tends to redistribute income and therefore reduce efficiency. Representative legislatures allow well-organized interest groups to lobby and legally appropriate resources at the expense of other groups and society as a whole. Democratic governments that try to maximize tenure tend to respond to popular demands for greater immediate consumption and spending at the expense of future growth. This line of argument echoes Friedrich Hayek's insights (1960) that while basic human rights and property rights have a positive effect on welfare and growth, a high degree of social rights (positive rights) could become counterproductive, even when democratically decided.

The question of the utilitarian value of civil rights and political liberties in the perspective of development is therefore of an empirical nature. Although the empirical studies on the relationship between civil and political rights and economic development are far from conclusive, many of them conclude that freedom in all its economic, civil, and political dimensions tends to favor economic growth and stability. Chong and Calderón (2000) show that improvements in the institutional framework have a positive influence on economic growth, especially in poor countries. Sah (1991) observes that authoritarian regimes exhibit a larger variance in economic performance than democracies, whereas Isham, Kaufman, and Pritchett (1997) find that substantial violations of civil and political rights

83

are related to lower economic growth. More recently, Blume and Voigt (2004), using a comprehensive set of human rights data, show that high levels of human rights are significantly conducive to economic growth and welfare. None of the four groups of rights they use (derived from economic freedom and civil and political rights) is ever found to have a significant negative effect on their various economic variables. Basic human rights and property rights are conducive to investment, whereas property rights, civil rights, and emancipatory rights are found to have a discernible effect on productivity gains. Robert Barro (1997) observes that democracy has a nonlinear effect on growth. Any increase in political rights initially increases growth, but this tends to ease off once a certain level of democracy is attained. His own interpretation of these results is that, in the strictest dictatorships, increased freedom stimulates growth by limiting government abuse. But after achieving some degree of political freedom, further increases in democracy hinder growth by intensifying the redistribution of resources. Economists Tavares and Wacziarg (2001) find that democracy hinders growth because it reduces investment in physical capital and raises the ratio of public consumption to GDP. In their survey on economic freedom, Hanke and Walters (1997) conclude that while both economic freedom and civil and political freedom contribute significantly to prosperity, gains in economic freedom have a "prosperity dividend" that is three to six times greater than that which would be obtained from comparable gains in civil and political freedom.

Not only does the effect of civil rights and political liberties on economic growth seem more equivocal than the effect of economic freedom, but the causal relationship also seems more ambiguous. Vega-Gordillo and Alvarez-Arce (2003) found that economic growth fosters political freedom, thereby confirming Lipset's hypothesis (1959) on the reverse causality between civil and political freedom and economic development. However, they also found that, when combined with economic freedom, political freedom helps enhance economic growth, thus highlighting the complex dynamic relationships between the various types of freedoms. Economic freedom enhances political freedom at the same time as more political freedom provides for greater economic freedom and economic growth. The authors conclude that "the interplay between economic freedom, democracy, and economic growth can be said to form various cause and effect chains, which have been studied theoretically and empirically but are not fully understood" (Vega-Gordillo and Alvarez-Arce 2003, p. 205). Part of the explanation may lie in the fact that, like economic freedom, the notion of civil and political liberties is difficult to quantify and that attempts to grasp such a complex subject in one summary index can only be deceptive.[29] The attempt by Freedom House to survey the state of global civil and political freedom experienced by individuals has not escaped criticism. Minier (1998) and Freeman (2002) emphasize the subjectivity and bias involved in the building of the index, which is largely impervious to change in institutions and the interactions among them.[30] Durham (1999) criticizes the available indicators of political freedoms, because they focus on outcomes rather than institutions.

Although it may be difficult to come to any definite conclusion on whether civil and political rights foster or hinder development in the narrow sense of an increase in per capita income,[31] as soon as one broadens the concept of development to incorporate the general well-being of the population at large, including some basic civil and political freedoms, any democracy that ensures these freedoms is, almost by definition, more conducive to development on these counts than a nondemocratic regime (Bardhan 1993).

The Scope of the State

The protection and promotion of economic freedom, civil rights, and political liberties call for an effective but limited state. Since economic freedom is essentially restricted by the extent of state coercion (usually by means of taxation and regulation), the scope of the state should not trespass the level necessary for citizens to protect and maintain liberty itself. Since Adam Smith (1776), it is common to consider the core functions of the state as being to protect individuals against violence, theft, and fraud, and providing a limited set of goods and services that markets may find it difficult to provide for a variety of reasons.[32] In particular, the state should establish the legal system and institutions to provide for the enforcement of contracts, the mutually agreeable settlement of disputes, and the guarantee of and respect for the rule of law. Except in cases where freedom of exchange is exceedingly costly or practically impossible, such as in the situation of monopoly or similar market imperfections or in the presence of externalities, the state should give way to the market to determine, arbitrate, and enforce the rules of the game.

Ironically, while the Declaration on the Right to Development focuses on the primary responsibility of the state to ensure the achievement of many economic, social, and cultural goals, including by means of redistribution, a human rights approach to development based on economic freedom would require the state to refrain from many activities, in particular those that interfere with personal choice, voluntary exchange, and the freedom to enter and compete in labor and product markets. When governments tax people in order to provide transfers to others, they reduce the freedom of individuals to keep what they earn. When government spending increases relative to spending by individuals, households, and businesses, government decisionmaking is substituted for personal choice, and economic freedom is reduced. In the same vein, economic freedom is reduced when government enterprises increase their share of total output, as government enterprises play by rules different from those to which private enterprises are subject, and often operate in protected markets.[33] Restrictions limiting entry into occupations and business activities would also hinder economic freedom and impede the market redistribution of income and wealth.

At a more conceptual level, a liberal philosophy of the state holds that the powers of any state should be circumscribed by individual natural rights that exist independently of the human mind (e.g., to life, liberty, and property) and overrule any social contract that is not arrived at by consensus.[34]

Such a philosophy of the state would seem consistent with different underlying ideas of human nature. Whether one's conception of the nature of man is that of active and resourceful individuals animated by unlimited altruistic and selfish motives (as discussed earlier) or whether one conceives of human beings in opposing terms as essentially passive and inert individuals unable to escape their own predetermined fate,[35] the trust placed in the state to solve social problems through coercion seems largely misplaced. In the former instance, classical liberals would maintain that, free from interference, human beings have the capacity to secure for themselves what they need to flourish in their own lives, while also coming to the aid of those in need in those exceptional cases where people are indeed incapacitated, irresponsible, or in a state of emergency. As

Machan (2006b, p. 278) points out, assuming otherwise, that is, assuming that "human beings aren't generally going to be kind, generous, and charitable of their own volition, as they are exposed to peer pressure and their own conscience, then there are scant grounds to believe that those administering governments are going to be that way."[36] In the latter instance, if most human beings are simply helpless and too ill-equipped to get ahead on their own, it would be quite paradoxical to believe that the very same inert human beings, once in a position of government control, are able to trigger all kinds of moves in society that are progressive, helpful, and proactive.

Not only does state coercion conflict with human rights in a normative way, but it also tends to be largely ineffective and, at times, even counterproductive in achieving its declared utilitarian social objectives. For instance, price controls are introduced on basic foodstuffs and other goods deemed of importance to the poor, on housing rents, or on public utilities. Interest rates are controlled and credits channeled to promote rural employment and other priority activities. A minimum wage, unemployment benefits, and other legislation for the protection of employment are introduced to increase workers' standards of living. Tariff and nontariff barriers, such as quotas, are imposed on imports to encourage local production, import substitution, and employment. Current and capital account transactions, including foreign direct investment, are made subject to restrictions to regulate domestic markets or control the use of foreign exchange. One could cite many more examples.

However, notwithstanding the good intention of protecting the poor, it is fair to say that government intervention rarely delivers the results intended and often has the perverse effect of delivering the opposite, thereby confirming over and over again Merton's law of the unintended consequences of policy actions. Instead, the state should be guided by the principles of economic freedom and civil and political liberties. In particular, the principle of nondiscrimination obliges the state not to distort further a system already loaded with various determinisms, but rather to promote a level playing field aimed at offering equal opportunities for all responsible individuals.[37] Furthermore, beyond the state, a free society is a system of natural liberty, where people are free to form innumerable voluntary associations in the pursuit of their common interests, including those in favor of the poor. As noted by American philosopher Michael Novak (1990, pp. 21–22), "such freely chosen associations are prior to the state. . . . They are prior philosophically and practically. . . . They are defenses against the state."

Of course, the problem of when exactly government coercion starts interfering in the market and consequently with economic freedom is open to reasoned debate. In the final analysis, while the scope of the state is a matter for the democratic process to decide, the latter should be exercised within constitutional boundaries that preserve individual fundamental freedoms. All the same, while societies may reveal different preferences as to the tradeoff between state intervention and economic freedom, the majority rule does not usually lead to the optimal state either from a normative or utilitarian perspective, especially when it violates the freedom of minorities (e.g., discrimination, expropriation, confiscatory taxation). Nobel laureate economist Milton Friedman (1962) noted that *market* solutions (i.e., voluntary cooperation among responsible individuals) permitted "unanimity without conformity" (i.e., a system of effective proportional representation), whereas *political* solutions (even in proportional representation) typically tended to produce the opposite, that is, "conformity without unanimity." From this he concluded that the wider the range of activities covered by the market, the fewer the issues on which explicitly political decisions were needed and, hence, required agreement. In turn, the fewer the issues on which agreement was necessary, the greater the likelihood of reaching agreement while maintaining a free society.

Accordingly, state coercion or constraint on the production, distribution, or consumption of goods and services should be limited to matters where effective market solutions are genuinely difficult or impossible to achieve, such as in the provision of indivisible public goods (e.g., national defense, public infrastructure, macroeconomic management), in the face of natural monopolies and other market imperfections (e.g., antitrust regulation, utility regulation, financial regulation), and in the presence of externalities (e.g., environmental protection, some elements of education, and public health).[38] When market solutions exist but have been rendered imperfect because of preexisting state regulations or institutional imperfections, further state coercion or constraint would only compound the problem and lead to further market distortions and inefficiencies. In such cases, instead of expanding the scope of the state to deal with these imperfections, they should be dealt with at their source. For instance,

Polish economist Leszek Balcerowicz (2004) notes that regulations aimed at controlling prices, wages, rents, interest rates, and so on invariably lead to shortages and the rationing of goods, employment, housing, and credit, which in turn prompt public intervention to fill the void and correct a so-called market failure. However, in such instances, the void does not preexist the public intervention; it is created by it. Typical examples are housing where rent controls generate demand for "social" housing, or employment where ill-designed labor market regulations generate massive structural unemployment. Indeed, the deadly effect of government failure on freedom and prosperity can affect the whole character of an economy—even of a people. While this lesson was drawn during the time of the cold war (Hayek 1960), it remains valid in many parts of the world, in developed and developing countries alike. In short, there may be fewer externalities, public goods, and market failures in real life than typically assumed, and, as a result, the necessary (or desirable) scope of the state's activity may be narrower, too.

As to whether the optimal scope of the state would be different in developed and developing countries, Balcerowicz (2004) opines that there are "sufficiently strong motivational and cognitive invariants constituting human nature, so that the optimal scope of the state is broadly similar across communities." Indeed, policies based on the opposite view—for instance, the suggestion that poorer societies need a more interventionist state, say, because poor farmers do not respond well to the standard economic incentives—have been a major reason for the perpetuation of poverty in the Third World (Bauer 1976; Schultz 1980).

Although economic freedom sets limits on the functions and goals assumed by governments, it also requires states to be effective in delivering those core activities of government responsibility. Far from requiring a weak state, securing economic freedom and civil and political rights necessitates a strong state with effective institutional capacities and instruments to maintain the rule of law and other core functions, such as the protection of people, contracts, and properties, or the provision of basic public goods. Ineffective states tend to take on an ambitious range of activities that they cannot perform well. At the extreme, weak and failing states commit human rights abuses, provoke humanitarian disasters, drive massive waves of immigration, and attack their neighbors (Fukuyama 2004). It is now conventional wisdom to say that building appropriate institutions, in particular institutions for markets, is the critical variable in development and a whole host of studies have provided empirical documentation that this is the case (World Bank 2002).

6. Institutions

Economic freedom and civil and political liberties can be seen as the most fundamental elements of a society's organizational framework. Being nothing less than "the humanely devised constraints that shape human interaction" in the broadest sense of Douglass North's understanding of institution,[1] freedom, in all its dimensions, shapes the rules and norms applicable in society and the nature of institutions. In particular, freedom principles influence a country's macroeconomic institutions in four key dimensions: they delineate the relationship between individuals and the state (i.e., the rule of law); they determine the relationship between individuals and the objects that they see as being their own (i.e., the property regime); they define the relationship among individuals in reaching agreement on collective matters (i.e., the participatory process); and they determine the relationship between individuals and their representatives in the use of public resources (i.e., governance). All four relationships capture the extent to which a country's institutional framework is consistent with a free society.[2] They are discussed in turn in the next few pages.

Rule of Law

The rule of law is fundamental in its own right for advancing freedom and needs no further justification. As stated in the Universal Declaration of Human Rights, "Human rights should be protected by the rule of law." In particular, the rule of law and its related legal infrastructure should protect and enforce property and contract rights.[3] Freedom to exchange, for example, is meaningless if individuals do not have secure rights to property, including the fruits of their labor. The failure of a country's legal system to provide for the security of people and property rights, enforcement of contracts, and the mutually agreeable settlement of disputes undermines a free society and the operation of a market-exchange system.[4] It encourages violence in conflict resolution and threatens social peace.

91

Beside its normative motive, the rule of law also serves a broader utilitarian one. Well-functioning legal institutions and a government bound by the rule of law are usually considered important to economic development.[5] If individuals and businesses lack confidence that contracts will be enforced and the fruits of their productive efforts protected, their incentive to engage in productive activity and invest will be eroded. In contrast, legal systems that provide solid protection for investors have allowed for the development of sophisticated financial markets, enhanced the ability of economies to bear risk, and encouraged entrepreneurship and economic growth through the spread of risk over a multitude of investors.

The power of legal and judicial reform to spur economic development is supported by a growing body of research showing that economic development is strongly affected by the quality of a nation's legal institutions, including the system of checks and balances (e.g., Knack and Keefer 1995). Actually, the capacity of national legal institutions to protect property rights, reduce transaction costs, and prevent coercion may be decisive in determining whether economic development takes place. According to the Economic Freedom of the World index, which indicates the consistency of a nation's legal structure with respect for the rule of law, unbiased enforcement of contracts, independence of the judiciary, and protection of property rights, all countries with sound legal systems achieved positive real gross domestic product growth per capita over the period 1980–2000. In contrast, countries with poor legal systems had per capita income and growth performance of only one-eighth that of countries with sound legal systems. A major explanatory factor is that without a legal system capable of enforcing contracts and protecting property rights, trade will occur mostly among mutually trusting parties and cover only a relatively small geographic or market area. The gains from what Douglass North (1990) called "depersonalized exchange," that is, trade between parties that do not know each other and will probably never meet, then go unrealized.

Of course, correlation does not equal causation. While there are strong reasons to suppose that a strong legal system facilitates development, it is also plausible that high levels of economic growth spur the development of better institutions. Indeed, many researchers believe that the causality runs in both directions, thus suggesting "multiple institutional equilibria" (Chong and Calderón 2000). Furthermore, although one can safely conclude that institutions "matter" in a broad sense, it is difficult to assess institutional quality in practice as the economic effect of a particular set of (often complex) institutions depends on context. For example, certain institutions make it difficult for the government to institute policy changes. In some contexts, this is beneficial for economic development, since it makes government commitments more credible (Brunetti and Weder 1994; Henisz 2000). On the other hand, in times of economic crisis or rapid change, these same institutions can hinder a government's ability to respond effectively (Tsebelis 1995). Similarly, scholars have been arguing about the relative effect of the common law system, with its priority given to jurisprudence, and the civil law system on economic growth.[6]

The effect of the rule of law on economic development has also to do with the actual content and enforcement of the law. Bad governance and corruption render codified law ineffective and can be detrimental to development. While enforcement of the law is usually said to mean "good laws," a legal system does more than enforce contract and property rights; it may also enforce bad laws that reduce economic freedom and economic efficiency. In those circumstances, corruption may be preferable to honest enforcement of bad rules (Barro 2000). For example, economic outcomes may be worse if a regulation that prohibits some useful economic activity is thoroughly enforced rather than circumvented through bribes. Since informal markets are the direct result of some kind of government intervention in the marketplace,[7] the existence of an informal market is positive to the extent that economic actors can engage in entrepreneurship or obtain scarce goods and services that would otherwise not exist. Of course, many societies outlaw activities such as trafficking in illicit drugs, but others frequently limit individual liberty by outlawing more benign activities, such as private transportation, education, and construction services. Furthermore, a government regulation or restriction in one area may create an informal market in another. For example, a country with high barriers to trade may have laws to protect its domestic market and prevent the import of foreign goods, but these barriers create incentives for smuggling and an informal market for the barred products. In addition, governments that have only weak protection for items like intellectual property, or that do not enforce existing laws, encourage piracy and the theft of these products. Protecting people from the threat of government confiscation is another critical enforcement issue. As noted by law professor Richard Posner (1998, pp. 7–8), "It is all very well to have well-defined private property rights determine legal remedies against the invasion of those rights by private parties, but these rights will mean nothing if the state can simply seize the fruits of successful investments."

Judicial reforms in developing countries should be part of a larger effort to make legal systems more market-friendly. The core of such judicial reforms would typically consist of measures to strengthen the judicial branch of government and make it independent, facilitate access to dispute resolution mechanisms, speed the processing of cases, and professionalize the bench and bar (Messik 1999).[8] It would also encompass everything from writing, or revising, commercial codes, bankruptcy statutes, and company laws through overhauling regulatory agencies and teaching justice ministry officials how to draft legislation to foster private investment. However, in contrast to the "law and development model" developed in the 1970s, the state should not be expected to be the direct protagonist of social change.[9] Instead, the state should simply enforce the rule of law to prevent the actions of different individuals from interfering with each other, including the drawing of boundaries. This would entail first and foremost the enforcement of private property rights.

Property Regime

Freedom, prosperity, and property rights are inextricably linked. From a human rights perspective, private property provides "the key to the emergence of political and legal institutions that guarantee liberty" (Pipes 1999, p. xii). From an economic perspective, it provides "the most appropriate permanent framework which will secure the smoothest and most efficient working of competition" (Hayek 1948, p. 135).[10] The stronger the set of property rights, the stronger the incentive to work, save, and invest, and the more effective the operation of the economy.[11] In the broader sense, the property rights system in a society defines the permissible forms of competition. For Austrian economist and philosopher Ludwig von Mises (1966), economic competition based on secured property rights is a system of social cooperation.[12] Such a system prohibits force, threat, and violence and encourages cooperation. In contrast, unsecured private property is cause for corruption (Chafuen and Guzmán 2000). In a narrower sense, Peruvian economist Hernando de Soto (2000) observes that, in essence, a well-integrated legal property system does two things: first, it tremendously reduces the costs of knowing the economic qualities of assets by representing them in a way that our senses can pick up quickly; and second, it facilitates the capacity to agree on how to use assets to create further production and increase the division of labor.[13]

Property rights have been neglected both in human rights discourse and, until quite recently, in the development economic literature as well. As noted earlier, although the right to property was stated in the Universal Declaration of Human Rights, it has remained largely peripheral to the human rights discourse in United Nations debates of the past 60 years, including those on the right to development. More surprisingly perhaps, a similar judgment could be made about the economics profession (O'Driscoll and Hoskins 2003), which has long been concerned with proximate causes of economic growth, such as material factors contributing to economic development (e.g., capital accumulation and technological progress), and has only recently rediscovered the key role played by property rights and incentives toward economic development (Pipes 1999).[14]

Although Harold Demsetz (1967) and a few other economists have theorized about the circumstances leading to the assignment and formation of property rights,[15] the importance of secured property rights was largely omitted from the development consensus until the 1980s.[16] Few studies provide a formal empirical analysis of the causal relationship between property rights and economic development and how one leads to the other. Economic professors Daron Accmoglu and Simon Johnson (2003) found evidence that property rights institutions have a major influence on long-run economic growth, investment, and financial development. Using an international cross section of countries, economist Bernhard Heitger (2004) also found that the overall effect of property rights and the rule of law on economic development was considerable. More secure property rights significantly raise the accumulation of physical and human capital. Furthermore, rising income levels lead to further improvements in the quality of property rights, implying that property rights and economic development are determined simultaneously. These authors lend strong support to the views of Olson

(1996) and de Soto (2000) that there are "big bills left on the sidewalk" and the unrealized gains from secure property rights and a transparent legal framework could amount to trillions of dollars.

Indeed, the lack of legal protection for private property has blocked the democratization of both property and capitalism in many developing countries.[17] In his seminal work, Hernando de Soto (2000) found that the major stumbling block preventing the rest of the world from benefiting from capitalism was its inability to transform assets into capital.[18] Although most of the poor already possess the assets they need to make a success of capitalism,[19] they typically hold these assets in defective forms (e.g., houses, but no titles; crops, but no deeds; businesses, but no statutes of incorporation).[20] Because the rights to these assets are not properly registered, they cannot readily be turned into capital, traded outside narrow local circles where people know and trust one another, used as collateral for a loan, or used as a share against investment.[21] The result is that most people's resources are commercially and financially invisible. Nobody really knows who owns what or where, who is accountable for the performance of obligations, who is responsible for losses and fraud, or what mechanisms are available to enforce payments for the delivery of goods and services. It is a world in which ownership of assets is difficult to trace and to validate and that is governed by no legally recognizable set of rules. At times, this state of deprivation has even been the direct—albeit unintended—result of government interventions to "protect" certain segments of the population.[22] Without an integrated formal property system, a modern market economy is simply inconceivable.

Building strong systems of property rights in poor countries is no easy task, and each country needs to evolve the appropriate property rights institution in terms of its own history.[23] This evolution has little to do with technology (although technology can play a very important supporting role). The crucial change has to do with adapting the law to the social and economic needs of the majority of the population. Such adaptation generally requires the integration of all property systems for a given type of property (e.g., real property, personal property) under one formal property law, so that the legitimacy of owners' rights is shifted from the politicized context of local communities to the impersonal context of law. Such reform of the law and property system would tend to facilitate the division of labor. Ordinary people would be able to specialize in ever-widening markets, increase capital formation, and raise their productivity with living standards to match. Releasing owners from restrictive local arrangements and bringing them into a more integrated legal system also facilitates their accountability and respect for the law.

Although the right to property is recognized by many national legal regimes, there often remains an enormous gap between what the content of the law demands and what has to be done for the law to work in practice. Again, Hernando de Soto (2000) expressed confidence that the extralegal social contracts currently prevailing in developing countries are a solid enough foundation for creating modern official property laws. As governments of the West succeeded in formally rooting property law in social contracts to which people were already committed, developing countries should also be able to develop an official legal framework based on their own circumstances, so as to achieve the widespread popular acceptance required to overcome any resistance.

While assigning property rights would seem straightforward in most instances, there are economic areas where identifying, enforcing, and securing property rights are more challenging, such as with respect to the economic use of natural resources, protection of the environment, and especially with intellectual property. In the case of natural resources and environmental preservation, the issue is essentially that of externalities resulting from a "missing" market. It is the absence of private property rights (e.g., over land, forest, livestock, water, etc.) that often leads to predatory behavior and negative externalities (e.g., deforestation, resource depletion). Indeed, the core of many environmental disputes—over wetlands, endangered species, zoning, and land preservation—involves the lack of proper property rights. However, while the institution of private property should, in theory, foster conservation as a result of the owner's own self interests (Mises 1966), it is not always possible to find consensus across peoples or nations on how to define and enforce such property rights. A human rights approach to environmental conservation should thus focus on the need to promote property rights wherever they are absent and only to constrain these rights through the legal system in case of externalities.

Arguments about the rationale, scope, and implications of intellectual property raise a number of even more challenging normative issues.[24] Intellectual property can be seen as the extension of property to cover the territory of ideas and should therefore not be regarded as fundamentally different from physical property.[25] Because each person has the right to the fruits of his or her own labor, the argument is that the creativity that goes into an intellectual product does indeed create a property right. This would be consistent with a Lockean interpretation of intellectual property as a natural right. Ownership of one's own self and effort is the most basic of human rights. Inventors and authors mix their efforts with their creations and thereby enjoy natural rights to their intellectual property. Indeed, in looking at how patent rights relate to competition, economic freedom, and economic growth, Economists Park and Ginarte (1997) found that, from a causal point of view, economic freedom determines patent rights. Countries with high levels of economic freedom are more likely to provide intellectual property protection.

However, as with all liberties, intellectual property rights should not create unjustifiable limits on others' enjoyment of their own freedoms, including the right to learn, to borrow ideas, to imitate; in other words, what is known in human rights terms as the right of everyone to "enjoy the benefits of scientific progress and its applications." Although intellectual property is generally supported by advocates of economic freedom, it has been challenged, inter alia, by a number of libertarian-minded critics, who consider intangible property, such as patents and copyrights, being different from tangible property, in that ideas (i.e., intellectual property) are not scarce resources in the economic sense (Kinsella 2001b). The argument goes that since the use of another's idea does not deprive him of its use, then no conflict over its use is possible, thereby undermining the natural law justification for property rights. To paraphrase Thomas Jefferson, you can light your candle from mine without taking my light.[26] Indeed, even advocates of intellectual property do not maintain that the legal system must reward everyone for every single useful idea.[27] For example, philosophical, mathematical, or scientific truths are usually not protected. This, in turn, raises the issue of the consistency and fairness of a system that rewards certain types of creators (e.g., practical creators and entertainment providers) but not others (e.g., more theoretical science and math researchers and philosophers).

On the whole, the difficulty in dealing with intellectual property from a human rights perspective stems from this original ambiguity.[28] On the one hand, intellectual property could be interpreted as the prolongation of the fundamental human right to property. On the other, it could be seen as yet another piece of state coerciveness in people's freedom to enter into contracts with the adverse side effect of discriminating between classes of intellectual creators.[29] Intellectual property may skew research and development to favor practical inventions rather than more fundamental and theoretical ones, but it is not clear whether this kind of institutional arrangement is better suited to society. The ambiguity is further complicated by the fact that, like property rights over physical assets, and perhaps even more so, the concept of intellectual property tends to evolve with time in light of technological change (Bell and DeLong 2002).[30] In other words, the right to property should not be regarded as some eternal and unchanging essence, but as something in need of redefinition in keeping with changing social needs (Hayek 1944).

The utilitarian point of view usually considers intellectual property as having two conflicting effects on economic welfare.[31] In the short run, it confers monopoly power on rights holders, thereby reducing competition and diffusion and increasing prices.[32] In the long run, it provides the right kind of incentive for creators to engage in research and development activities, which benefit society as a whole in terms of improved technology and better products.[33] On balance, the relationship between market power, innovation, and diffusion is a difficult theoretical matter (Branstetter and Sakakibara 2001; Helpman 1993; Quirmbach 1986; Reinganum 1981). Whether intellectual property unintentionally advances the common good by providing incentives for investment, wealth creation, and the provision of employment has become an empirical question.[34] Investigating the effect of intellectual property right protection on the international diffusion of new products and technology in the film industry, McCalman (2005) found that the relationship is surprisingly complex. While raising the intellectual property protection standard from a "low" to a "moderate" level of protection promotes diffusion, a further increase from "moderate" to "high" decreases it. This implies that a country would benefit most from maintaining a minimum level of protection that covered basic rights, whereas raising standards higher would require careful attention to the specificities of the sector concerned as well as the country's environment.

Whether one takes a normative or utilitarian approach to intellectual property, the challenge in both cases is to strike the right balance between protecting the individual right to the fruits of one's labor and the individual right to learn from others; in other words, the right balance between promoting creation and innovation on the one hand, and encouraging diffusion and dissemination on the other. While it is unlikely that governments can measure all the relevant economic, legal, technological, and cultural factors that go into calculating the optimal level of intellectual property protection in each particular sector of the economy, instruments of international norms and standards (such as those developed by the World Intellectual Property Organization) could help establish basic national intellectual property legislation and procedures and facilitate the resolution of private intellectual property disputes.[35]

Participation

The call for participation is commonplace in both human rights and development discourses. It refers to the process by which all stakeholders, including the have-not citizens usually excluded from the political and economic processes, influence and share control of policymaking, including priority setting, resource allocations, and program implementation and monitoring. For instance, the Declaration on the Right to Development declares that "states should encourage popular participation in all spheres as an important factor in development and in the full realization of all human rights." Similarly, in the development discourse, participation is a core principle underlying the poverty reduction strategy paper (PRSP) approach, where the coordinated participation of development partners (government, domestic stakeholders, and external donors) should provide policymakers with concrete inputs into their decisionmaking and policy implementation through information dissemination, dialogue, and participatory monitoring and evaluation.

Although the concept of participation resonates with the development notions of empowerment and ownership, and the human rights principles of economic freedom and civil and political rights, it has remained vague and controversial in its application.[36] Alston (2004) found that too many of the discussions on the need for "participation" in the development process were "hollow and tokenistic." Without spelling out what participation actually means, particularly

100

how it relates to civil and political rights and the democratic process, and how it might be translated into concrete law or policy, participatory processes tend to be open-ended, to supplant or bypass existing institutional structure, to benefit vocal and organized groups (at the expense of individual citizens), or to result in generalities and vague recommendations that do not directly influence policy choices and policymaking.[37] Peter Uvin (2002) goes one step further by denouncing the rhetorical, manipulative, and high moral ground discourse of the human rights language in development policies, which merely provides a fig leaf for the continuation of the status quo instead of reconceptualizing the practice of development.[38] A more benign interpretation might stress that the wordplay could constitute the first step toward a true shift in vision.[39] Indeed, an external evaluation of the International Monetary Fund's role in PRSPs concluded that "participation in the formulation of PRSPs was generally more broadly based than in previous approaches, and most stakeholders involved in the process viewed this as a significant improvement" (IMF 2004, p. 3). Yet it also found that, although of benefit on the microeconomic side, the PRSPs process has had "limited impact in generating meaningful discussions, outside the narrow official circle, of alternative policy options with respect to the macroeconomic framework and macro-relevant structural reforms" (IMF 2004, p. 3).

This being said, formulating and achieving genuine participatory outcomes at the macroeconomic level are fraught with difficulties.[40] It raises the question of how the participation process is supposed to mesh with existing domestic political processes (and when these processes would be judged sufficient in and of themselves), the level at which meaningful input from individuals can contribute to macroeconomic decisionmaking, and how to reconcile different views.[41] Given the ultimate responsibility of government officials to be accountable to those whom they represent, how much participation is needed? In making difficult societal choices in the face of budget constraints that not only span the country's economy but also reach across generations, how many voices need to be heard and whose voices are they? Should nonelected nongovernmental organization representatives have a say in making very difficult, complex, and sensitive macroeconomic policy choices?

Ultimately, the concept of participation raises the broader issue of the system of government representation and the criterion for social choice. While it is widely accepted that democratic systems (i.e., systems ruled by the people) offer the best guarantees for people's participation and sovereignty over their own affairs, different democratic systems (e.g., representative democracy, direct democracy, participatory democracy, liberal democracy) provide different levels of participation. In particular, the extent of the majority's ruling over the minority or even over the individual would seem a key determinant of the genuineness of the participatory process. From the perspective of this book, any meaningful participatory process should be firmly established on the basis of civil and political rights (e.g., the right to freedom of speech, to a free press, to associate freely) and the protection of fundamental freedoms, including economic freedom. This would be consistent with a liberal democratic system where the ability of elected representatives to exercise decisionmaking power is subject to the rule of law and moderated by a constitution that emphasizes the protection of the rights and freedoms of individuals and minorities and that places strict constraints on the extent to which the will of the majority can be exercised. In particular, majorities and special-interest coalitions that form majorities should be prevented from violating the freedom and sovereignty of the individual and from interfering coercively with the peaceful and voluntary relationships of the market.

In a free society, it is liberty in all its dimensions—and first and foremost the freedom to participate in the marketplace—that is primary, with democratic rule but a byproduct. Participation cannot be limited to the notion that everyone has a right to take part in public decisionmaking and then the obligation to accept the rule of the majority. As has long been argued by early liberals, such a concept of participation carries the risk of despotism.[42] As Machan (2003) put it, "Whereas the original classical liberal idea is that we are free in all realms and democracy concerns mainly who will administer a system of laws that are required to protect our liberty, the corrupt version of this idea is that democracy addresses everything in our lives and the only liberty we have left is to take part in the decision-making about whatever is taken to be a so called 'public matter.'"[43]

Indeed, such a concept of democratic participation can only be deceptive because of the "rational ignorance" of voters. Observing that each voter is faced with an infinitesimally small probability that his vote will change the result of the elections and that gathering the relevant information necessary for a well-informed voting decision requires substantial time and effort, Anthony Downs concludes in his 1957 seminal work that the rational decision for each voter is to be generally ignorant of politics and perhaps even abstain from voting. Democratic systems are also vulnerable to the "capture" of government officials by special-interest groups to support inefficient policies or policies that are not in the greater public interest (Stigler 1971).[44] These public-choice arguments have long challenged the possible use of voting to make collective decisions that please everyone when people have different goals (Arrow 1951)[45] and, more generally, the fairness of the collective decisionmaking process based on majority rule (Buchanan and Tullock 1962).

A logical conclusion is that genuine participation in the sense of effective citizen control (Arnstein 1969) calls for a liberal society, which reduces the necessity of agreement to a minimum compatible with the diversity of individual opinions (Hayek 1944).[46] In other words, participation can be genuine only if citizens accept the fact that their shared consensus would inevitably remain limited, and therefore, that the purposes for which government can be used are limited as well. When the system of government does not limit the range of questions that can be decided through the political process, it is the right to participate itself that is threatened, as one economic interest group after another can make demands on politicians in the name of social justice and other self-serving motives at the expense of the rest of society.

Governance

Underlying the call for participation is the implicit notion that participation will bring about improved governance at all levels of society—that is, improved processes and systems by which an organization or a society operates for the common good, in particular in the area of public-sector management.[47] Although the very notion of governance has remained rather fuzzy,[48] World Bank economists Kaufmann, Kraay, and Mastruzzi (2005) identify three main dimensions of governance: the political dimension (i.e., the process by which those in authority are selected, monitored, and replaced); the economic dimension (i.e., the government's capacity to effectively

103

manage its resources and implement sound policies); and the institutional dimension (i.e., the respect of citizens and the state for the country's institutions), all of which call for a strong public system of integrity based on participation, transparency, accountability, the rule of law, and the fight against corruption.[49] Given that these key principles share a great deal of common ground with human rights concepts, it has been suggested that the two concepts of good governance and human rights are mutually reinforcing (Cockroft 1998; UN Economic and Social Council 2004b).

Yet notwithstanding the multifaceted linkage between governance and human rights, there has been little interface between the development and human rights communities (even within the UN system) on these issues.[50] In the development community, the concept of governance has often played a proxy role as a means of avoiding a more direct addressing of issues related to democracy and human rights.[51] Governance is typically addressed through the lens of corruption and its adverse effect on economic growth. In the human rights community, despite the analytical evidence linking governance and corruption issues with human rights issues,[52] as well as the incipient empirical evidence, human rights instruments do not refer explicitly to the right to good governance and to freedom from corruption.

The theoretical literature on the economic consequences of corruption has focused on the detrimental effect of corruption on economic growth, efficiency, equity, and welfare (Dabla-Norris 2000).[53] By weakening property rights, corruption deprives investors of compensation for risk taking and increases uncertainty about potential investment payoffs. This reduces the incentive to invest, which in turn dampens economic growth.[54] It can also be expected to lower the quality of public infrastructure and services, reduce public revenues, misallocate talent to rent-seeking activities, and distort the composition of government expenditures and tax revenues (Abed and Gupta 2002). In particular, corrupt governments divert resources and tend to shift spending away from productive activities (such as health and education or high-quality physical infrastructure) toward the construction of ''white elephant'' projects or other low-quality investment projects (Gupta, Davoodi, and Tinogson 2000; Mauro 1998; Tanzi and Davoodi 1997). Higher levels of corruption also tend to be associated with rising military spending (Gupta, de Mello, and

Saran 2000). Because corruption exacerbates unequal distribution of wealth and access to education, as well as other means of increasing human capital, it can be expected to increase income inequalities and poverty (Gupta, Davoodi, and Alonso-Terme 1998). In particular, the distributional effects of tax evasion and corruption have been found to be unambiguously regressive (Hindriks, Keen, and Muthoo 1999).

As to the causes of corruption, the economic literature considers that corruption results from a combination of opportunities and incentives. Opportunities to indulge in the abuse of power are prevalent in areas where government restrictions and intervention lead to the availability of rents, such as large public sectors, complex tax and customs systems, exchange rate controls and financial market regulations, trade restrictions, windfall gains from natural resources, privatization decisions, and discretionary public spending (Tanzi 1998).[55] When corruption is widespread, incentives may even exist for individuals at all levels to acquiesce in it, even if everybody would be better off without it. This can lead countries to be stuck in a vicious circle of widespread corruption cum slow economic growth, from which they cannot escape without outside intervention (Mauro 2004). When corruption is systemic, the likelihood of detection and punishment decreases and incentives created for corruption increase further. Eradication of corruption would thus be particularly costly in countries with weak institutions and fragile economic environment (Dabla-Norris and Freeman 1999). This leads to the important policy implication that anti-corruption policy must be sustained to be effective. Ad hoc, anti-corruption campaigns have generally little effect in eliminating corruption.

Taking a step back to look at what might create incentives to engage in corrupt behavior in the first place, the literature points to the quality of institutions and the political economy of corruption. Corruption may be endogenous to institutional factors, such as cultural heritage, the political structure, the quality and effectiveness of the rule of law, the degree of transparency in government operations, and, more generally, the respect for human rights. In a preliminary empirical study to explore the links between governance and human rights, Daniel Kaufmann (2004) found illuminating results—especially in light of the overall thesis defended in this book.[56] First, bad governance and high levels of corruption are associated with, and possibly result from, the nonrespect of civil and political rights, as measured by the level of killings, torture, disappearances, imprisonment, women's political rights, political participation, government censorship, and voice, civil liberties, and accountability.

Second, good governance is not a luxury that only rich countries can afford. The causal relation is more in the direction of better governance and greater respect for civil and political rights to higher economic growth, rather than the other way around.[57] A country that improves its governance from a relatively low level to an average level could be expected to almost triple its population's per capita income in the long term, and reduce infant mortality and illiteracy by the same amount. Third, progress in the realization of economic and social aspirations is found to be dependent on respect for civil and political rights. In particular, good governance and the fight against corruption appear to be an important link between both sets of rights. Fourth, echoing an earlier point, official development assistance policies need to consider the role of civil and political rights for enhancing aid effectiveness in a deeper and more integral fashion.

Improving transparency and accountability in the public sector would seem key to curbing both the demand- and supply-side of corruption and bribery. Transparency and accountability presuppose the securing of people's freedom of expression[58] and right to information.[59] While freedom of expression and an unfettered media play a critical role in disseminating ideas, shaping public opinion, and providing a public forum for debate, the right to information is no less crucial to challenging corruption and enhancing transparency, thereby creating a more open and democratic society. As emphasized by UNDP (2004, p. 9): ''A secretive government is nearly always inefficient in that the free flow of information is essential if problems are to be identified and resolved. Furthermore, a secretive governing culture fosters suspicion and encourages rumors and conspiracy theories. In such a culture, the public is likely to treat all government information with skepticism, including public education campaigns, such as those dealing with important health issues like HIV/AIDS or those which may be particularly sensitive. People are more likely to be politically malleable, skeptical of government and its intentions, and resistant to change unless sanctioned by informal opinion leaders.'' Right-to-information laws are therefore critical tools in the fight against corruption.

While a growing number of countries have adopted comprehensive laws to facilitate access to state records,[60] the right to information and the system of formal recordkeeping remain poor in many developing countries. As noted by the UNDP (2004), in many instances an informal system of recordkeeping has emerged, leading to gaps in information, slow retrieval time, and opportunities to manipulate information. In addition, inadequate information systems tend to trigger informality in the public sector that leads to unfair treatment of citizens and difficult performance monitoring, auditing, and fraud detection. Policy is not evidence based, and legal compliance cannot be demonstrated. Adopting and implementing right-to-information legislation would therefore seem paramount to build up public trust in government and improve governance. This can be done in different ways. When the legal system has matured enough to give effect to constitutional rights in law, the right to information can be provided in the form of constitutional provision. In other cases, legal guarantees can be directly provided in right-to-information legislation. Such legislation should presume, inter alia, that all information held by public bodies is open,[61] that any exception should be defined in law rather than left ambiguous, and that an effective and efficient appeals mechanism is available in the event of a request for information being denied. Furthermore, an effective implementation of right-to-information legislation would require action on the part of the state to develop an efficient and well-organized information management system, to build public awareness of the right to information, and to train civil servants on the legislation's implications.[62]

7. Macroeconomic Policies

Achieving a critical comprehension of development as freedom entails that macroeconomic policymaking be consistent with the economic paradigm and institutions of a free society discussed in previous chapters. This requires notably that fiscal policy, monetary and exchange rate policy, competition and trade policy, and other macroeconomic policies, such as those governing the business and employment climates, be formulated with a view to respecting, enforcing, and promoting economic freedom and civil and political rights. Contrary to a view held in a number of human rights circles, standard market-oriented macroeconomic policies based on macro-economic stability, fiscal discipline, monetary prudence, openness to trade and investment, and competitive product and factor markets are the only policies consistent with the promotion and protection of human rights. Furthermore, these policies are typically pro-growth and good for the poor. As researched by World Bank economists David Dollar and Aart Kraay (2002), they raise the income of the poor proportionately with average incomes and tend to improve income distribution. This growth-poverty relationship has also proved to be resilient, even during crises, and is generally the same for rich countries as for poor. This last chapter will therefore review the relationship between freedom and the main dimensions of macroeconomic policymaking.

Fiscal Policy

Fiscal policy is the central macroeconomic policy instrument of a state's financial intrusiveness in society. It involves governments' raising resources from individuals to fund government expenditures. Both the revenue and the expenditure components of fiscal policy are deemed to affect economic development and human rights. Sound fiscal policy fosters macroeconomic stability and economic development, and well-designed revenue and expenditure reforms may directly promote growth as well as enhance the economy's supply-side response, particularly in low-income countries (Abed 1998). The extent to which government expenditures place emphasis on delivering core public goods and services and the way these expenditures are financed—by current taxation, future taxation (debt issuance or money creation), or varying amounts of both—also directly affect human rights. Contrary to a view commonly held by human rights advocates, a pro–human rights fiscal policy has little to do with extending government spending on social services, transfers, and subsidies; increasing tax on international trade; granting tax exemptions; or accumulating debts and deficits. Instead, human rights pointers should be expenditure restraint, fairness of the tax system, fiscal discipline, transparency, accountability, and debt sustainability.

Government expenditures constitute the most complete measure of a state's burden on the economy. As we have seen earlier, both the protection of human rights and promotion of economic growth call for a limited, but effective state. When a government expends money, it acquires resources, diverting them from potentially more productive private choices and goals. This is true whether the expenditure is to acquire resources for its own purposes (government consumption) or for transfer payments among citizens for collective social purposes (social security). As a government increases expenditures beyond its core functions and the provision of key public goods, it necessarily reduces the level of economic freedom in a society. It also hinders economic development in at least three other ways. First, extension beyond the core activities will most likely be detrimental to its delivery of core public goods and services, which most benefit the poor.[1] This is especially true for low-income countries with little institutional and administrative capacity. Second, increased expenditures in noncore activities will tend to be regressive and benefit higher-income groups, rather than the poor. Third, public expenditures that substitute for private-sector outlays are likely to be less efficient in producing the kinds of goods and services that people want in the long run. More than the size of government, it is the quality and efficiency of government expenditures in its core functions that are key to creating the enabling environment for growth-promoting investment in human and physical capital.

The financing of government expenditures—even when limited to the core functions of the state—also affects human rights and economic development. States typically levy a wide range of taxes on individuals or associations of individuals (e.g., corporations) on their income, wealth, and transactions (both domestic and international); they inflate away part of their liabilities (inflation tax); issue bills, bonds, and other debt instruments both domestically and internationally; and from time to time accumulate domestic and external payment arrears or even default on their obligations. All these financing devices tend to discriminate against individuals, whether residents or nonresidents, within and across generations and to badly distort economic incentives. Eventually, the normative approach to taxation is fraught with unintended consequences and the overall effect of the state finance on economic growth, poverty, and income redistribution becomes largely unknown and unobservable.[2] In particular, the greatest gap in knowledge seems to relate to the incidence question: who in a given tax system really bears the burden of taxation? Notwithstanding the lack of transparency and apparent complexity of state-financing devices, the analytical issue of state finance boils down to that of taxation, primarily the issue of current vs. future taxation (debt) and explicit vs. implicit taxation (inflation tax).

All coercive taxation is a prima facie interference with economic freedom and the right of enjoyment of property. Although the right to property is largely muted in international human rights law,[3] to be deprived of one's property by means of taxation or expropriation, including inflation, constitutes a fundamental threat to economic freedom. Yet as we have seen, to protect freedom itself and to enjoy the use of a number of goods and services that the market may find difficult to provide, the state cannot avoid levying taxes to finance its core functions. While still a potential breach of the right not to be deprived of property,[4] coercive taxation would need to satisfy other human rights principles, most notably the principles of non-discrimination and equity. These principles also refer to the ability-to-pay and benefit principles of taxation, according to which people should be taxed according to the benefit they receive from the government services financed by the tax revenues raised. Taxation must be imposed according to law, it must serve a valid purpose in the interest of the general public, and the provisions adopted must be a reasonable and proportionate means to achieve that end. Given that all citizens stand to benefit from the core functions of the state as discussed earlier, the main issue for discussion becomes that of the ability-to-pay principle, or what is sometimes referred to as the fairness of the tax system.

The fairness of taxation is usually discussed in terms of two concepts of equity: (a) horizontal equity—the equal treatment of equals; and (b) vertical equity—the unequal tax treatment of unequals. While horizontal equity is essentially agnostic about the distribution of wealth in society, vertical equity provides the moral rationale to achieve distributive justice. Although each concept has a voluminous literature that raises either philosophically complex and/or technically demanding questions (Zee 2005),[5] a human rights approach to fair taxation would tend to resonate with the concept of horizontal equity. Indeed, although all human beings are intrinsically unique (both genetically and culturally) and therefore unequal in many respects, the human rights philosophy is to consider and treat all (responsible) human unequals as equal human beings, regardless of their various individual determinisms and capabilities.[6] In terms of tax policy, this means that although human beings are unequal in their financial capabilities, they are considered as equal human beings to be treated equally according to the principle of nondiscrimination.[7] As opposed to vertical equity and its complex, costly, and opaque system of social redistribution, the concept of horizontal equity has the additional advantage of making the tax system simpler, more efficient, and more transparent—three other major features limiting the threat of taxation on human rights.

Although fair taxation involves equal individuals' making an equal "sacrifice" (loss of utility) to finance the core functions of the state, the operationalization of the concept of fairness in the sense of horizontal equity requires a clarification of the exact meaning of equal sacrifice, that is, an equal absolute sacrifice (poll tax), an equal proportional sacrifice (linear tax), or an equal marginal sacrifice (nonlinear tax). As we have seen, a progressive income tax, whereby citizens and corporations with higher incomes pay tax at a higher rate than those with lower incomes, threatens individual freedom and self-reliance, violates the human rights principle of nondiscrimination, and abridges the benefit principle of taxation. Not to mention that, from a utilitarian viewpoint, high tax rates foster tax avoidance and evasion to the point of nullifying in many instances the intended progressivity of the tax system (Owens and Hamilton 2004). At the other extreme, a poll or head tax (a tax of a uniform, fixed amount per individual) fully satisfies the benefit principle as people pay only for the public goods and services they consume from society. Since people consume roughly the same amount of public goods and services (e.g., national defense, police, public transport infrastructure, basic health and education, and policy formulation) regardless of their wealth or earnings, the rationale of the poll tax is to levy the same absolute amount of taxes on citizens. While the poll tax would not seem to be inconsistent with human rights principles,[8] it would not ensure, however, that people in similar income circumstances (i.e., equals in terms of income) bear equal tax burdens. This could be ensured only by a linear or flat tax, where all taxable entities in a class (typically either citizens or corporations) are taxed at the same rate as a proportion of income.

If one were to seek an argument for linearity from the optimal tax literature, IMF economists Keen, Kim, and Varsano (2006) observe that it would be that since views and circumstances point in principle to quite different forms of nonlinearity,[9] and we have relatively little idea about which best represent reality, linearity may be a reasonable choice.[10] The principle of equity embodied in a flat tax is that every taxpayer pays taxes in direct proportion to his income. As incomes double, triple, or grow tenfold, tax obligations rise accordingly. Those who earn more pay more, while low-income families are generally exempted.[11] Also, given its overall simple administration, a flat tax system increases the likelihood that people in similar *ex ante* income circumstances actually support equal *ex post* tax burdens. It makes the "price" of government more visible to average citizens.[12] More than any other alternative therefore, the flat tax would meet the tests of equity, transparency, efficiency, predictability, simplicity, and, more generally, human rights consistency.[13]

Taxation—including a flat tax system—distorts incentives and leads to economic inefficiencies and welfare losses.[14] In general, the higher the tax rate, the narrower the tax base, the larger the distortions, inefficiencies, and welfare losses. High tax rates reduce incentives for work, entrepreneurial activity, and capital formation, thereby adversely affecting national output and the standard of living.[15] High tax rates also increase incentives for tax evasion, corruption, and underground activities. Tax loopholes and shelters in the form of exemptions (e.g., allowance for each member of a taxpaying household), deductions (e.g., mortgage interest, charitable contributions, and so on), exclusions (e.g., retirement contributions), and credits (sums that can be credited against tax liabilities) have the effect of narrowing the tax base and directing resources to investments designed to generate deductions (e.g., real estate) rather than to produce goods and services. This is much the same as the government's reimbursing those taxpayers (often special-interest groups) to conduct these unproductive activities.[16] As economics professor Steven Landsburg (1993, p. 67) so crisply put it, ''The true economic cost of a taxation is that people take costly actions to avoid it, and these actions benefit nobody.''[17]

Although there seems to be a strong congruence between the economic arguments in favor of low, broad-based taxation and the human rights principle of equality and nondiscrimination, human rights seem rather agnostic on the nature of the taxable base. Is a corporate income tax more pro–human rights than a consumption tax (e.g., value-added tax)? From a rights-based approach to development, the only thing that should matter is that individuals (consumers, investors, stockholders, interest and dividend earners, or a combination of these) should not be discriminated against on the basis of their status and that the tax system be conducive to achieving the highest possible economic growth. The first point to make is that only individuals can bear the burden of taxes. A corporate income tax should not be seen as a tax on some anonymous entity. Although the corporate income tax is collected from the owners of the business, its true incidence lies with stockholders and owners of capital through depressed rates of return, consumers through higher prices, workers in the form of lower wages, or some combination of these groups. Accordingly, the corporate income tax, while possibly a useful tax collection device from a tax administration standpoint, is largely opaque on its final effect on individuals and therefore at odds with human rights principles.[18] In the final analysis, behind the corporate veil stand only people; individuals are taxed, not businesses.

The second point to make is that exempting savings from taxation generally encourages investment and economic growth. The usual justification for a consumption tax rests on its built-in incentives to save and invest. For those who worry that a consumption tax would be especially regressive and unfair because it is unrelated to income levels, it should be noted that a consumption tax is nothing but a flat tax on income net of savings. Both encourage investment and discourage consumption. Human rights practitioners could remain agnostic in principle about the comparative merits of a broad-based consumption tax and a flat tax on income net of savings. There is no need for both and the one to keep is essentially an empirical question, one that depends on the capacity of the institutional tax administration and other country-specific characteristics. Given the considerable difficulties that developing countries experience in levying an effective personal income tax, a broad-based consumption tax, such as a modern value-added tax, with a single tax rate in the 15–20 percent range and the broadest possible coverage of goods and services, is usually considered to be the most effective and fair income taxation (Ebrill and others 2001).

Monetary Policy

Monetary policy is the other main instrument of macroeconomic policymaking by which the state, through the process of managing a country's money supply, can weaken or strengthen a free society and affect its economic development. It involves setting the level of interest rates, the supply of money, and other monetary parameters (e.g., reserve requirements for banks) to achieve certain goals, such as containing inflation, promoting economic growth, or achieving full employment. Given that the state's power over money is a potent coercive tool for controlling and shaping the economy,[19] the conduct of monetary policy inevitably interferes with human rights. However, contrary to a view occasionally held by human rights advocates and others,[20] this interference has little to do with pursuing price stability, establishing an independent central bank, or limiting the amount of central bank financing available for government spending. The real threat to human rights is that a sovereign's discretion in monetary matters can erode the value of property held in monetary instruments and confiscate people's wealth through inflation, notably unexpected inflation.

When governments use money creation to finance expenditures, they are in effect expropriating the property and violating the economic freedom of their citizens. They are also breaching the principle

115

of nondiscrimination, as the poor are most heavily taxed in an inflationary environment. From time immemorial, the control of money has enabled sovereigns to exact heavy taxes from the populace. As John Maynard Keynes (1919, p. 235) observed, "By a continuing process of inflation, governments can confiscate, secretly and unobserved, an important part of the wealth of their citizens." Short of removing the control of the money supply from the government's hands altogether,[21] the main issue becomes one of establishing the kind of institutional monetary arrangement that will "enable government to exercise responsibility for money, yet at the same time limit the power thereby given to government and prevent this power from being used in ways that will tend to weaken rather than strengthen a free society" (M. Friedman 1962, p. 39).

The fundamental function performed by a monetary framework is to facilitate monetary exchange while preserving the trust in price stability, or, more precisely, in the predictability of the future price level. In a free-market economy, the price system is a key public good. It allows scarce resources to be allocated to their most productive use. Prices act as signals to economic agents (e.g., producers and consumers, workers and entrepreneurs, lenders and borrowers, and so on) by conveying information that would otherwise be prohibitively costly to obtain. As Friedrich Hayek (1948) put it, "We must look at the price system as . . . a mechanism for communicating information if we want to understand its real function—a function which, of course, it fulfills less perfectly as prices grow more rigid." Monetary frameworks that jeopardize the integrity of the price system will therefore hinder the freedom of exchange. In particular, high rates of monetary growth invariably lead to high and volatile rates of inflation, which, in turn, distort relative prices, resulting in the misallocation of resources, alteration in the fundamental terms of long-term contracts, and making it virtually impossible for individuals and businesses to plan, save, and invest sensibly for the future. Similarly, when governments mandate wage, price, and interest rate controls, including futile attempts to rein in inflation, they further inhibit information, restrict economic activity, and curtail economic freedom.

While it is generally accepted that inflation has a negative effect on medium- and long-term economic growth,[22] the exact threshold above which inflation significantly slows growth has been the subject of theoretical and empirical debate.[23] A number of empirical studies have tested the possibility of a nonlinear relationship between inflation and long-run growth; that is, a positive relationship at low rates of inflation and a negative one above a certain threshold (Fischer 1993). While it has been difficult to pinpoint the exact inflation threshold above which inflation negatively affects growth, it is generally found in the low single digits for industrial countries and in the high single digits for developing or transition economies.[24]

Although there is no single accepted theory of the right monetary institutions to deliver low inflation in a free society, the evolution of monetary frameworks during the last few decades provides useful lessons on the institutional arrangements best able to protect people from monetary policy abuses.[25]

First, rules are better than discretion in monetary policymaking. With the abandonment of the gold standard in the mid-1970s, and as developments in the macroeconomic environment, economic theory, and popular preferences unfolded, institutional frameworks based on monetary rules (i.e., monetary aggregates or exchange rate anchors) emerged as superior to discretion-based monetary frameworks as a way of protecting people and their monetary assets from surprise inflation (Barro and Gordon 1983; Kydland and Prescott 1977). Notably, among rules-based frameworks, exchange rate anchors have proved particularly popular among developing countries for keeping inflation expectations in check (see the discussion on exchange rate below).

Second, credibility is even more important than rules in monetary policymaking. Given that preannounced rules are not always necessarily credible, monetary frameworks in the last 25 years have aimed at establishing credible institutional mechanisms for convincing private agents that discretion in monetary management would not be exploited by those in charge of monetary policy, whether to achieve transitory welfare gains, or to pursue private interests, such as electoral gains or seigniorage revenue (Cottarelli and Giannini 1997). Although credibility is a rather elusive notion, countries have sought to establish this long-run anti-inflationary commitment in various ways but most prominently through the delegation of monetary policy to an independent central bank or to an outside source of credibility (e.g., International Monetary Fund–supported programs),[26] through a front-loaded investment in an anti-inflationary reputation on the part of the monetary authorities, and/or through the increased accountability and transparency of the monetary policy process (Schelling 1982). In particular, making a nation's central bank institutionally independent of the rest of the executive with sole responsibility for setting policy instruments to maintain price stability has proved to be an effective way of freeing the central banks in many developed countries of any obligation to finance either the government or government-controlled bodies and to foster people's access to sound money with apparently no cost in economic growth, or growth variability (Alesina and Summers 1993).

Credible institutional arrangements to deliver low inflation are more difficult to establish in developing countries, especially when the rule of law is flouted and financial markets are undeveloped. In authoritarian regimes, the delegation of monetary power to an independent domestic institution would simply be noncredible and therefore ineffective (Elster 1994). Similarly, most developing countries with undeveloped and unreactive financial markets would find it hard to establish and maintain an anti-inflationary reputation. However, even when the monetary authorities lack a clear framework, mandate, or credibility to pursue price stability as their primary monetary policy objective, it is still crucial that people's access to sound currency be preserved and property rights protected. Banks should be allowed to offer savings and checking accounts in foreign currencies, and citizens should be able to open foreign bank accounts.

Central banks and governments are also responsible for fostering the soundness of the banking system and ensuring the smooth operation of the financial system. The expansion in the variety of intermediaries and financial transactions has major benefits, which include reducing the transaction costs of investing, expanding access to capital, allowing more diverse opinions to be expressed in the marketplace, and permitting better risk sharing (Rajan 2005). While these changes have made society better off, they have also created opportunities to make things worse; hence the importance of the government's prudential supervision and regulation aimed at ensuring the stability and soundness of the financial system. The prudential regulation and supervision of banks and other financial services (e.g., on capital adequacy, asset quality, earnings and profitability, liquidity, sensitivity to market risk, and so on) fall under the duty of a government to enforce contracts, ensure that banks and other financial institutions do not behave recklessly or fraudulently, and protect citizens against systemic risks. As for central banking, the establishment of an independent financial services agency is a credibility-enhancing device aimed at ensuring that the state will not manipulate regulatory tools to effect political goals, such as reelecting the current government. However, like with all government regulations, bank regulation should remain mindful of the risk of regulatory failure. Barth, Caprio, and Levine (2006) observe that, although much bank regulation is introduced for the best of reasons—for instance, to tackle market failures such as bank runs—it tends to be written without due consideration for the risk of regulatory failure. As a result, such failure often occurs and frequently has worse consequences than the market failings it is supposed to address.[27]

The government's prudential regulation of the financial system should not be confused with the burdensome government restrictions that interfere with the market provision of financial services to consumers. It is the latter, not the former, that interferes with economic freedom. While the effective prudential regulation and supervision of the financial system require a degree of control and coercion by the state, it is important that the state's coercive power in this area not be used in ways that weaken rather than strengthen a free society. In most countries, notably developing countries with undeveloped financial markets, banks provide the essential financial services that facilitate economic growth; that is, they furnish a safe place in which individuals can keep their earnings (time and savings deposits), lend money to start businesses, purchase homes, and secure credit that is used to buy durable consumer goods. The more banks are restricted coercively by the state in their asset and liability management (e.g., mandatory requirement to hold government paper, finance state-owned enterprises, extend subsidized credits, and so on), the less free they are to engage in profitable activities and to channel savings toward their most profitable uses (Beach and Miles 2005). In particular, public banks, like other state-owned commercial enterprises, do not respond to market incentives and play by rules that are highly discriminatory. Similarly, the more governments interfere with the pricing of assets and intervene in the stock market and other nonbanking parts of the financial services industry (i.e., mutual funds, pension funds, hedge funds, insurance companies, and other forms of private equity), the less free investors are to allocate capital resources to their highest valued uses.

Some critics have pointed out that institutional devices aimed at limiting the government's policy space, such as an independent central bank or independent financial services agency, run into a conceptual difficulty as they can conflict with people's will and the democratic process. Given that institutional devices aim at improving economic performance by raising the costs for policymakers deviating from the institutionalized policy course, one may question the legitimacy of such devices when there is a democratic majority in favor of the deviation's desirability. As noted by IMF economists Cottarelli and Giannini (1997), if the inflation bias is ultimately rooted in democratic policymaking, as is widely agreed to be the case (M. Smith 1992), how can democratic institutions be expected to enforce the set of rules meant to eradicate the inflation bias itself?[28] Although the answers are usually rooted in a positive argument about the need to educate people about the economic superiority of the institutional arrangement in question, a more immediate answer would simply be to recognize the fundamental obligation of democracies to protect civil and political rights and economic freedom in all circumstances. In the same way that a society committed to preserving human rights cannot simply decide to violate people's right to life, freedom of association, and freedom of the press on the basis of a mere democratic majority ruling, it can no more threaten the fundamental elements of freedom of exchange and the right to property.

Exchange Rate Policy

A country's exchange arrangement is another important dimension of macroeconomic policymaking that affects human rights and development. The exchange arrangement determines the nature of the exchange rate regime and the scope of exchange controls on international transactions (e.g., exports, imports, remittances, foreign direct investment, and other capital transactions). Although the choice of an exchange rate regime per se is unlikely to have any major effect on human rights—unless the regime leads to a major crisis—the extension of exchange controls can severely reduce economic freedom. Again, contrary to the popular view, the threat to human rights is not in the international liberalization and free movement of capital, but in the very foreign exchange regulations constraining people's freedom to exchange currencies.[29]

From an economic standpoint, there is a strong theoretical presumption about the potential benefits of integration into global capital markets—including the benefits of allowing foreign competition in the financial sector (Fischer 1998). Greater financial integration, especially in the form of foreign direct investment, would provide improved technology and management techniques, as well as access to international networks, all of which would further increase productivity and growth. It could also increase market discipline and facilitate the diversification of risks, thereby leading to a more efficient allocation of capital and higher productivity growth. Although empirical macroeconomic analysis has yet to yield robust, conclusive results on the effects of financial globalization for developing countries (Eichengreen 2002),[30] there appears to be empirical support that developing countries can take a number of steps to increase the benefits from capital account liberalization and reduce the risks— such as preserving macroeconomic stability, building strong institutions, improving the quality of governance, strengthening financial systems, enacting sound regulations and prudential supervision, and, more generally, enforcing a strong rule of law (Prasad and others 2003).

Exchange controls are nothing more than a ring fence within which governments can expropriate people's property (Hanke 1999).[31] First, the imposition of restrictions on making payments and transfers for current and capital international transactions considerably narrows economic opportunities for residents and nonresidents alike and lowers the net present value of income that could be derived from domestic and foreign assets, thereby reducing people's wealth. Second, varying degrees of restrictions on external current and capital transactions are by definition highly discriminatory and create multitier currency markets prone to black market premium, crony capitalism, and corruption. Third, exchange controls, like most government discriminatory actions, are subject to unintended consequences. They tend to promote rather than obstruct capital flight, as asset holders seek to preserve the foreign-denominated value of their assets, further compounding the problem. In addressing the symptoms rather than the cause of the problem—which often lies in the unsustainability of the authorities' macroeconomic policy mix—

exchange controls have the effect of delaying difficult policy correc-
tions and contributing to the accumulation of macroeconomic
imbalances.[32]

In contrast to exchange control, human rights can be rather agnostic about the choice of an exchange rate regime, insofar as the regime
protects the freedom to exchange currencies (i.e., full convertibility).[33]
The greater the overall flexibility of the economy, the less likely it
is for any exchange rate system to have a major effect on human
welfare, unless that system leads to a major crisis (Stockman 2000).
This being said, the actual policy choice of many countries is de facto
restricted by Mundell's impossible trinity—the fact that a country
cannot, at the same time, have a fixed exchange rate, capital mobility,
and monetary policy dedicated to domestic goals. In a free society,
that is, in an environment of full capital mobility, countries must
choose between a fixed exchange rate (i.e., hard pegs) or an independent monetary policy (i.e., free float), the so-called corner solutions.
Indeed, in practice, intermediate exchange rate regimes representing
a variety of soft-pegging exchange rate arrangements have proved
unsustainable and prone to crisis (Fischer 2001).[34] They give the
illusion of flexibility and autonomy (e.g., through capital controls
or discrete monetary intervention) with the effect of delaying adjust-
ments in the real exchange rate and causing extensive economic and
social damage when the crisis erupts.

Although fixed and floating exchange arrangements appear to be
dissimilar, they are both free-market mechanisms for international
payments (Hanke 1999). Under both regimes, market forces act to
automatically rebalance financial flows and avert balance-of-
payment crises. Under a floating rate, the exchange rate automatically adjusts to preserve external viability, with the degree of
the exchange rate change reflecting the tightness of monetary and
fiscal policies. Under a fixed-rate regime, money supply automatically adjusts to preserve external viability, with the extent of the
adjustment in money supply and interest rates reflecting changes
in the country's foreign exchange position, itself reflecting the tightness of fiscal policy. Both regimes allow the economy to adjust
continuously to its environment through gradual changes in the real
exchange rate. Eventually, they are more likely to be sustainable
and politically acceptable than pegged regimes.[35] The choice between
a hard peg and floating arrangement depends therefore on the characteristics of the economy, including its size, its inflationary history,

and the nature of its potential shocks. A hard peg makes sense for countries with a long history of monetary instability, dominant money demand shocks, and/or for small open economies closely integrated in both their capital and current account transactions with the rest of the world.

For low-income countries, the choice between a fixed and floating exchange arrangement is usually further constrained by difficulties in conducting an effective monetary policy.[36] Few low-income countries have the institutional monetary arrangements and depth of financial system necessary to effectively control money supply and inflation. Exchange rate movements directly affect the price level, and money velocity is difficult to predict (owing to the important role played by monetary assets as a store of value in undeveloped financial environments). Accordingly, the exchange rates tend to exhibit a tighter relation with inflation than monetary aggregates, and hard pegs become the most natural regime for preserving financial stability. Furthermore, the choice of a fixed exchange rate regime may be explained by political and external sector factors that go beyond the monetary sphere and the role of these hard pegs as credibility-enhancing devices (S. Edwards 1995). Changes in the exchange rate may have a powerful effect on the wealth of domestic citizens and on the allocation of resources, which may have not only economic but also political effects. Policymakers in most developing countries are therefore usually concerned with the behavior of the exchange rate, which is seen as a target in itself, irrespective of monetary policy considerations (Cottarelli and Giannini 1997).

Competition and Trade Policy

Competition and trade policy delineate the freedom of exchange within and across national boundaries, which, in turn, directly affect human rights and development. Provided that the exchange between two parties does not adversely affect a third party,[37] any restriction on the free will of individuals to enter into a mutually beneficial exchange—domestic or international—should be regarded as a threat to human rights and economic growth. Contrary to a view expressed by the Office of the High Commissioner on Human Rights (OHCHR 2003) and other human rights advocates, human rights ought not to be neutral with regard to trade liberalization or trade protectionism. At the national level, government restrictions that prevent the functioning of a single market, where competition is free and undistorted, constitute a threat to the principle of freedom of exchange and nondiscrimination. Similarly, at the international level, trade restrictions in the form of tariff and nontariff barriers (e.g., quotas, licenses, marketing restrictions, exchange rate controls) and preferential trade agreements or regimes have the effect of limiting, reducing, or delaying the ability of individuals to pursue their economic goals and constitute a similar threat to the principle of freedom of exchange and nondiscrimination.[38]

Ironically, while trade liberalization and the pursuit of open trade are often presented as threats to human rights by anti-globalization activists and others,[39] it is the very restrictions and discriminations that liberalization seeks to remove that constitute the true threat to human rights. The degree to which government hinders access to the free flow of domestic and international trade discourages individuals from applying their talents and skills in a manner that they know or believe will be better for them. In addition, it limits consumers' choices, thereby also limiting their well-being. These threats are not limited to the freedom to trade in goods and services, but encompass restrictions on the free flow of capital, technological knowledge, know-how, and ideas more generally.

Freedom of exchange is also a conduit to promoting all other dimensions of freedom. As pointed out by Sykes (2003), openness to trade likely begets a higher rate of interchange of ideas and information among countries. In turn, as people in nations with fewer rights and freedoms become aware of conditions elsewhere, internal pressures for improvement may grow. Isolated societies, by contrast, may be more subject to human rights abuses. Empirical evidence tends to confirm the positive link between openness of trade, the level of civil liberties and political rights, and democracy (Hamilton 2002). Looking at the spatial dependence in economic freedom between geographic neighbors and trade partners, Sobel and Leeson (2007) found evidence that economic freedom does indeed spread through both geography and trade, but modestly.[40] By liberalizing their trade with foreign nations, economically free countries can exert at least a modest positive effect on economic freedom in less free nations. In turn, the more trade there is between two states or the more they are economically interdependent, the less likely military conflict between them becomes. From a human rights perspective, the avoidance of war is a paramount concern, given the frequency of human rights abuses and war crimes committed during conflicts. Whether assessed by financial market openness, trade, or property rights, economic freedom contributes to peace (Gartzke 2005; Harrelson-Stephens and Callaway 2001).

Freedom of exchange is not only an end to advance human rights but also a means to spur economic growth and reduce poverty. With freedom of exchange, individuals are able to produce more and achieve a higher income level than would otherwise be possible. Since Ricardo (1817), most economists would agree that "there is essentially only one argument for free trade or freer trade, but it is an exceedingly powerful one, namely: free trade promotes a mutually profitable division of labor, greatly enhances the potential real national product of all nations, and makes possible higher standards of living all over the globe" (Samuelson 1973, p. 651). Trade liberalization promotes economic growth by raising productivity through static and dynamic gains from trade. Static gains accrue through a more efficient allocation of resources as lower trade restrictions reduce the bias against investment in the tradable goods and services sectors of the economy,[41] and through economies of scale to producers of exported goods and services who benefit from increased market opportunities abroad. Dynamic gains accrue from faster rates of capital accumulation and technical progress that are encouraged when the economy is opened up to increased competition as well as to flows of knowledge and investment from abroad (WTO 2005). Openness is particularly important for developing economies and less populous countries. These propositions have been confirmed by an amount of seminal empirical research showing that more open trading systems experience higher rates of economic growth.[42] Trade liberalization can promote not only faster economic growth, but also more robust economic growth that helps improve the economy's resilience to external shocks and its capacity to service external debt. In particular, it was observed that the predictability provided by the multilateral trading system helped ensure that the emerging markets' financial crisis of the late 1990s did not degenerate into a trade shock for the economies that were affected (WTO 2002).

While open economies tend to invest more, exchange more ideas, and grow faster, it is also widely recognized that openness to trade is an opportunity for development, not a guarantee. Trade liberalization is rarely implemented in isolation and needs to be accompanied by other policy reforms. In particular, as noted earlier, without a strong institutional framework, including respect of property rights and the rule of law, it is unlikely that the development benefits of freedom of exchange can be reaped in many instances. Indeed, a positive (two-way) relationship seems to exist between openness to trade and the quality of institution. Rodrik, Subramanian, and Francesco (2002) find that trade does not so much affect income level and growth directly as indirectly through its positive effect on institutional quality.[43] Professor Alan Winters (2004) observes that trade liberalization is unlikely to boost economic growth in an economic environment that is not conducive to investment. He identifies corruption and lack of, or poor-quality, trade-related institutions as particular obstacles to raising growth and notes that trade liberalization can itself contribute to the fight against corruption, because the less restrictive, more transparent and nondiscretionary trade policy is, the lower the incentives and opportunities for corruption. This reflects the fact that restrictions on freedom of exchange give rise to rents and rent-seeking behaviors of a variety of forms. Even when rent seeking does not directly take the form of bribery, corruption, smuggling, or black markets, it is detrimental to economic growth, as people use their energy and creativeness to compete for rents instead of creating value added.[44]

From a development perspective, the pursuit of freedom of exchange is best achieved through the realization of reciprocal and nondiscriminatory open trade at the multilateral level. While issues related to the relationship between trade and development are at the core of the current round of multilateral trade liberalization under the Doha Development Agenda, these issues have unfortunately not been addressed exclusively with the aim of creating a rules-based multilateral trading system free of distortions and discriminations. In particular, although the current level of trade distortion and discrimination in developing and least developed countries is one factor explaining their lack of development, a number of these countries have sought to avoid or delay liberalization commitments in the current negotiations, calling instead for special and differential treatment, protection of the home market, preferences on export markets, or policy space.[45] However, adding new distortions and discriminations to an already loaded system would just have the effect of further restraining the freedom of exchange of many poor people in developing countries, thereby maintaining them in poverty. Like technological progress (albeit to a much lower degree), trade liberalization is both a challenge to the economic and societal status quo and the engine of development. In the same way that it is self-defeating to refuse the advance of technological progress or to introduce it only gradually (based on some bureaucratic notion of what constitutes the right form, pace, and sequencing), it is also self-defeating to slow trade liberalization and to ignore its potential macroeconomic benefits because of its possible adverse effect on some individuals and groups in the short run.[46]

Arguably, a Doha Round agreement that would be supportive of human rights and development would have three main features. It would remove all forms of foreign barriers to trade for products originating in poor countries; lower all forms of domestic barriers that raise the prices and reduce the variety of goods and services consumed by firms and households in poor countries; and support the adoption of complementary regulations and institutions to enhance development, all the while avoiding burdening developing countries with unaffordable implementation costs (Hoekman 2005). In that sense, most Doha Round simulations suggest that developing countries—both as a whole and most subgroups—have much to gain from an ambitious Doha outcome. The lion's share of these gains would result from liberalization by and among developing countries themselves. From this perspective, a strategy that focuses on avoiding liberalization commitments would seem counterproductive. Trade liberalization is not a concession and economic development is not a zero-sum game. As already noted, those countries that have taken most advantage of the international economy are also the ones that have experienced the greatest advances in poverty reduction (Gwartney, Skipton, and Lawson 2001).

Other Macroeconomic Policies

States are responsible for a host of other macroeconomic policies with a bearing on human rights and economic development. Most of these policies are associated with government regulation of economic sectors (i.e., agriculture, industry, and services), economic agents (i.e., producers, consumers, workers, entrepreneurs, and so on), and economic spaces (i.e., local, national, regional). Restrictive or prohibitive regulations of product and factor markets are likely to threaten human rights and to impinge on the free character of society. Certainly, as pointed out by Friedrich Hayek as early as 1944 (p. 95): "Economic control is not merely control of a sector of human life which can be separated from the rest; it is the control of the means for all our ends. And whoever has sole control of the means must also determine which ends are to be served, which values are to be rated higher and which lower—in short, what men should believe or strive for."

From an economic standpoint, government regulations can be assimilated to a form of taxation and, like taxation, can run the risk beyond a certain threshold of distorting economic incentives and discriminating against individuals, both residents and nonresidents, within and across sectors and regions. When government regulations provide for the necessary basic institutional infrastructure to strengthen a free society and are applied evenly, transparently, and predictably, they ensure the "rules of the game" and help establish the necessary level playing field for a market economy to flourish. Sound regulation and supervision also address the market failures and externalities present in some sectors and therefore provide an important public good. However, when regulations and restrictions are excessive, when they are applied selectively, nontransparently, and inconsistently, they have the effect of discriminating among individuals, stimulating rent-seeking behaviors, fostering the informal economy, and supporting corruption. Eventually, the overall effect of government regulations on economic growth and income redistribution is likely to be unknown, unobservable, and fraught with unintended consequences. While it is beyond the scope of this book to go over the range of sectoral economic policies and outcomes that are shaped by government controls and regulations (e.g., agriculture, fisheries, energy, telecommunications, financial services, and so on), it could still be illustrative to elaborate on two areas of government intervention critical to economic freedom and prosperity: the business climate and the employment climate.

A good investment climate provides opportunities and incentives for firms—from microenterprises to multinationals—to invest productively, create jobs, and expand. In turn, private firms provide the goods and services needed to sustain life; improve living standards; and progressively achieve various economic, social, and cultural goals. The investment climate is thus key for economic growth and poverty reduction.[47] Governments influence the investment climate through the effects of various regulations on economic freedom and economic competition. In particular, government regulations affect the costs, risks, and barriers to competition facing firms. The World Bank (2005) estimates that the costs of contract enforcement difficulties, inadequate infrastructure, crime, corruption, and burdensome regulation could amount to over 25 percent of sales—or more than three times what firms typically pay in taxes. Costs also have a time dimension, for example, the time needed to obtain a license and register a new company or business, to clear goods through customs, and to obtain basic infrastructure.[48] More generally, the time taken to navigate red tape may be the most detrimental to growth. Heightened risks to businesses related to policy uncertainty, macroeconomic instability, and arbitrary regulation also mask opportunities and freeze incentives to invest.[49] In addition to high costs and risks, government regulation can influence barriers to competition directly through their regulation of market entry and exit and their response to anti-competitive behavior by firms. In sum, to foster a pro–human rights, pro-development investment climate, developing countries should strive to streamline excessive government regulations and tackle the various sources of policy failures related to the regulatory environment of firms.

In the same way, a sound employment climate should help people get a job—whether through self-employment or from wages—so they can work their way out of poverty.[50] While it is usually considered that the labor market will not function well without proper institutions (Blanchard 2004),[51] labor-market regulations have come to exemplify what can go wrong with government regulation and restrictions. First, many types of labor-market regulations and institutions infringe on the economic freedom of employees and employers to enter into voluntary contracts. The right to attempt to earn a living is one of the most basic human rights. Any law that restricts this ability or prevents people from voluntarily selling their own labor violates this right. As noted long ago, "The property which every man has is his own labour, as it is the original foundation of all other property, so it is the most sacred and inviolable" (A. Smith 1776, p. 143). Among the more prominent threats to the right to work are minimum wages, limits on working hours, dismissal regulations, centralized wage setting, extensions of union contracts to nonparticipating parties, unemployment benefits that undermine the incentive to accept employment, labor tax distortions, and conscription. When employers and employees are not free to engage in collective bargaining free of government interference, contract rights are violated.

129

The rights of either the workers or the employers are violated if some law prevents them from giving or receiving something they would otherwise be inclined to give or receive.[52] In that sense, well-intentioned affirmative action programs to remedy racial, gender, or class inequalities in employment should be seen for what they are: policy-induced discrimination, that breach the equality principle in human rights, especially when these policies are perpetuated. Not only is the theory of affirmative action flawed from a human rights perspective but also such programs have in practice at best negligible effect on the groups they are intended to assist (Sowell 2005).

Second, although regulation of labor markets is usually intended to help workers, the economic consequences of these often ill-designed regulations are to discourage firms from creating jobs and workers from seeking them, to segment the labor market, to create structural unemployment, to distort the determination of labor costs, to lower labor-market participation, to create regional disparities, and to contribute to a swelling of the informal workforce (which often lacks statutory protection), not to mention the broader noneconomic adverse effect of mass unemployment on the individuals affected, on their families, and on societies at large.[53] In other words, active labor-market policies are simply unable to raise labor standards for all peoples in a sustainable fashion—either at home or abroad (McGee and Yoon 2003). Only the persuasion of markets, technical progress, and productivity gains can do so.

Labor-market institutions that are supportive of human rights and development would thus provide the necessary regulatory framework to protect civil and political rights[54] and preserve economic freedom, including allowing market forces to determine wages and establish the conditions of dismissal, avoiding excessive unemployment benefits that undermine work incentives, eliminating labor tax distortions, and refraining from the use of conscription.[55] The restated Jobs Strategy (2006) of the Organisation for Economic Co-operation and Development provides an updated blueprint for labor-market reforms that aim at promoting economic dynamism while protecting workers' rights. Based on the experience of successful labor-market performers,[56] the four pillars of the strategy are to (a) set appropriate macroeconomic policy, (b) remove impediments to labor-market participation as well as job search, (c) tackle labor- and product-market obstacles to labor demand, and (d) facilitate the development of labor-force skills and competencies.

Conclusion

What this book has sought to demonstrate, above all else, is the centrality of freedom for both the human rights agenda and the development agenda. Although innocuous on the surface, this proposition challenges a number of human rights and development orthodoxies as well as practices developed over the last 60 years. For the human rights community, it challenges the notion that all human rights proclaimed in the various instruments of international human rights law are "interrelated, interdependent, and indivisible" for developmental purposes. It conjectures that this original inconsistency undermines the principle of freedom for all and explains why the Declaration on the Right to Development has remained an irrelevance since its inception 20 years ago. For the development community, it challenges the notion that economic development could be brought about by a grand design of social engineering that ignores or even undermines the main root of development that constitutes people's freedom. It conjectures that the debilitating outcomes of traditional development policies in many low-income countries are often the direct, albeit unintended, result of a disregard for freedom in development.

Although the energy invested by the international community in the promotion of a development agenda and a human rights agenda since the adoption of the United Nations Charter in 1945 has resulted in products that have deliberately been kept entirely separate (Alston 2004), the good news is that a reconciliation between them is conceptually possible, and actually necessary if real effect is to be given to either the human rights or the development agenda. It would require critical and uncompromising self-examination by all the actors involved—individuals, associations, civil society, states, and international institutions—on the place of freedom in their purpose. A number of development agencies have already begun to reflect the importance of economic freedom and the protection of fundamental civil and political liberties in their programs. Building on this emerging trend, as well as the daily lessons from successful emerging countries, the proposition in this book is that all development actors should engage more incisively in upstream economic policy debates that shape opinion and policy choice, including those related to the norms and values applicable in society, and embed their activities more directly into a human rights framework to promote freedom.

Mainstreaming freedom in development means that the development process is itself elevated to the exercise of freedom. It requires, first, that public institutions, whether they relate to the relationship between individuals and the state (the rule of law), individuals and their assets (the property regime), individuals and their collective choices (participation), or individuals and their representation (governance), be governed by the liberal principles of economic freedom and civil and political liberties. In turn, this implies that the scope for government actions be limited to matters for which consensus can be achieved among free individuals. Second, mainstreaming freedom in development requires the implementation of macroeconomic policies that are consistent with a free society. Whether these policies regulate the fiscal system, the monetary and exchange regime, the labor, or any other product or factor market, they would seem the most effective in the quest for inclusive and sustainable development when they protect economic freedom, notably personal choice, voluntary exchange, and the freedom to compete.

To be sure, development as freedom is no quick fix, but rather a long and winding road. Contrary to most beliefs, while classical liberal tradition has a rationalistic strain that posits man as a highly integrated will that acts purposively through time, it also incorporates human frailty, prejudice, and error into economic ideas; into the economic theory of the market process; and into the theory of government behavior. Like individuals, societies are highly prone to developing bad habits and prejudices, to erring on the side of self-delusion, but also to gradually engaging in self-reform. Indeed, the classical liberal tradition argues that liberty accords people ownership of their experience, including their errors and vices, and thereby allows them to learn the contours of action, and consequence; that liberty engenders the institutions, practices, and attitudes that heighten the individual's discovery of the worthiness of actions and of ways to refine his habits and control his impulses; and that liberty in the end simply affirms the dignity of the human being (Klein 2004).

A final point on two issues that have not been discussed in this book. The proposition made at the outset—that liberty in all its dimensions is the only matrix for thinking about development and human rights in an internally consistent and mutually supportive way—is unlikely to satisfy at least two groups of critics: those who challenge the universalist claims of human rights in the name of ethical, moral, or cultural relativism, and those who challenge the presumed objective character of human rights principles.[1]

On the former, it is true that human rights remain philosophically grounded within a mostly Western or Christian individualist moral doctrine and that its fundamental moral beliefs, principles, and practices undeniably conceive of the individual person as the principal bearer of human rights.[2] However, it is also true that the idea of freedom, or at least many of its basic precepts, are found in all the great philosophical and religious traditions, and are therefore equally relevant in non-Western settings.[3] As these cross-cultural universals, values, and beliefs (as far as fundamental freedoms are concerned) acquire wider acceptance in the global village to the detriment of moral relativism, one remains hopeful that the globalization of ideas, principles, and practices will also serve the broader utilitarian motive of economic development.[4]

As to the more epistemological critic of freedom, according to which moral principles and concept are inherently subjective in character,[5] the philosophical debate would seem to have few practical implications. While the debate on whether freedom can be rationalized by appeal to self-interest, the will, the universality of the human spirit, or something else continues unabated, the power of freedom will remain at the center of any sustainable enterprise to unite human rights and development.

References

Abed, George T. 1998. "Fiscal Reforms in Low-Income Countries: Experience under IMF-Supported Programs." Occasional Paper no. 160, International Monetary Fund, Washington. www.imf.org/external/pubs/cat/longres.cfm?sk=2609.0.

Abed, George T., and Sanjeev Gupta. 2002. *Governance, Corruption, and Economic Performance*. Washington, DC: International Monetary Fund. www.imf.org/external/pubs/cat/longres.cfm?sk=15667.0.

Acemoglu, Daron, and Simon Johnson. 2003. "Unbundling Institutions." Working Paper no. 9934, National Bureau of Economic Research, Cambridge, MA. http://web.mit.edu/sjohnson/www/attach/unbundlingfinal%20August%204%202003.pdf.

Acemoglu, Daron, and James Robinson. 2004. "Institutions as the Fundamental Cause of Long-Run Growth," Working Paper no. 10481, National Bureau of Economic Research, Cambridge, MA. www.nber.org/papers/w10481.

ActionAid. 2006. "Tackling Political Barriers to End AIDS," ActionAid International.

Alesina, Alberto, and David Dollar. 1998. "Who Gives Foreign Aid to Whom and Why?" Working Paper no. 6612, National Bureau of Economic Research, Cambridge, MA. http://papers.nber.org/papers/W6612.

Alesina, Alberto, and Lawrence H. Summers. 1993. "Central Bank Independence and Macroeconomic Performance: Some Comparative Evidence." *Journal of Money, Credit and Banking* 25 (2): 151–62. www.jstor.org/view/00222879/di975232/97p00191/0.

Alston, Philip. 1988. "Making Space for New Human Rights: The Case of the Right to Development." *Harvard Human Rights Journal* 1 (Spring): 3–40.

———. 2004. "A Human Rights Perspective on the Millennium Development Goals." Paper prepared as a contribution to the work of the Millennium Project Task Force on Poverty and Economic Development. www2.ohchr.org/english/issues/millennium-development.docs/alston.doc.

———. 2005. "Ships Passing in the Night: The Current State of the Human Rights and Development Debate Seen through the Lens of the Millennium Development Goals." *Human Rights Quarterly* 27 (3): 755–829. http://muse.jhu.edu/search/pia.cgi.

Alston, Philip, and Gerard Quinn. 1987. "The Nature and Scope of State Parties' Obligations under the International Covenant on Economic, Social and Cultural Rights." *Human Rights Quarterly* 9 (2): 156–229.

Alston, Philip, and Henry Steiner. 2000. *International Human Rights in Context: Law, Politics, Morals*. Oxford, U.K.: Oxford University Press.

An-Na'im, Abdullah A. 1990. *Toward an Islamic Reformation: Civil Liberties, Human Rights, and International Law*. Syracuse, NY: Syracuse University Press.

Annan, Kofi. 2005. "In Larger Freedom: Towards Development, Security, and Human Rights for All: Report of the Secretary General." Report presented at the 59th Session of the United Nations General Assembly, March 21, New York.

135

——— . 2006. Address of United Nations Secretary-General Kofi Annan to the Human Rights Council. Geneva: United Nations Office at Geneva.

Arbour, Louise. 2005. Statement to the Open-Ended Working Group established by the Commission on Human Rights to consider options regarding the elaboration of an optional protocol to the International Covenant on Economic, Social and Cultural Rights. www.unhchr.ch/huricane/huricane.nsf/view01/ECAE2629449C1EBCC1256F8C0035047D?opendocument.

Arnstein, Sherry R. 1969. "A Ladder of Citizen Participation." *Journal of the American Institute of Planners* 35 (4): 216–24. http://lithgow-schmidt.dk/sherry-arnstein/ladder-of-citizen-participation.html.

Arrow, Kenneth J. 1951. *Social Choice and Individual Values.* New York: Wiley.

——— . 1962. "Economic Welfare and the Allocation of Resources for Invention. In *The Rate and Direction of Inventive Activity: Economic and Social Factors.* A Conference of the Universities–National Bureau Committee for Economic Research, pp. 609–26. Princeton, NJ: Princeton University Press.

Auty, Richard M. 1993. *Sustaining Development in Mineral Economies: The Resource Curve Thesis.* New York: Routledge.

Azam, Jean-Paul, Shantayanan Devarajan, and Stephen A. O'Connell. 1999. "Aid Dependence Reconsidered." Policy Research Working Paper no. 2144, World Bank, Washington. http://econ.worldbank.org/external/default/main?pagePK=64165259&theSitePK=469382&piPK=64165421&menuPK=64166093&entityID=000094946_99073007343382.

Balcerowicz, Leszek. 2004. "Toward a Limited State." *Cato Journal* 24 (3): 185–204. www.catojournal.com/pubs/journal/cj24n3/cj24n3-1.pdf.

Bardhan, Pranab. 1993. "Symposium on Democracy and Development." *Journal of Economic Perspectives* 7 (3): 45–49.

Barro, Robert J. 1991. "Economic Growth in a Cross-Section of Countries." *Quarterly Journal of Economics* 106 (2): 407–43. http://ideas.repec.org/a/tpr/qjecon/v106y1991i2p407-43.html.

——— . 1997. *Determinants of Economic Growth: A Cross-Country Empirical Study.* Cambridge, MA: MIT Press.

——— . 2000. "Rule of Law, Democracy, and Economic Performance." In *2000 Index of Economic Freedom,* ed. Gerald O'Driscoll Jr., Kim Holmes, and Melanie Kirkpatrick, 31–49. Washington: Heritage Foundation.

Barro, Robert J., and David Gordon. 1983. "Rules, Discretion, and Reputation in a Model of Monetary Policy." *Journal of Monetary Economics* 12 (1): 101–21.

Barth, James, Gerard Caprio Jr., and Ross Levine. 2006. *Rethinking Bank Regulation: Till Angels Govern.* Cambridge, U.K.: Cambridge University Press.

Bauer, Peter T. 1976. *Dissent on Development.* Cambridge, MA: Harvard University Press.

——— . 1981. *Equality, the Third World, and Economic Delusion.* Cambridge, MA: Harvard University Press.

Beach, William, and Marc Miles. 2005. "Explaining the Factors of the Index of Economic Freedom." In *2005 Index of Economic Freedom,* 55. Washington: Heritage Foundation and Dow Jones.

Bell, Michael, Hoe Ee Khor, and Kalpana Kochhar. 1993. "China at the Threshold of a Market Economy." Occasional Paper no. 107, International Monetary Fund, Washington.

Bell, Tom W., and James V. DeLong. 2002. "The Great Debate on Intellectual Property." *Cato Policy Report* 24 (1): 8. www.catojournal.com/pubs/policy_report/v24n1/property.pdf.

Bengoa, José. 2005. "Economic, Social, and Cultural Rights: The Social Forum Report of the Chairman-Rapporteur, José Bengoa, in accordance with Sub-Commission Resolution 2004/8." Report presented at the 57th Session of the United Nations Economic and Social Council, August 2.

Bentham, Jeremy. 1816. Anarchical Fantasies in A. Melden (ed.) Human Rights (1970).

Berggren, Niclas. 2003. "The Benefits of Economic Freedom: A Survey." *Independent Review* 8 (2): 193–211. www.freetheworld.com/papers/berggren_review.pdf.

Berlin, Isaiah. 2002. "Two Concepts of Liberty." In *Liberty: Incorporating Four Essays on Liberty*, ed. Henry Hardy, pp. 166–217. Oxford, U.K.: Oxford University Press, 2002.

Bertocchi, Graziella, and Chiara Strozzi. 2005. "Citizenship Laws and International Migration in Historical Perspective." Discussion Paper no. 4737, Center for Economic Policy Research, London.

Bethell, Tom. 1998. *The Noblest Triumph: Property and Prosperity through the Ages.* New York: St Martin's Press.

Bhagwati, Jagdish. 1993. *India in Transition.* Oxford, U.K.: Clarendon.

———. 1999. "Economic Freedom: Prosperity and Social Progress." Keynote address at the Conference on Economic Freedom and Development, Tokyo. www.columbia.edu/~jb38/freedom_tokyo.pdf.

———. 2006. "A Cocktail for Success." *Wall Street Journal Europe*, February 28.

Blanchard, Olivier. 2004. "Designing Labor Market Institutions." Lecture given at the Seventh Annual Conference of the Central Bank of Chile on Labor Markets and Institutions, Santiago, Chile, November 6–7. http://econ-www.mit.edu/files/687.

Blume, Lorenz, and Stefan Voigt. 2004. "The Economic Effects of Human Rights." Working Paper no. 66/04, University of Kassel, Germany.

Boadway, Robin, Katherine Cuff, and Maurice Marchand. 2000. "Optimal Income Taxation with Quasi-Linear Preferences Revisited." *Journal of Public Economic Theory* 2 (4): 435–60.

Branstetter, Lee, and Marik Sakakibara. 2001. "Do Stronger Patents Induce More Innovation? Evidence from the 1988 Japanese Patent Law Reforms." RAND *Journal of Economics* 32 (1): 77–100.

Brunetti, Aymo, and Beatrice Weder. 1994. "Political Credibility and Economic Growth in Less Developed Countries." *Constitutional Political Economy* 5 (1): 23–43.

Bruno, Michael, and William Easterly. 1998. "Inflation Crises and Long-Run Growth." *Journal of Monetary Economics* 41 (1): 3–26.

Buchanan, James, and Gordon Tullock. 1962. *The Calculus of Consent: The Logical Foundations of Constitutional Democracy.* Ann Arbor, MI: University of Michigan Press.

Burke, Edmund. 1790. Reflections on the Revolution in France. Published by J. Dodsley.

Burke, Edmund. 1795. Thoughts and Details on Scarcity, Rivington and Hatchard.

Burnside, Craig, and David Dollar. 2000. "Aid, Policies, and Growth." *American Economic Review* 90 (4): 847–68.

Card, David, and Alan B. Krueger. 1994. "Minimum Wages and Employment: A Case Study of the Fast-Food Industry in New Jersey and Pennsylvania." *American Economic Review* 84 (4): 772–93.

Chafuen, Alejandro, and Eugenio Guzmán. 2000. "Economic Freedom and Corruption." In *2000 Index of Economic Freedom*, ed. Gerald O'Driscoll Jr., Kim Holmes, and Melanie Kirkpatrick, 51–63. Washington: Heritage Foundation.

Chauffour, Jean-Pierre. 2005. "International Accountability in Pro–Human Rights Growth Policies: The IMF Perspective." Working draft, Commission on Human Rights, Social Forum. www.ohchr.org/english/issues/poverty/docs/3sfMrChauffour IMF.pdf.

———. 2006. "Pro–Human Rights Growth Policies." *Development Outreach* (October): 12–14.

Chong, Alberto, and Cesar Calderón. 2000. "Causality and Feedback between Institutional Measures and Economic Growth." *Economics and Politics* 12 (1): 69–81.

Christoffersen, Peter F., and Peter Doyle. 1998. "From Inflation to Growth: Eight Years of Transition." Working Paper no. 98/100, International Monetary Fund, Washington. www.imf.org/external/pubs/ft/wp/wp98100.pdf.

Clemens, Michael, Steven Radelet, and Rikhil Bhavnani. 2004. "Counting Chickens When They Hatch: The Short-Term Effect of Aid on Growth." Working Paper no. 44, Center for Global Development, Washington. http://cgdev.org/content/ publications/detail/2744.

Coase, Ronald H. 1976. "Adam Smith's View of Man." In *Essays on Economics and Economists*, p. 116. Chicago: University of Chicago Press.

Cockcroft, Laurence. 1998. "Corruption and Human Rights: A Crucial Link." Working paper, Transparency International. www.transparency.org/working_papers/ cockcroft/cockcroft.html.

Cole, Julio H. 2003. "The Contribution of Economic Freedom to World Economic Growth, 1980–99." *Cato Journal* 23 (2): 189–98. www.catojournal.com/pubs/ journal/cj23n2/cj23n2-3.pdf.

Cottarelli, Carlo. 2005. "Efficiency and Legitimacy: Trade-Offs in IMF Governance." Working Paper no. 05/107, International Monetary Fund, Washington. www.imf.org/external/pubs/ft/wp/2005/wp05107.pdf.

Cottarelli, Carlo, and Curzio Giannini. 1997. "Credibility without Rules? Monetary Frameworks in the Post–Bretton Woods Era." Occasional Paper no. 154, International Monetary Fund, Washington.

Dabla-Norris, Era. 2000. "Corruption." Research Summary. *IMF Research Bulletin* 1 (3): 5–7. www.imf.org/external/Pubs/FT/irb/2000/eng/03/4a#4a.

Dabla-Norris, Era, and Scott Freeman. 1999. "The Enforcement of Property Rights and Underdevelopment." Working Paper no. 99/127, International Monetary Fund, Washington.

Dalton, Russell J., Wilhelm F. Burklin, and Andrew Drummond. 2001. "Public Opinion and Direct Democracy." *Journal of Democracy* 12 (4): 141–53.

Debrun, Xavier. 2003. "Unemployment and Labor Market Institutions: Why Reforms Pay Off." In *World Economic Outlook*, pp. 129–50. Washington: International Monetary Fund.

Demsetz, Harold. 1967. "Toward a Theory of Property Rights." *American Economic Review* 57 (2): 347–59.

de Schweinitz, Karl Jr., 1959. "Industrialization, Labor Controls, and Democracy." *Economic Development and Cultural Change* 7: 385–404.

de Soto, Hernando. 2000. *The Mystery of Capital*. New York: Bantam Press.

Diamond, Jared. 1997. *Guns, Germs, and Steel: The Fate of Human Societies*. New York: Norton.

Dichter, Thomas. 2005. "Time to Stop Fooling Ourselves about Foreign Aid: A Practitioner's View." Foreign Policy Briefing no. 86, Cato Institute, Washington. www.cato.org/pub_display.php?pub_id=4653.

Dollar, David. 1992. "Outward-Oriented Developing Economies Really Do Grow More Rapidly: Evidence from 95 LDG, 1976–95." *Economic Development and Cultural Change* 40 (April): 523–44.

Dollar, David, and Aart Kraay. 2002. "Growth Is Good for the Poor." *Journal of Economic Growth* 7 (3): 195–225. www.worldbank.org/research/growth/pdfiles/growthgoodforpoor.pdf.

Domar, Evsey. 1946. "Capital Expansion, Rate of Growth, and Employment." *Econometrica* 14 (2): 137–47.

Donnelly, Jack 1982. "Human Rights as Natural Rights." *Human Rights Quarterly* 4 (3): 391–405.

———. 1985. "In Search of the Unicorn: The Jurisprudence and Politics of the Right to Development." *California Western International Law Journal* 15: 473–509.

Downs, Anthony. 1957. *An Economic Theory of Democracy.* New York: Harper and Row.

Duflo, Esther, and Michael Kremer. 2003. "The Use of Randomization in the Evaluation of Development Effectiveness." Paper prepared for the World Bank Operations Evaluation Department, Conference on Evaluation and Development Effectiveness, July 15–16, Washington.

Dundes Renteln, Alison. 1988. "Relativism and the Search for Human Rights." *American Anthropologist* 90 (1): 56–72.

Durham, J. Benson. 1999. "Economic Growth and Political Regimes." *Journal of Economic Growth* 4 (1): 81–111.

Dworkin, R. 1977. *Taking Rights Seriously.* Cambridge, MA: Harvard University Press.

Easterly, William. 2001. *The Elusive Quest for Growth: Economists' Adventures and Misadventures in the Tropics.* Cambridge, MA: MIT Press.

———. 2003. "Can Foreign Aid Buy Growth?" *Journal of Economic Perspectives* 17 (3): 23–48.

———. 2005. "The Utopian Nightmare." *Foreign Policy* (September/October): 150.

Easterly, William, Ross Levine, and David Roodman. 2003. "New Data, New Doubts: A Comment on Burnside and Dollar's Aid, Policies, and Growth." Working Paper no. 9846, National Bureau of Economic Research, Cambridge, MA.

Easton, Stephen T., and Michael A. Walker. 1997. "Income Growth and Economic Freedom." *American Economic Review* 87 (2): 328 32.

Ebrill, Liam, Michael Keen, Jean-Paul Bodin, and Victoria Summers. 2001. *The Modern VAT.* Washington: International Monetary Fund. www.imf.org/external/pubs/nft/2001/VAT/index.htm.

Edwards, Chris, 2006. "Income Tax Rife with Complexity and Inefficiency." Tax and Budget Bulletin, no. 33, Cato Institute, Washington.

Edwards, Sebastian. 1995. "Exchange Rate Anchors and Inflation: A Political Economy Approach." In *Positive Political Economy: Theory and Evidence*, ed. Sylvester Eijffinger and Harry Huizinga. New York: Wiley.

———. 1998. "Openness, Productivity, and Growth: What Do We Really Know." *The Economic Journal* 108 (447): 393–98.

Eichengreen, Barry. 2002. "Capital Account Liberalization: What Do Cross-Country Studies Tell Us?" *World Bank Economic Review* 15 (3): 341–65.

———. 2003. *Capital Flows and Crises.* Cambridge, MA: MIT Press.

Elster, Jon. 1994. "The Impact of Constitutions on Economic Performance." Proceedings of the World Bank's Annual Conference on Development Economics, April 28–29, Washington.

Farr, W. Ken, Richard A. Lord, and J. Larry Wolfenbarger. 1998. "Economic Freedom, Political Freedom, and Economic Well-Being: A Causality Analysis." *Cato Journal* 18 (2): 247–62. www.catojournal.com/pubs/journal/cj18n2/cj18n2-5.pdf.

Finnis, John. 1980. *Natural Law and Natural Rights*. Oxford, U.K.: Clarendon Press.

Fischer, Stanley. 1983. "Inflation and Growth." Working Paper no. 1235, National Bureau of Economic Research, Cambridge, MA.

———. 1993. "The Role of Macroeconomic Factors in Growth." *Journal of Monetary Economics* 32 (3): 485–512.

———, ed. 1998. "Capital-Account Liberalization and the Role of the IMF." In *Should the IMF Pursue Capital-Account Convertibility? Essays in International Finance* no. 207, pp. 1–10. Princeton, NJ: Princeton University Press.

———. 2001. "Exchange Rate Regimes: Is the Bipolar View Correct?" Paper presented at the Meeting of the American Economic Association, January 6, New Orleans. www.imf.org/external/np/speeches/2001/010601a.htm.

Forbes, Kristin J. 2005. "Capital Controls: Mud in the Wheels of Market Efficiency." *Cato Journal* 25 (1): 153–66. www.catojournal.com/pubs/journal/cj25n1/cj25n1-16.pdf.

Frankel, Jeffrey, and David Romer, 1999. "Does Trade Cause Growth." *American Economic Review* 89 (3): 379–99.

Frankovits, André. 1995. "The Rights Way to Development: A Human Rights Approach to Development Assistance." Human Rights Council of Australia, North Sydney.

Freedom House. 2005. "Freedom in the World: The Annual Survey of Political Rights and Civil Liberties, 2005." www.freedomhouse.org/template.cfm?page= 35&year=2005.

Freeman, Richard. 2002. "Institutional Differences and Economic Performance among OECD Countries." Discussion Paper no. 557, Centre for Economic Performance, London.

Friedman, Benjamin M. 2005. *The Moral Consequences of Economic Growth*. New York: Knopf.

Friedman, Milton. 1962. *Capitalism and Freedom*. Chicago: University of Chicago Press.

Friedman, Thomas L. 2006. "The First Law of Petropolitics." *Foreign Policy* (May/ June): 28.

Fukuyama, Francis. 1992. *The End of History and the Last Man*. Washington: Free Press.

———. 2004. *State-Building: Governance and World Order in the 21st Century*. Ithaca, NY: Cornell University Press.

Gartzke, Erik. 2005. "Freedom and Peace." In *Economic Freedom of the World: 2005 Annual Report*, ed. James Gwartney and Robert Lawson, 29–44. Vancouver, BC: Fraser Institute.

Ghosh, Atish, and Steven Phillips. 1998. "Warning: Inflation May Be Harmful to Your Growth." *IMF Staff Papers* 45 (4): 672–710. www.imf.org/external/Pubs/FT/staffp/1998/12-98/pdf/ghosh.pdf.

Gilabert, Pablo. 2005. "The Duty to Eradicate Global Poverty: Positive or Negative?" *Ethical Theory and Moral Practice* 7 (5): 537–50.

Glick, Reuvan, and Michael Hutchinson. 2000. "Stopping 'Hot Money' or Signaling Bad Policy? Capital Controls and the Onset of Currency Crises." Working paper no 00-14, Economic Policy Research Unit, Department of Economics, University of Copenhagen, Copenhagen.

Goodman, Ryan, and Derek Jinks. 2003. "Measuring the Effects of Human Rights Treaties." *European Journal of International Law* 14 (1): 171–83.

Granger, Clive W. J. 1969. "Investigating Causal Relations by Econometric Models and Cross-Spectral Methods." *Econometrica* 37 (3): 424–38.

Gupta, Sanjeev, Hamid Davoodi, and Rosa Alonso-Terme. 1998. "Does Corruption Affect Income Inequality and Poverty?" Working Paper no. 98/76, International Monetary Fund, Washington.

Gupta, Sanjeev, Hamid Davoodi, and Irwin Tinogson. 2000. "Corruption and the Provision of Health Care and Education Services." Working Paper no. 00/116, International Monetary Fund, Washington.

Gupta, Sanjeev, Luiz de Mello, and Rajii Saran. 2000. "Corruption and Military Spending." Working Paper no. 00/23, International Monetary Fund, Washington.

Gupta, Sanjeev, Robert Powell, and Yongzheng Yang. 2005. "The Macroeconomic Challenges of Scaling Up Aid to Africa." Working Paper no. 05/179, International Monetary Fund, Washington.

Gwartney, James, and Robert Lawson. 2003. *Economic Freedom of the World: 2003 Annual Report*. Vancouver, BC: Fraser Institute.

———. 2004. *Economic Freedom of the World: 2004 Annual Report*. Vancouver, BC: Fraser Institute.

Gwartney, James, Charles Skipton, and Robert Lawson. 2001. "Trade Openness, Income Levels, and Economic Growth, 1980–98." In *Economic Freedom of the World: 2001 Annual Report*, ed. James Gwartney and Robert Lawson, 23–70. Vancouver, BC: Fraser Institute.

Haan, Jakob de, and Clemens L. J. Siermann. 1998. "Further Evidence on the Relationship between Economic Freedom and Economic Growth." *Public Choice* 95 (3–4): 363–80.

Haan, Jakob de, and Jan Sturm. 2000. "On the Relationship between Economic Freedom and Economic Growth." *European Journal of Political Economy* 16 (2): 215–41.

Haan, Jakob de, Erik Leertouwer, and Jan Sturm. 2002. "Which Economic Freedoms Contribute to Growth? A Comment." *Kyklos* 55 (3): 403–16.

Habermas, Jurgen. 1976. *Legitimation Crisis*. London: Heinemann Educational Books.

Hall, Robert E., and Alvin Rabushka. 1983. *Low Tax, Simple Tax, Flat Tax*. New York: McGraw-Hill.

Hamilton, Carl B. 2002. "Globalization and Democracy." Discussion Paper no. 3653, Center for Economic Policy Research, Washington. http://ssrn.com/abstract=366681.

Hanke, Steve H. 1999. "Reflections on Exchange Rate Regimes." *Cato Journal* 18 (3): 335–44. www.catojournal.com/pubs/journal/cj18n3/cj18n3-4.pdf.

Hanke, Steve, and Stephen Walters. 1997. "Economic Freedom, Prosperity, and Equality: A Survey." *Cato Journal* 17 (2): 117–46. www.cato.org/pubs/journal/cj17n2-1.html.

Hansen, Henrik, and Finn Tarp. 2001. "Aid and Growth Regressions." *Journal of Development Economics* 64 (2): 547–70.

Harrelson-Stephens, Julie, and Callaway, Rhonda L. 2001. "Does Trade Openness Promote Security Rights in Developing Countries?" *International Interactions* 29 (2): 143–58.

Hathaway, Oona. 2002. "Do Human Rights Treaties Make a Difference?" *Yale Law Journal* 111 (8): 1935–2042.

Hayek, Friedrich A. 1944. *The Road to Serfdom.* Chicago: University of Chicago Press.
———. 1948. "The Use of Knowledge in Society." In *Individualism and Economic Order.* Chicago: University of Chicago Press.
———. 1960. *The Constitution of Liberty.* Chicago: University of Chicago Press.
———. 1973. *Law, Legislation and Liberty, vol. 1: Rules and Order.* Chicago: University of Chicago Press.
———. 1976. *Law, Legislation and Liberty, vol. 3: The Mirage of Social Justice.* Chicago: University of Chicago Press.
———. 1978a. *Denationalization of Money: The Argument Refined: An Analysis of the Theory and Practice of Concurrent Currencies,* 2nd ed. London: Institute of Economic Affairs.
———. 1978b. *Law, Legislation and Liberty, vol. 2: The Mirage of Social Justice.* Chicago: University of Chicago Press.
Heitger, Bernhard. 2004. "Property Rights and the Wealth of Nations: A Cross-Country Study." *Cato Journal* 23 (3): 381–402. www.catojournal.com/pubs/journal/cj23n3/cj23n3-7.pdf.
Helfer, Laurence R. 2003. "Human Rights and Intellectual Property: Conflict or Co-existence?" *Minnesota Intellectual Property Review* 5 (1): 47–61. http://ssrn.com/abstract=459120.
Heller, Peter S. 2005. "Pity the Finance Minister: Issues in Managing a Substantial Scaling Up of Aid Flows." Working Paper no. 05/180, International Monetary Fund, Washington.
Helpman, Elhanan. 1993. "Innovation, Imitation and Intellectual Property Rights." *Econometrica* 61 (6): 1247–80.
Henisz, Witold J. 2000. "The Institutional Environment for Economic Growth." *Economics and Politics* 12 (1): 1–31.
Henkin, L. 1990. *The Age of Rights.* New York: Columbia University Press.
Hindriks, Jean, Michael Keen, and Abhinay Muthoo. 1999. "Corruption, Extortion, and Evasion." *Journal of Public Economics* 74 (3): 395–430.
Hoekman, Bernard. 2005. "Making the WTO More Supportive of Development." *Finance and Development* 42 (1): 14–18.
Holmes, Stephen, and Cass R. Sunstein. 2000. *The Cost of Rights: Why Liberty Depends on Taxes.* New York: W. W. Norton.
Huntington, Samuel P. 1968. *Political Order in Changing Societies.* New Haven, CT: Yale University Press.
International Labour Organization. 1998. *Declaration on Fundamental Principles and Rights at Work.* Geneva: International Labour Organization.
International Monetary Fund, Independent Evaluation Office. 2004. *Evaluation of the IMF's Role in Poverty Reduction Strategy Papers and the Poverty Reduction and Growth Facility.* Washington: International Monetary Fund.
International Monetary Fund. 2006. *Global Monitoring Report: Strengthening Mutual Accountability—Aid, Trade, and Governance.* Washington: International Monetary Fund and World Bank.
———. 2008. *Global Monitoring Report, MDGs, and the Environment: Agenda for Inclusive and Sustainable Development.* Washington: International Monetary Fund and World Bank.
Isham, Jonathan, Daniel Kaufman, and Lant Pritchett. 1997. "Civil Liberties, Democracy and the Performance of Government Projects." *World Bank Economic Review* 11 (2): 219–42.

Isham, Jonathan, Deepa Narayan, and Lant Pritchett. 1995. "Does Participation Improve Performance? Establishing Causality with Subjective Data." *World Bank Economic Review* 9 (2): 175–200.

Jahan, Selim. 2002. "Human Development and Millennium Development Goals (MDGs): Analytical Linkages and Policy Issues." United Nations Development Programme, New York. www.inwent.org/ef-texte/human_rights/jahan.htm.

Jayawickrama, Nihal. 1998. "Corruption—A Violation of Human Rights?" Working paper, Transparency International, Berlin. www.transparency.org/working_papers/jayawickrama/jayawickrama.html.

Jensen, Michael C., and William H. Meckling. 1994. "The Nature of Man." *Journal of Applied Corporate Finance* 7 (2): 4–19. http://ssrn.com/abstract=5471.

Jones, Peter. 1994. *Rights.* London: Macmillan.

Jonsson, Urban. 2004. "Human Rights Approach to Development Programming." United Nations Children's Fund, New York. www.nutrition.uio.no/iprfd/Encounterdocuments/DocO25-G24.html.

Kant, Immanuel. 1795. *Perpetual Peace: A Philosophical Sketch.* Indianapolis, IN: Hackett. www.mtholyoke.edu/acad/intrel/kant/kant1.htm.

Karatnycky, Adrian. 2002. *Freedom in the World 2001–2002: The Annual Survey of Political Rights and Civil Liberties.* Piscataway, NJ: Transaction Publishers.

Kaufmann, Daniel. 2004. "Human Rights and Governance: The Empirical Challenge." Paper presented at the Conference on Human Rights and Development: Towards Mutual Reinforcement, Ethical Globalization Initiative and the NYU Center for Human Rights and Global Justice, New York University Law School, March 1, New York.

———. 2005. "10 Myths about Governance and Corruption." *Finance and Development* 42 (3): 41–43.

Kaufmann, Daniel, Aart Kraay, and Massino Mastruzzi. 2005. "Governance Matters IV." Policy Research Working Paper no. 3630, World Bank, Washington.

Kaufmann, Daniel, Aart Kraay, and Pablo Zoido-Lobaton. 1999. "Governance Matters." Policy Research Working Paper no. 2196, World Bank, Washington.

Keen, Michael, Yi Tae Kim, and Recard Varsano. 2006. "The 'Flat Tax(es)': Principles and Evidence." Working Paper no. 06/218, International Monetary Fund, Washington.

Keith, Linda Camp. 1999. "The United Nations International Covenant on Civil and Political Rights: Does It Make a Difference in Human Rights Behavior?" *Journal of Peace Research* 36 (1): 95–118.

Keller, Linda M. 2003. "The American Rejection of Economic Rights as Human Rights and the Declaration of Independence: Does the Pursuit of Happiness Require Basic Economic Rights?" *New York Law School Journal of Human Rights* 19 (2): 557–614. http://ssrn.com/abstract=541722.

Keynes, Maynard J. 1919. *The Economic Consequences of the Peace.* London: Macmillan.

Khan, Mohsin S., and Abdelhak S. Senhadji. 2000. "Threshold Effects in the Relationship between Inflation and Growth." Working Paper no. 00/110, International Monetary Fund, Washington. www.imf.org/external/pubs/ft/wp/2000/wp00110.pdf.

Kinsella, Stephen N. 2001a. "Against Intellectual Property." *Journal of Libertarian Studies* 15, no. 2 (Spring): 1–53.

———. 2001b. "Is Intellectual Property Legitimate?" Federalist Society for Law and Public Policy Studies, Washington.

Klein, Daniel B. 2004. "Statist Quo Bias." *Econ Journal Watch* 1 (2): 260–71.

Knack, Stephen, and Philip Keefer. 1995. "Institutions and Economic Performance: Cross-Country Tests Using Alternative Institutional Measures." *Economics and Politics* 7 (3): 207–27.

Krueger, Anne O. 1974. "The Political Economy of the Rent-Seeking Society." *American Economic Review* 64 (3): 291–303.

———. 2005a. "From Despair to Hope: The Challenge of Promoting Poverty Reduction." Annual Boehm-Bawerk Lecture, University of Innsbruck, Innsbruck, Austria. www.imf.org/external/np/speeches/2005/111705.htm.

———. 2005b. "Tis Not Too Late to Seek a Newer World: What Globalization Offers the Poor." Address to Oxford Union, Oxford, UK. www.imf.org/external/np/speeches/2005/050905.htm.

Kydland, Finn E., and Edward C. Prescott. 1977. "Rules Rather than Discretion: The Inconsistency of Optimal Plans." *Journal of Political Economy* 85 (3): 473–91.

Landsburg, Steven E. 1993. *The Armchair Economist: Economics and Everyday Life*. New York: Free Press.

La Porta, Rafael, Florencio Lopez-de-Silanes, Andei Shleifer, and Robert W. Vishny. 1988. "Law and Finance." *Journal of Political Economy* 106 (6): 1113–55.

Leite, Sergio Pereira. 2001. "Human Rights and the IMF." *Finance and Development* 38 (4). www.imf.org/external/pubs/FT/tandd/2001/12/leite.htm.

Leite, Carlos, and Jens Weidmann. 1999. "Does Mother Nature Corrupt? Natural Resources, Corruption, and Economic Growth." Working Paper no. 99/85, International Monetary Fund, Washington.

Lin, Justin Y., Fang Cai, and Zhou Li. 2003. *The China Miracle: Development Strategy and Economic Reform*. Hong Kong: Chinese University Press.

Lincoln, Abraham. 1859. Second lecture on Discoveries and Inventions, Jacksonville, Illinois, February 11, 1859. In *Complete Works*, Vol. 1, ed. John Nicolay and John Hay. New York: The Century Co.

Lindahl, Eric. 1919. "Just Taxation: A Positive Solution." In *Classics in the Theory of Public Finance*, ed. Richard A. Musgrave and Alan T. Peacock, 168–76. London: Macmillan, 1958.

Lipset, Seymour M. 1959. "Some Social Requisites of Democracy: Economic Development and Political Legitimacy." *American Political Science Review* 53 (1): 69–105.

Luce, Edward. 2006. *In Spite of the Gods: The Strange Rise of Modern India*. London: Little and Brown.

Machan, Tibor R. 2001. "The Perils of Positive Rights." *The Freeman: Ideas on Liberty* 51 no. 4 (April): 49–52. www.fee.org/Publications/the=Freeman/article.asp/aid=2993.

———. 2003. "The Value and Limits of Democracy." Working paper, Ludwig von Mises Institute, Auburn, AL. www.mises.org/workingpapers.asp.

———. 2006a. "Human Rights and Poverty." In *Encyclopedia of World Poverty*, ed. Mehmet Odekon. Thousand Oaks, CA: SAGE Publications.

———. 2006b. *Libertarianism Defended*. Burlington, VT: Ashgate.

Maddison, Angus. 1998. *Chinese Economic Performance in the Long Run*. Paris: OECD Development Center.

Mahoney, Paul G. 2000. "The Common Law and Economic Growth: Hayek Might Be Right." Legal Studies Working Paper no. 00-8, University of Virginia Law School, Charlottesville, VA. http://ssrn.com/abstract=206809.

Marks, Stephen. 2003a. "The Human Rights Framework for Development: Seven Approaches." Working Paper no. 18, Bagnoud Center for Health and Human Rights, Boston. www.hsph.harvard.edu/fxbcenter/FXBC_WP18—Marks.pdf.

144

———. 2003b. "Obstacles to the Right to Development." Working Paper no. 17, Bagnoud Center for Health and Human Rights, Boston. www.hsph.harvard.edu/fxbcenter/FXBC_WP17—Marks.pdf.

———. 2004. "The Human Right to Development: Between Rhetoric and Reality." *Harvard Human Rights Journal* 17 (Spring): 137–68.

Martin, Diarmuid. 2003. "Comprehensive Development Strategies and the Right to Development." In *The Right to Development: Reflections on the First Four Reports of the Independent Expert on the Right to Development*, ed. Franciscans International. New York: Franciscans International.

Mauro, Paolo. 1995. "Corruption and Growth." *Quarterly Journal of Economics* 110 (3): 681–712.

———. 1998. "Corruption and the Composition of Government Expenditure." Working Paper no. 9/98, International Monetary Fund, Washington.

———. 2004. "The Persistence of Corruption and Slow Economic Growth." *IMF Staff Papers* 51 (1): 1–18.

M'Baye, Kéba. 1972. "Le droit au développement comme un droit de l'homme." *Human Rights Journal* 5 (2–3): 505–34.

McCalman, Phillip. 2005. "International Diffusion and Intellectual Property Rights: An Empirical Analysis." *Journal of International Economics* 67 (2): 353–72.

McGee, Robert W., and Yeomin Yoon. 2003. "Labor Standards and Human Rights Abuses: A Look at Some Neglected Rights Issues." Paper presented at the 13th International Conference of the International Trade and Finance Association, May 28–31, Vaasa, Finland. http://papers.ssrn.com/sol3/papers.cfm?abstract_id=409040.

Merton, Robert. 1936. "The Unanticipated Consequences of Purposive Social Action." In *Sociological Ambivalence and Other Essays*. New York: Free Press, 1976.

Messick, Richard E. 1999. "Judicial Reform and Economic Development: A Survey of the Issues." *World Bank Research Observer* 14 (1): 117–36.

Minier, Jenny A. 1998. "Democracy and Growth: Alternative Approaches." *Journal of Economic Growth* 3 (3): 241–66.

Mirrlees, James. 1971. "An Exploration in the Theory of Optimum Income Taxation." *Review of Economic Studies* 38 (2): 175–208.

Mises, Ludwig von. 1966. *Human Action: A Treatise on Economics*, 3rd rev. ed. Chicago: Henry Regnery.

Muller, Jerry Z. 2002. *The Mind and the Market: Capitalism in Modern European Thought.* New York: Knopf.

Mussa, Michael, Paul Masson, Alexander Swoboda, Esteban Jadresic, Paolo Mauro, and Andrew Berg. 2000. "Exchange Rate Regimes in an Increasingly Integrated World Economy." Occasional Paper no. 193, International Monetary Fund, Washington. www.imf.org/external/pubs/ft/op/193/index.htm.

Narayan, Deepa. 2000. *Voices of the Poor: Can Anyone Hear Us?* New York: Oxford University Press (for the World Bank).

Neumark, David, and William Wascher. 1995. "The Effect of New Jersey's Minimum Wage Increase on Fast-Food Employment: A Re-Evaluation Using Payroll Records." Working Paper no. W5224, National Bureau of Economic Research, Cambridge, MA.

Neumayer, Eric. 2005. "Do International Human Rights Treaties Improve Respect for Human Rights?" *Journal of Conflict Resolution*, 49 (16): 43–63.

Nickel, James W. 2004. "The Indivisibility of Human Rights: Is it True? Is it Relevant to Developing Countries?" Lecture at the Law Faculty, Cambridge, U.K.

Norberg, Johan. 2003. *In Defense of Global Capitalism*. Washington: Cato Institute.

North, Douglass C. 1981. *Structure and Change in Economic History.* New York: W. W. Norton.

―――. 1990. *Institutions, Institutional Change, and Economic Performance.* New York: Cambridge University Press.

North, Douglass C., and Robert P. Thomas. 1973. *The Rise of the Western World: A New Economic History.* London: Cambridge University Press.

Novak, Michael. 1982. *The Spirit of Democratic Capitalism.* New York: Simon & Schuster.

―――. 1990. *This Hemisphere of Liberty: A Philosophy of the Americas.* Washington: AEI Press.

Nozick, Robert. 1974. *Anarchy, State, and Utopia.* New York: Basic Books.

O'Driscoll, Gerald P. J., and Lee Hoskins. 2003. ''Property Rights: The Key to Economic Development.'' Policy Analysis no. 482, Cato Institute, Washington. www.cato.org/pubs/pas/pa482.pdf.

OECD (Organisation for Economic Co-operation and Development). 2006. ''Employment Outlook: Boosting Jobs and Incomes—Policy Lessons from Reassessing the OECD Jobs Strategy.'' Paris. www.oecd.org/document/56/0,2340,en_2649_34731_36998072_1_1_1_1,00.html.

―――. 2007. ''DAC Action-Oriented Policy Paper on Human Rights and Development.'' Development Assistance Committee, Paris.

―――. 2008. ''OECD Journal on Development: Development Co-Operation Report 2007.'' Paris. www.oecd.org/document/32/0,3343,en_2649_37413_40056608_1_1_1_37413,00.html#SummaryEngl.

OHCHR (Office of the High Commissioner for Human Rights). 1986. ''The Position of Aliens under the Covenant.'' General Comment No. 15, Geneva. www.unhchr.ch/tbs/doc.nsf/0/bc561aa81bc5d86ec12563ed004aaa1b?Opendocument.

―――. 2003. ''Human Rights and Trade.'' Statement to the 5th WTO Ministerial Conference, September 10–14, Cancún, Mexico.

―――. 2004. *Human Rights and Poverty Reduction: A Conceptual Framework.* Geneva: OHCHR.

Olson, M. 1996. ''Big Bills Left on the Sidewalk: Why Some Countries Are Rich, and Others Poor.'' *Journal of Economic Perspectives* 10 (2): 3–24.

Osmani, Siddiq. 2003. ''Some Thoughts on the Right to Development.'' In *The Right to Development: Reflections on the First Four Reports of the Independent Expert on the Right to Development,* ed. Franciscans International, 34–45. New York: Franciscans International.

Owens, Jeffrey, and Stuart Hamilton. 2004. ''Experiences and Innovations in Other Countries.'' In *The Crises in Tax Administration.* Washington: Brookings Institution Press.

Ozden, Caglar, and Maurice Schiff, eds. 2006. *International Migration, Remittances and the Brain Drain.* Washington: World Bank and Palgrave Macmillan.

Park, Walter G., and Juan Carlos Ginarte. 1997. ''Intellectual Property Rights and Economic Growth.'' *Contemporary Economic Policy* 15 (3): 51–61.

Pipes, Richard. 1999. *Property and Freedom.* New York: Knopf.

Piron, Laure Hélène. 2002. ''The Right to Development: A Review of the Current State of the Debate for the Department for International Development.'' Report for the Department for International Development, London.

―――. 2003. ''Are Development Compacts Required to Realise the Right to Development?'' In *The Right to Development, Reflections on the First Four Reports of the Independent Expert on the Right to Development,* ed. Franciscans International, 46–61. New York: Franciscans International.

_____ . 2004. "The Right to Development: Study on Existing Bilateral and Multilateral Programmes and Policies for Development Partnership." Paper submitted to Commission on Human Rights, E/CN.4/Sub.2/2004/15. www.odi.org.uk/rights/Publications/RTD&DevPart.pdf

Plant, Mark. 2005. "Human Rights and the Role of the IMF." In *Poverty Reduction Strategies: Towards Mutual Reinforcement in Human Rights and Development*, ed. Philip Alston and Mary Robinson, 498–508. Oxford, UK: Oxford University Press.

Pogge, Thomas. 2003. "The First UN Millennium Development Goal: A Cause for Celebration?" Paper presented at the Oslo Lecture in Moral Philosophy at the University of Oslo, September 11, Oslo. www.etikk.no/globaljustice/.

_____ . 2005a. "Recognized and Violated by International Law: The Human Rights of the Global Poor." *Leiden Journal of International Law* 18 (4): 717–45.

_____ . 2005b. "Severe Poverty as a Violation of Negative Duties." *Ethics and International Affairs* 19 (1):

Popper, Karl Raimund. 1957. *The Poverty of Historicism*. Boston: Beacon Press.

Posner, R. 1998. "Creating a Legal Framework for Economic Development." *World Bank Research Observer* 13 (1): 1–11.

Prasad, Eswar, Kenneth Rogoff, Shang-Jin Wei, and M. Ayhan Kose. 2003. "Effects of Financial Globalization on Developing Countries: Some Empirical Evidence." Occasional Paper no. 220, International Monetary Fund, Washington. www.imf.org/external/np/res/docs/2003/031703.htm.

Przeworski, Adam, and Fernando Limongi. 1993. "Political Regimes and Economic Growth." *Journal of Economic Perspectives* 7 (3): 51–69.

Quirmbach, Herman 1986. "The Diffusion of New Technology and the Market for an Innovation." *RAND Journal of Economics* 17 (1): 33–47.

Rajan, Raghuram. 2005. "Has Financial Development Made the World Riskier?" Working Paper no. 11728, National Bureau of Economic Research, Cambridge, MA.

Rajan, Raghuram, and Arvind Subramanian. 2005a. "What Undermines Aid's Impact on Growth?" Working Paper no. 05/126, International Monetary Fund, Washington.

_____ . 2005b. "Aid and Growth: What Does the Cross-Country Evidence Really Show?" Working Paper no. 05/127, International Monetary Fund, Washington.

Rajan, Raghuram, and Luigi Zingales. 2003. *Saving Capitalism from the Capitalists: Unleashing the Power of Financial Markets to Create Wealth and Spread Opportunities*. New York: Random House.

Rao, Vaman. 1984. "Democracy and Economic Development." *Studies in Comparative International Development* 19 (4): 67–81.

Ratha, Dilip. 2005. "Workers' Remittances: An Important and Stable Source of External Development Finance." In *Remittances: Development Impact and Future Prospects*, ed. Samuel Maimbo and Dilip Ratha, 19–52. Washington: World Bank.

_____ . 2008. "World Banker and His Cash Return Home." *New York Times*, March 17.

Rawls, John. 1971. *A Theory of Justice*. Cambridge, MA: Harvard University Press.

Reinganum, Jennifer. 1981. "Market Structure and the Diffusion of New Technology." *Bell Journal of Economics* 12 (2): 618–24.

Ricardo, David. 1817. *On the Principles of Political Economy and Taxation*. London: John Murray. www.econlib.org/LIBRARY/Ricardo/ricP.html.

Richardson, Craig J. 2005. "The Loss of Property Rights and the Collapse of Zimbabwe." *Cato Journal* 25 (3): 541–65.

Robinson, Mary. 2003. *Human Rights Perspectives on the Millennium Development Goals: Conference Report*. New York: New York University School of Law.

Rodrik, Dani. 2000. "Institutions for High-Quality Growth: What They Are and How to Acquire Them." Working Paper no. 7540, National Bureau of Economic Research, Cambridge, MA.

Rodrik, Dani, and Arvind Subramanian. 2004. "From Hindu Growth to Productivity Surge: The Mystery of the Indian Growth Transition." IMF Working Paper no. 04/77, International Monetary Fund, Washington. www.imf.org/external/pubs/ft/wp/2004/wp0477.pdf.

Rodrik, Dani, Arvind Subramanian, and Trebbi Francesco. 2002. "Institutions Rule: The Primacy of Institutions over Geography and Integration in Economic Development." Working Paper no. 9305, National Bureau of Economic Research, Cambridge, MA.

Romer, Paul. 1989. "What Determines the Rate of Growth and Technical Change?" Research Working Paper no. 279, World Bank, Washington.

———. 1990. "Endogenous Technological Change." *Journal of Political Economy* 98 (5): 571–602.

Roosevelt, Franklin Delano. 1941. "The Four Freedoms." Address to Congress, January 6. www.libertynet.org/~edcivic/fdr.html.

Rorty, Richard. 1993. "Human Rights, Rationality, and Sentimentality." In *On Human Rights: The Oxford Amnesty Lectures*, ed. Stephen Shute and Susan Hurley, 132–36. New York: Basic Books.

Rosenberg, Nathan, and L. E. Birdzell Jr. 1986. *How the West Grew Rich.* New York: Basic Books. www.perseusbooksgroup.com/basic/book_detail.jsp?isbn=0465031099.

Rothbard, Murray. 1978. *For a New Liberty.* New York: Collier Macmillan.

Rummel, Rudolph J. 1994. "Power, Genocide, and Mass Murder," *Journal of Peace Research* 31 (1): 1–10.

Sachs, Jeffrey D. 2001. "The Strategic Significance of Global Inequality." *Washington Quarterly* 24 (3): 187–98.

Sachs, J. D., and A. H. Warner. 1995. "Economic Reform and the Process of Global Integration." Brookings Paper on Economic Activity: 1–118.

———. 2005. *The End of Poverty: Economic Possibilities for Our Time.* New York: Penguin Press.

Sah, Raaj K. 1991. "Fallibility in Human Organizations and Political Systems." *Journal of Economic Perspectives* 5 (2): 67–88.

Sally, Razeen. 2005. "The Future of Trade, Development, and International Institutions: 2005 and Beyond." *Cobden Paper* no. 2, Globalisation Institute, London. www.globalisationinstitute.org/publications/2005.pdf.

Salman, Salman M. A., and Siobhan McInerney-Lankford. 2004. *The Human Right to Water: Legal and Policy Dimensions.* Washington: World Bank.

Samuelson, Paul A. 1973. *Economics,* 9th ed. New York: McGraw-Hill/Irwin.

Sarel, Michael. 1996. "Nonlinear Effects of Inflation on Economic Growth." *IMF Staff Papers* 43 (1): 199–215.

Schelling, Thomas. 1982. "Establishing Credibility: Strategic Considerations." *American Economic Review* 72 (1): 77–80.

Senate of Canada. 2007. "Overcoming 40 Years of Failure: A New Road Map for Sub-Saharan Africa." Standing Senate Committee on Foreign Affairs and International Trade, Ottawa.

Schultz, Theodore W. 1980. "Nobel Lecture: The Economics of Being Poor." *Journal of Political Economy* 88 (4): 639–51.

Sen, Amartya. 1981. *Poverty and Famines.* Oxford, U.K.: Oxford University Press.

———. 1999. *Development as Freedom.* Oxford, U.K.: Oxford University Press.

———. 2000. "Consequential Evaluation and Practical Reason." *Journal of Philosophy* 97 (9): 447–502.

Sengupta, Arjun. 1999. "Study on the Current State of Progress in the Implementation of the Right to Development." Commission on Human Rights, 56th Session, Open-Ended Working Group on the Right to Development, Economic and Social Council, OHCHR, Geneva. www.unhchr.ch/Huridocda/Huridoca.nsf/TestFrame/ 0b1c308a59eacdbb80256842003d857e?Opendocument

———. 2000. "The Right to Development as a Human Right." Working Paper no. 7, Bagnoud Center for Health and Human Rights, Boston. www.hsph.harvard.edu/ fxbcenter/working_papers.htm.

Sfeir-Younis, Alfredo. 2003. "The Right to Development: The Political Economy of Implementation." In *The Right to Development: Reflections on the First Four Reports of the Independent Expert on the Right to Development,* ed. Franciscans International pp 7-19. New York: Franciscan International.

Shue, Henry. 1996. *Basic Rights,* 2nd ed. Princeton, NJ: Princeton University Press.

Smith, Adam. 1776. *An Inquiry into the Nature and Causes of the Wealth of Nations,* 5th ed. Cannan, Edwin, ed. London: Methuen and Co., Ltd., 1904.

Smith, Michael R. 1992. *Power, Norms and Inflation: A Skeptical Treatment.* New York: Aldine de Gruyter.

Sobel, Russel, and Peter Leeson. 2007. "The Spread of Global Economic Freedom." In *Economic Freedom of the World: 2007 Annual Report,* ed. James Gwartney and Robert Lawson, 29–37. Vancouver, BC: Fraser Institute.

Solow, Robert M. 1956. "A Contribution to the Theory of Economic Growth." *Quarterly Journal of Economics* 70 (1): 65–94.

Sowell, Thomas. 2005. *Affirmative Action around the World: An Empirical Study.* New Haven, CT: Yale University Press.

Sterba, James P., ed. 1998. "From Liberty to Welfare." In *Ethics: The Big Questions.* Malden, MA: Blackwell.

Stern, Nicholas, Jean-Jacques Dethier, and F. Halsey Rogers. 2005. *Growth and Empowerment: Making Development Happen.* Cambridge, MA: MIT Press.

Stigler, George. 1971. "The Theory of Economic Regulation." *Bell Journal of Economics and Management Science* 2 (1): 3–21.

Stockman, Alan C. 2000. "Exchange Rate Systems in Perspective." *Cato Journal* 20 (1): 115–22. www.catojournal.com/pubs/journal/cj20n1/cj20n1-14.pdf.

Sykes, Alan O'Neil. 2003. "International Trade and Human Rights: An Economic Perspective." Olin Working Paper no. 188, University of Chicago Law School, Chicago. http://ssrn.com/abstract=415802.

Tanzi, Vito. 1998. "Corruption around the World: Causes, Consequences, Scope and Cures." *IMF Staff Papers* 45 (4): 559–594.

Tanzi, Vito, and Hamid Davoodi. 1997. "Corruption, Public Investment and Growth." IMF Working Paper no. 97/139, Washington: International Monetary Fund.

———. 2000. "Corruption, Growth, and Public Finances." IMF Working Paper no. 00/182. Washington: International Monetary Fund.

Tavares, Jose, and Romain Wacziarg. 2001. "How Democracy Affects Growth." *European Economic Review* 45 (8): 1341–78.

Transparency International. 2005. *Corruption Perception Index.* London: Transparency International.

Tsebelis, George. 1995. "Decision Making in Political Systems: Veto Players in Presidentialism, Parliamentarism, Multicameralism and Multipartyism." *British Journal of Political Science* 25 (3): 289–325.

Tseng, Wanda, and Markus Rodlauer, eds. 2003. *China: Competing in the Global Economy*. Washington: International Monetary Fund.

UNDP (United Nations Development Programme). 2003. "Millennium Development Goals: A Compact among Nations to End Human Poverty." In *Human Development Report 2003*, 1–13. Oxford, U.K.: Oxford University Press. http://hdr.undp.org/reports/global/2003/.

———. 2004. "Right to Information: A Practical Guidance Note." Bureau for Development Policy, Democratic Governance Group, New York. www.undp.org/governance/docs/A2I%20-%20Guides%20-%20RighttoInformation.pdf.

———. 2005. "International Cooperation at a Crossroads: Aid, Trade and Security in an Unequal World." In *Human Development Report* 2005. Oxford, UK: Oxford University Press. http://hdr.undp.org/en/reports/global/hdr2005/.

United Nations. 1987. "Indivisibility and Interdependence of Economic, Social, Cultural, Civil and Political Rights." New York. www.un.org/documents/ga/res/42/a42r102.htm.

———. 2000. "Millennium Declaration." New York. www.un.org/millennium/declaration/ares552e.htm.

———. 2002. "Report of the International Conference on Financing for Development" (Monterrey Consensus). New York. www.un.org/esa/ffd/aconf198-11.pdf.

———. 2005a. "Larger Freedom: Towards Development, Security, and Human Rights for All." New York. www.un.org/largerfreedom/contents.htm.

———. 2005b. "World Summit Outcome." A/RES/60/1, New York. http://daccessdds.un.org/doc/UNDOC/GEN/N05/487/60/PDF/N0548760.pdf?OpenElement.

———. 2006. "International Migration." Department of Economic and Social Affairs, Population Division, New York.

United Nations Committee on Economic, Social and Cultural Rights. 2002. "Substantive Issues Arising in the Implementation of the International Covenant on Economic, Social and Cultural Rights." General Comment no. 15, The Right to Water, Geneva.

United Nations Commission on Human Rights. 2001. "The Right to Development." Resolution 2001/9,e/CN.6/RES/2001/9.

United Nations Economic and Social Council. 1998. "Report of the Intergovernmental Group of Experts on the Right to Development on Its Second Session." November 7, New York. www.unhchr.ch/Huridocda/Huridoca.nsf/TestFrame/a3d16232ae8c9bb4c125660a0058bdb1?Opendocument.

———. 2004a. "Report of the Working Group on the Right to Development on Its Fifth Session." E/CN.4/2004/23/Add.1, New York. www.unhchr.ch/Huridocda/Huridoca.nsf/(Symbol)/E.CN.4.2004.23.Add.1.En?Opendocument.

———. 2004b. "Promotion and Protection of Human Rights." New York. http://daccessdds.un.org/doc/UNDOC/GEN/G04/168/12/PDF/G0416812.pdf?OpenElement.

United Nations General Assembly. 1999. "The Right to Development." Resolution adopted by the General Assembly. A/RES/53/155, February 25, New York.

———. 2000. "The Right to Development." Resolution adopted by the General Assembly. A/RES/54/175, September 15, New York.

———. 2002. "The Right to Development." Resolution adopted by the General Assembly. A/RES/56/150, February 8, New York.

_____. 2004. "The Right to Development." Resolution adopted by the General Assembly. A/RES/58/172, March 11, New York.

_____. 2005. "The Right to Development." Resolution adopted by the General Assembly. A/RES/59/185, March 8, New York. http://daccessdds.un.org/doc/ UNDOC/GEN/N04/487/36/PDF/N0448736.pdf?OpenElement.

Uvin, Peter. 2002. "On High Moral Ground: The Incorporation of Human Rights by the Development Enterprise." *Fletcher Journal of Development Studies* 17.

_____. 2004. *Human Rights and Development.* Bloomfield, CT: Kumarian Press.

Van de Walle, Nicolas. 2005. *Overcoming Stagnation in Aid-Dependent Countries.* Washington, DC: Center for Global Development. http://cgdev.org/content/publications/ detail/2871.

Vasak, Karel. 1977. "Human Rights: A Thirty-Year Struggle: The Sustained Efforts to Give Force of Law to the Universal Declaration of Human Rights." *UNESCO Courier* 30: 11, Paris.

Vásquez, Ian. 1998. "Official Assistance, Economic Freedom, and Policy Change: Is Foreign Aid Like Champagne?" *Cato Journal* 18 (2): 275–86.

Vega-Gordillo, Manuel, and José Alvarez-Arce. 2003. "Economic Growth and Freedom: A Causality Study." *Cato Journal* 23 (2): 199–215. www.catojournal.com/pubs/ journal/cj23n2/cj23n2-4.pdf.

Vizard, Polly. 2005. "The Contributions of Professor Amartya Sen in the Field of Human Rights." CASE Paper no. 91, London School of Economics and Political Science, London.

Walmsley, Terrie, and L. Alan Winters. 2005. "Relaxing the Restrictions on the Temporary Movements of Natural Persons: A Simulation Analysis." *Journal of Economic Integration* 20 (4): 688–726.

Weede, Erich. 2008. "Human Rights, Limited Government, and Capitalism." *Cato Journal* 28 (1): 35–52.

Weigel, George. 2001. "Two Ideas of Freedom." The Inaugural William E. Simon Lecture, Washington, DC.

Weston, Burns H. 2002. "Human Rights." *Encyclopaedia Britannica,* 15th rev. ed. Chicago: Encyclopaedia Britannica.

White, Lawrence H. 1984. "Competitive Payments Systems and the Unit of Account." *American Economic Review* 74 (4): 699–712.

Wicksell, Knut. 1896. "A New Principle of Just Taxation." In *Classics in the Theory of Public Finance*, ed. Richard A. Musgrave and Alan T. Peacock, 1958, 72–119. London: Macmillan.

Williamson, John. 1990. "What Washington Means by Policy Reform." In *Latin American Adjustment: How Much Has Happened?* ed. John Williamson, 5–20. Washington: Institute for International Economics.

Winters, Alan. 2004. "Trade Liberalization and Economic Performance: An Overview." *The Economic Journal* 114 (493): 4–21.

Wolf, Martin. 2005. "Business Squeals about Tax but It Is People Who Feel the Pain." *Financial Times* (London), December 7.

World Bank. 1998. *Assessing Aid: What Works, What Doesn't, and Why.* Washington: World Bank.

_____. 2002. *Building Institutions for Markets: World Development Report 2002.* Washington: World Bank.

_____. 2005. *World Development Report 2005: A Better Investment Climate for Everyone.* Washington: World Bank.

————. 2008a. *Doing Business in 2008*. Washington: World Bank.

————. 2008b. *Migration and Remittances Factbook*. Washington: World Bank.

WTO (World Trade Organization). 2002. ''The Relationship between Trade and Finance: A Review of Selected Literature Related to Financial Crises in the 1990s.'' Note by the Secretariat, WT/WGTDF/W/4, Geneva.

————. 2005. ''Trade Liberalization as a Source of Growth.'' Note by the Secretariat, WT/WGTDF/W/31, Geneva.

Zee, Howell H. 2005. ''Personal Income Tax Reform: Concepts, Issues, and Comparative Country Developments.'' Working Paper no. WP/05/87, International Monetary Fund, Washington.

Notes

Introduction

1. At the conceptual level, one can define development and human rights with a sufficient degree of abstraction as to be virtually identical and essentially unimpeachable (Marks 2003a).

2. According to the most recent *Global Monitoring Report* (IMF 2008), halfway to 2015, most countries are off track to meet most of the MDGs. At a regional level, sub-Saharan Africa lags on all MDGs and South Asia on most human development goals.

3. This failure was illustrated by the declining credibility of the UN Commission on Human Rights and its replacement by the Human Rights Council to improve the effectiveness of the human rights treaty bodies.

Part I

1. For Frankovits (1995), the essential definition of this approach is "that a body of international human rights law is the only agreed international framework which offers a coherent body of principles and practical meaning for development cooperation which provides a comprehensive guide for appropriate official development assistance, for the manner in which it should be delivered, for the priorities that it should address, for the obligations of both donor and recipient governments and for the way that official development assistance is evaluated." (cited in Marks 2003, p. 5).

2. Easterly (2001) provides an illuminating discussion of why the myriad development remedies that have been tried to make poor countries richer (aid, investment, education, conditionality-based policy reform, debt relief, debt forgiveness, and so forth) have not delivered as promised.

3. Marks (2003a) identified seven different human rights approaches relevant to human development: the holistic approach, the rights-based approach, the social justice approach, the capabilities approach, the responsibilities approach, the human rights education approach, and the right to development approach.

4. The human person is proclaimed to be the central subject of development, in the sense of being the active participant and beneficiary of the right to development. It involves not just economic growth, but equitable distribution, enhancement of people's capabilities, and widening of their choices. It gives top priority to poverty elimination, integration of women into the development process, self-reliance and self-determination of people and governments, and protection of the rights of indigenous people.

5. In a rights-based approach, only those kinds of capability failures that are deemed to be basic in some order of priority would count as poverty, for example, "being adequately nourished, being adequately clothed and sheltered, avoiding preventable morbidity, taking part in the life of a community, and being able to appear in public with dignity" (OHCHR 2004, p. 7).

6. This argument may miss the broader point that if the political opponent cannot speak freely, society will be deprived of the kind of exchange of views and ideas and checks and balances that challenge the status quo and generate changes, innovation, and creation.

Chapter 1

1. The Declaration on the Right to Development was adopted by the UN General Assembly on December 4, 1986, by a vote of 146 to 1 (the United States) with 8 abstentions (Denmark, the Federal Republic of Germany, Finland, Iceland, Israel, Japan, Sweden, and the United Kingdom).

2. The UN machinery for the promotion of the right to development involves the General Assembly and, under its authority, the Economic and Social Council, the Human Rights Council, the High Commissioner for Human Rights, and the Office of the High Commissioner for Human Rights. In 1998, the Open-Ended Working Group on the Right to Development was established and an Independent Expert on the Right to Development appointed. In 2004, the High-Level Task Force on the Implementation of the Right to Development was set up to provide expertise to the working group on how to promote the realization of the right to development.

3. International standards in the form of treaties, declarations, guidelines, and bodies of principles are public and readily accessible tools describing in detail the institutional and developmental requirements of the various guaranteed rights, including the requirements of, for example, health, education, housing, and governance.

4. For instance, in the quest to have basic social services given priority over military expenditure, or in sounding the alarm when "progressive realization" of economic and social rights stalls, is reversed, or is compromised by conflicting trade agreements or economic adjustment programs (OHCHR 2004).

5. In his address to the first session of the Human Rights Council, former UN Secretary-General Kofi Annan (2006, p. 3) noted that one of the urgent tasks that the new council inherited from the commission was "that of reaching agreement on issues where the Commission found consensus elusive, such as making the right to development clear and specific enough to be effectively enforced and upheld."

6. In his *Reflections on the Revolution in France*, Edmund Burke (1790, p. 53) criticized the drafters of the Declaration of the Rights of Man and the Citizen for proclaiming the "monstrous fiction" of human equality, which he argued, serves but to inspire "false ideas and vain expectations in men destined to travel in the obscure walk of laborious life." Jeremy Bentham, at the other end of the political spectrum, argued in his *Anarchical Fantasies* (1816, pp. 28, 30–34) that "rights is the child of law; from real law come real rights; but from imaginary laws, from the 'laws of nature' come imaginary rights."

7. See statement made by the United States at the 61st UN Commission on Human Rights on March 22, 2005, at http://geneva.usmission.gov/humanrights/2005/ 0322Item 7.htm. For an account of U.S. objections to the right to development, see Marks (2003b).

8. It is in that context that the United States supported the right to development in the 1993 Vienna Declaration.

9. For Sengupta (1999, website), the right to development emerged as "a human right that unified in itself the civil and political rights as well as the economic, social

and cultural rights," looking at the various components as an integrated whole of an international bill of rights.

10. Novak (1982) defines such a conception as one where the amount of resources is assumed to be fixed, so that whatever one person gains, another loses. This led to the socialist view that, first, capitalists become wealthy by exploiting workers; second, capitalist nations exploit Third World nations; and third, the elimination of private property will end such exploitation.

11. Western countries made a distinction between the two types of rights on the grounds that (a) human rights are individual rights; (b) human rights have to be coherent, in the sense that each right holder must have some corresponding duty holder whose obligation would be to deliver the right; and (c) human rights must be justiciable.

12. As noted by Jerry Muller (2002), professor of history, Hayek considered it analytically fallacious to separate "self-interest" from "purpose," not because all purposes are ultimately selfish, but because, whether conceptions of self-interest are egotistical or altruistic, materialistic or idealistic, they are best pursued through the market. "Those who want to earn money to raise their children, or to build a church to the greater glory of God, need to participate in the market as much as the fellow who earns money to acquire a flashy car that he hopes will attract women. The parent and the religious believer are acting on their interests no less than the would-be playboy; they merely have a different conception of their interests and purposes" (Muller 2002, pp. 366–67).

13. It would seem that the main quid pro quo of the right to development is to claim that the human being is the "central subject" of his own development (empowerment) while simultaneously describing the right as essentially a claim on others (entitlement). This boils down to a philosophical conflict of views on the essence of economic development: a matter of individual empowerment and creation or a matter of collective entitlement and redistribution.

14. Recalling the right of peoples to self-determination, by virtue of which they have the right freely to determine their political status and to pursue their economic, social, and cultural development, the declaration asserts that "states shall take resolute steps to eliminate the massive and flagrant violations of the human rights of peoples and human beings affected by situations such as those resulting from apartheid, all forms of racism and racial discrimination, colonialism, foreign domination and occupation, aggression, foreign interference and threats against national sovereignty, national unity and territorial integrity, threats of war and refusal to recognize the fundamental right of peoples to self-determination."

15. On the occasion of the 50th anniversary of the Bandung Conference, the 2005 Bandung Declaration on the New Asian-African Strategic Partnership states that the partnership will be based, inter alia, on "the promotion and protection of human rights and fundamental freedoms, including the right to development."

16. In UN debates and resolutions, it has taken the form of requiring a more favorable international environment, in particular in the areas of trade, debt, a more equitable environment for rules (e.g., intellectual property rights and special and differential treatment), and changes to the representation of developing countries in the decisionmaking mechanisms of the international financial institutions.

17. Other well-known UN declarations subsequent to the Universal Declaration on Human Rights have addressed the right to self-determination of countries and peoples; the rights of disabled individuals; the elimination of all forms of intolerance

and discrimination based on religion or belief; the right of peoples to peace; the rights of individuals belonging to national, ethnic, religious, and linguistic minorities; and the elimination of violence against women.

18. Resolutions and declarations are not subject to signature and ratification, and therefore have no binding effect, though they may provide the impetus for subsequent binding instruments and advance the definition of policy and principle in a given area.

19. For others, because the Declaration on the Right to Development straddles all other rights, it then becomes the "superior value" in decisionmaking rather than just a material expression, or a residual notion, of yet another perception of socioeconomic development (United Nations 2004).

20. Scholars tend to view the history of the content of human rights as reflecting, on the one hand, evolving perceptions of values and capabilities most in need of responsible attention at any given period of time and, on the other, humankind's recurring need for continuity and stability.

Chapter 2

1. The precise origin of the concept of the right to development is usually traced back to the lecture by Judge Kéba M'Baye at the International Institute of Human Rights in 1972. It was first proclaimed by the Organization of African Unity and included in the African Charter on Human and Peoples' Rights in 1981. The idea of promoting all civil, political, economic, social, and cultural rights as an integrated whole was first promoted in the Philadelphia Declaration of the International Labour Conference in 1944.

2. Five other core UN human rights treaties elaborate on the provisions of the International Bill of Human Rights: the International Convention on the Elimination of All Forms of Racial Discrimination (1965), the Convention on the Elimination of All Forms of Discrimination against Women (1979), the Convention against Torture and Other Cruel, Inhuman or Degrading Treatment or Punishment (1984), the Convention on the Rights of the Child (1989), and the International Convention on the Protection of the Rights of All Migrant Workers and Members of Their Families (1990).

3. The two other purposes of the UN are to (a) maintain international peace and security, and (b) develop friendly relations among states based on respect for the principle of equal rights and self-determination of peoples.

4. The charter gives the Economic and Social Council a range of important functions that involve coordination, policy review, and policy dialogue, but no enforcement powers. It is the only UN organ explicitly mandated by the charter to coordinate the activities of the specialized agencies, such as the International Monetary Fund and the World Bank.

5. The position of human rights relative to sovereignty has undergone significant changes over the last half century. The distinction that existed between matters that were exclusively within the domestic purview and those that were legitimately within the remit of the international community has become blurred and prey to power politics. For a discussion of this issue, see Alston and Steiner (2000).

6. The Universal Declaration of Human Rights was adopted without dissent and proclaimed by the UN General Assembly on December 10, 1948. Although the declaration does not have the enforceable legal obligations of a treaty, it has acquired a juridical status greater than originally intended and is widely used, even by national courts, as a means of judging compliance with human rights obligations under the

UN Charter. As noted, it is usually recognized that, even in the absence of enforcement mechanisms, international law does matter by affecting actors' perceptions, calculations, reputations, incentive structures, and norms.

7. Both proclaim that men are born and remain free and equal in rights. The French Declaration states that men have certain "natural rights" that have "no limits except those which assure to the other members of the society the enjoyment of the same rights," whereas the Virginia Declaration prefers "inherent rights," so that "when they enter into a state of society, they cannot, by any compact, deprive or divest their posterity; namely, the enjoyment of life and liberty, with the means of acquiring and possessing property, and pursuing and obtaining happiness and safety."

8. These rights include the following: (a) freedom from slavery or servitude; from torture or cruel, inhuman, or degrading treatment or punishment; from arbitrary interference with one's privacy, family, home, or correspondence; (b) freedom of thought, conscience, and religion; freedom of opinion and expression; and (c) the right to life, liberty, and security; to peaceful assembly and association; to form and to join trade unions; to take part in the government, directly or through freely chosen representatives; to leave any country, including his own, and to return to his country; to seek and to enjoy in other countries asylum from persecution; to recognition everywhere as a person before the law; to a fair and public hearing by an independent and impartial tribunal; and to be presumed innocent until proved guilty.

9. In the French Declaration of the Rights of Man and of the Citizen (1789), the right to property is explicitly referred to as "an inviolable and sacred right," of which "no one shall be deprived except where public necessity, legally determined, shall clearly demand it, and then only on condition that the owner shall have been previously and equitably indemnified." The Universal Declaration incorporates the right to own property (alone as well as in association) and the right not to be arbitrarily deprived of it, adding the concept of intellectual property. Article 27(2) states that "everyone has the right to the protection of the moral and material interests resulting from any scientific, literary or artistic production of which he is the author."

10. Article 26(1) of the Universal Declaration states that "education shall be free, at least in the elementary and fundamental stages. Elementary education shall be compulsory. Technical and professional education shall be made generally available and higher education shall be equally accessible to all on the basis of merit."

11. Alongside the extensive catalog of rights, the Universal Declaration makes provision for duties in its Article 29(1): "Everyone has duties to the community in which alone the free and full development of his personality is possible."

12. The International Covenant on Civil and Political Rights and the International Covenant on Economic, Social and Cultural Rights were opened for signature in 1966 and entered into force in 1976 among the states that had become party to them. Thirty years later, 156 and 153 countries have become state parties to the ICCPR and ICESCR, respectively. When the Universal Declaration and the two covenants overlap, the latter are understood to explicate and help interpret the former.

13. While the Human Rights Committee is a treaty entity established explicitly under the ICCPR, no such mechanism is provided for under the ICESCR. The Committee on Economic, Social, and Cultural Rights was established by the Economic and Social Council rather than emanating from a specific provision of the ICESCR.

14. The covenant also calls for the establishment of a Human Rights Committee. State parties that become party to the covenant's First Optional Protocol further recognize the competence of the Human Rights Committee to consider and act on

communications from individuals claiming to be victims of covenant violations. Also noteworthy is the covenant's Second Optional Protocol, which is aimed at abolishing the death penalty worldwide. Adopted in 1989 and entered into force in 1991, it has been favorably received in most of western Europe and in many countries in the Americas, though not in the United States.

15. In contrast, the ICCPR obliges each state party to respect and to ensure to all individuals within its territory the rights recognized in the covenant. The only obligation subject to immediate application in the ICESCR is the prohibition of discrimination in the enjoyment of the rights enumerated on grounds of "race, colour, sex, language, religion, political or other opinion, national or social origin, property, and birth or other status."

16. As noted by law professor Burns Weston (2002), the Soviet Union wished to gain recognition of its western frontiers as established at the end of World War II, and the West sought concessions primarily on security requirements and human rights (largely in that order).

17. The basic principles embodied in the Helsinki Accords are widely considered to have strongly influenced the end of East-West confrontation and provided the impetus for democratic change that led to the end of the cold war.

18. In 1994, the CSCE was replaced by the Organization for Security and Cooperation in Europe.

19. In the Middle East and Asia, states have been more divided over the desirability of establishing regional human rights frameworks for the promotion, protection, and enforcement of human rights. The Arab Charter on Human Rights (1994) provides few instruments for monitoring human rights and no enforcement mechanism. In the Asian and Pacific region, the process of establishing a regional mechanism for the promotion and protection of human rights has remained largely at the exploratory stage.

20. The European Social Charter (1961) was established as a companion instrument to the European Convention to deal with the promotion of economic, social, and cultural rights. However, in contrast to the convention, and reflecting the increased emphasis on market-oriented economic policies in many European countries, the Social Charter and its revised version (1996) have never received the same political commitment as that received by the European Convention.

21. The United States is not a party to the Additional Protocol to the American Convention on Human Rights in the Area of Economic, Social, and Cultural Rights that was adopted in 1988.

Chapter 3

1. A negative right is a right, either moral or decreed by law, to not be subject to an action of another human being (usually abuse or coercion). In contrast, a positive right is a right to be provided with something through the action of another person or group of people (usually a state). The former proscribes action, whereas the latter prescribes it.

2. Some scholars would subdivide negative rights into liberty rights (i.e., the pure negative rights that one does not hold against anybody, for instance, of walking freely in the street) and negative claim rights (i.e., the negative rights that one holds against others' interfering in one's life or property). For a discussion, see Jones (1994).

3. While negative rights are mostly covered in the Universal Declaration of Human Rights and the International Covenant on Civil and Political Rights, they also include the right to own property and the right not to be deprived of it arbitrarily—rights that were fundamental to the interests fought for in the American and French Revolutions and to the rise of capitalism.

4. Positive rights are mostly covered in the Universal Declaration of Human Rights and the International Covenant on Economic, Social and Cultural Rights, including the right to social security; the right to work and to protection against unemployment; the right to rest and leisure, including periodic holidays with pay; the right to a standard of living adequate for the health and well-being of self and family; and the right to education.

5. Other solidarity rights include the right to political, economic, social, and cultural self-determination; the right to participate in and benefit from the common heritage of mankind (shared earth and space resources; scientific, technical, and other information and progress; and cultural traditions, sites, and monuments); the right to peace; the right to a healthy and sustainable environment; and the right to humanitarian disaster relief.

6. Alston and Quinn (1987, p. 184) note that "given that the chief difference is one of degree, it can be said in general terms that economic and social rights are, on average, somewhat more dependent for their full realization on positive state action than are civil and political rights."

7. Donnelly (1982, p. 401) notes that in the Universal Declaration of Human Rights: "Human rights are clearly and unambiguously conceptualized as being inherent to humans and not as the product of social cooperation. These rights are conceptualized as being universal and held equally by all, that is as natural rights." In that paradigm, human rights are only personal rights, based on negative freedom, such as the rights to life, liberty, and property, whereby the law prohibits others from killing, imprisoning, or silencing an individual who has a claim to such freedoms that the state is expected to protect. In contrast, economic and social rights are associated with positive freedoms that the state has to secure and protect through positive action. Therefore, according to this view, they are not natural rights. However, for Alston (1988), the Universal Declaration has many elements going beyond the principles of natural rights. In fact, it is firmly based on a pluralistic foundation of international law with many elements of economic and social rights, viewing an individual's personality as essentially molded by the community.

8. Negative rights have the additional characteristic of protecting the freedom of individuals, in particular minorities, against the will of the majority. For democracies, this implies that negative rights limit the scope of majority decisionmaking and create protected domains on which not even the state is allowed to trespass.

9. Alston (2004, p. 49) notes that "a (negative) approach is too often interpreted as requiring only abstention on the part of governments and does not attach sufficient importance to the need for positive, affirmative measures in many contexts."

10. Machan (2001) notes that "because it is itself arbitrary and incoherent, the doctrine of positive rights leaves government free to be arbitrary and incoherent."

11. Each right imposes three kinds of duties: (1) duties not to deprive the right-holder of the object of the right; (2) duties to protect right holders from such deprivations; and (3) duties to compensate those who have been deprived.

12. Although closely related, it would be wrong to assert that civil and political rights and other first-generation rights correspond completely to the concept of "negative" as opposed to "positive" rights. In the same way, all the rights embraced by

the second generation of economic, social, and cultural rights cannot properly be labeled positive rights. For example, the right to free choice of employment, the right to form and to join trade unions, and the right to participate freely in the cultural life of the community do not inherently require affirmative state action to ensure their enjoyment.

13. Under this logic, the "global rich" have an obligation to eradicate the radical poverty of the "global poor," because they have violated a principle of justice not to harm others unduly by imposing a coercive global order on them that reduces the security of their access to the objects of their human right to subsistence (Gilabert 2005).

14. As for all positive rights, this would require an elusive definition and delineation of what such a right would involve (e.g., the right to adequate medicine, the right to adequate health facilities, etc.).

15. One should recall that about 170 million people have been killed by states, quasi-states, and stateless groups in genocide, massacres, extrajudicial executions, and the like in the 20th century (Rummel 1994). As noted by sociology professor Erich Weede (2008), although the 20th century suffered two world wars and other bloody wars, fewer people died on the battlefield or because of bombing campaigns than have been murdered or starved to death by their own governments. Whoever wants to protect human rights should, therefore, first of all focus on the necessity of protecting people from the state and its abuse of power.

16. Death from starvation often arises when there is no overall decline in food availability but rather violation of fundamental freedoms, including that of trading one's labor power or skills. For instance, Sen (1981) shows that there have been many famines during which the food supply did not diminish—such as the one in Bangladesh in 1974, a peak year for food production. Famines are usually created by policies, not by pests or droughts.

17. Determinism theory states that the way things will be is a result of how things are and the work of natural laws.

18. The distinction between the two concepts of liberty is deeply embedded in the philosophical tradition, with the notion of negative liberty being associated with the classical English political philosophers such as Locke, Hobbes, Smith, and Mill, and positive liberty with thinkers such as Hegel, Rousseau, and Marx.

19. This philosophical debate finds concrete application in a number of societal debates, for instance, on the issue of drug consumption, road safety, or regular opening hours for shops.

20. "Once I take this view," Isaiah Berlin (2002, p. 180) says, "I am in a position to ignore the actual wishes of men or societies, to bully, oppress, torture in the name, and on behalf, of their 'real' selves, in the secure knowledge that whatever is the true goal of man . . . must be identical with his freedom."

21. Friedrich Hayek (1960) noted that competitive market allocations arise not as an "intended outcome" of some foreseen purpose or plan, but as a result of the actions of millions of self-interested economic agents acting independently, in a "self-generating" process of adaptation and cumulative growth. He argued that "unintended outcomes" of this type (a) fall outside the ambit of human responsibility, (b) cannot be categorized as just or unjust, and (c) fall outside the range of "freedom-restricting" conditions (see Vizard 2005).

22. In contrast, positive freedom would require that not only all individuals be provided with a similar level of command over economic resources but that the individual's capacity to convert these resources into *capabilities* be taken into account

in the social engineering (OHCHR 2004). For instance, people with different biological characteristics may require different amounts of food and health care to acquire the same degree of freedom to live a healthy life. Similarly, people living in different cultural environments might feel that they need different amounts of clothing to have the capability to be clothed at a minimally acceptable level.

23. An act of commission (e.g., killing someone) does not carry the same moral blame as a failure to intervene to rescue someone (e.g., a drowning person) or to take action to address a human disaster (e.g., a famine).

24. For instance, in his inaugural William E. Simon lecture on "Two Ideas of Freedom," George Weigel (2001) notes that "in the final analysis, Berlin's 'two concepts' are unsatisfactory because Berlin does not drive the analysis deeply enough, historically and philosophically." The main philosophical debate relates to the relationship between determinism and free will.

25. Egalitarians usually consider that the poor in a capitalist society are, as such, unfree, or that they are less free than the rich, in contrast to libertarians, who tend to see the poor in a capitalist society as being no less free than the rich.

26. A legally enforceable right should consist of four interrelated components: (a) the right holder (an individual or group of individuals), (b) the substantive content of the right, (c) a duty bearer (an individual or group of individuals), and (d) an enforcement mechanism.

27. Philosophical supporters of human rights are necessarily committed to a form of moral universalism, in contrast to moral relativists who would claim that universally valid moral truths do not exist since moral beliefs, principles, and practices tend to be socially and historically contingent.

28. For instance, the Child Rights Information Network, supported by the United Nations Children's Fund, has developed a human rights approach to development programming whereby human rights, in particular children's and women's rights, are mainstreamed into development through the identification of key claim holder and/or duty bearer relationships at all levels of society (Jonsson 2004).

29. While states are often the notional duty bearers (in the Declaration on the Right to Development "states should take steps to eliminate obstacles to development resulting from failure to observe civil and political rights, as well as economic, social and cultural rights"), economic and social rights would remain fictitious until they are protected in national law and are justiciable before national courts.

30. In the economic sphere, Blume and Voigt (2004) conjecture that a divergence between de jure and de facto rights could lead to lower levels of legitimacy of the state and its representatives, thereby imputing welfare costs on societies to provide the same level of collective goods, as more resources are necessary to achieve a given objective when the state enjoys less legitimacy.

31. While Neumayer (2005) shows that ratification of international human rights treaties can marginally improve a country's human rights record, Keith (1999) and Hathaway (2002) find that, if anything, ratification can often be connected with more, rather than less, abuses by governments. These latter findings were challenged by Goodman and Jinks (2003).

32. This credibility deficit of the Human Rights Commission has cast a shadow on the reputation of the UN system as a whole and prompted then UN Secretary-General Kofi Annan (2005) to propose replacing the commission by a smaller standing Human Rights Council aimed at abiding by the highest human rights standards.

33. Philip Alston does not go as far as Peter Uvin (2004, p. 44), who characterizes the UN's human rights mechanisms as "some of the most powerless, under-funded, toothless, formulaic, and politically manipulated institutions of the United Nations."

34. None of the international human rights instruments currently in force says anything about the legitimacy or priority of the rights it addresses, save possibly in the case of rights that are stipulated by international covenant to be "nonderogable" and therefore, arguably, more fundamental than others (e.g., freedom from arbitrary or unlawful deprivation of life, freedom from torture and from inhuman or degrading treatment and punishment, freedom from slavery, and so on).

35. In 1987, a specific resolution was adopted on the indivisibility and interdependence of economic, social, cultural, civil, and political rights (United Nations 1987). It recalled that "the ideal of free human beings enjoying freedom from fear and want can only be achieved if conditions are created whereby persons may enjoy their economic, social and cultural rights as well as their civil and political rights."

36. These freedoms include freedom of speech and expression; freedom of every person to worship God in his own way; freedom from want; and freedom from fear.

37. For instance, Salman Salman and Shiobhan McInerney-Lankford (2004) express the view that neither set of rights has a full meaning without the other, and that attempting to find a normative priority between them is a fruitless endeavor.

38. To be sure, some disagreements about legitimacy and priority could also derive from differences of definition and interpretation of negative rights (e.g., what is "torture" or "inhuman treatment" to one may not be so to another, as in the case of punishment by caning or by death).

39. The right to own property is stated in the Universal Declaration but is not included in either of the international covenants, and has thus remained outside the scope of the human rights monitoring system.

40. The right to property in UN instruments is often circumscribed to the rights of indigenous people or other vulnerable groups over their lands, territories, and other resources. The United Nations Economic and Social Council (1998) notes that "states should take measures to ensure that poor and vulnerable groups, including landless farmers, indigenous people and the unemployed, have access to productive assets such as land, credit and means for self-employment," or that "in areas where conflicts of any types have occurred or are occurring, States should ensure that the population living in the affected areas is able to retain the right to their property and legally acquired rights."

41. The Office of the United Nations High Commissioner for Refugees was established in 1950 to lead and coordinate international action to protect refugees and resolve refugee problems worldwide. Its primary purpose is to safeguard the rights and well-being of refugees, including the right to seek asylum and find safe refuge in another state.

42. International migration is dominated by voluntary movement of people. Refugees and asylum seekers represented 7 percent of global migrants in 2005 (World Bank 2008b).

43. According to International Migration (United Nations 2006), 191 million people, representing 3 percent of the world population, lived outside their country of birth in 2005. Almost 1 in every 10 people living in more developed regions is a migrant compared with 1 of every 70 people in developing regions. Sixty percent of the world's migrants currently reside in more developed regions.

44. Ironically, the perception that migration could pose a threat to political stability, economic welfare, social security, or cultural identity has more to do with the development of the welfare, paternalistic, at times nationalist, state than with actual migration flows.

45. According to the World Bank (2008b), the flow of recorded remittances from migrants to their relatives in their country of birth was estimated at $318 billion in 2007, of which $240 billion went to developing countries, thereby surpassing by far the total amount of official development assistance.

46. "It is not from the benevolence of the butcher, the brewer, or the baker that we expect our dinner, but from their regard to their own self-interest" (A. Smith 1776, p. 14).

47. Finnis (1980) and others have defended the philosophical foundations of human rights by an approach based on self-interest.

48. The authors argue that the Resourceful, Evaluative, Maximizing Model, as opposed to the Economic (or Money-Maximizing) Model, Psychological (or Hierarchy of Needs) Model, Sociological (or Social Victim) Model, and the Political (or Perfect Agent) Model, best describes the systematically rational part of human behavior. The model is based on four postulates: (a) every individual cares and is an evaluator, (b) each individual's wants are unlimited, (c) each individual is a maximizer, and (d) the individual is resourceful.

49. While it could be argued that the universal acceptance of a claim as a right is sufficient moral foundation for the concept of human rights, it does not imply that the particular right is relevant from a development perspective.

50. Sustainability is key, as the protection of today's economic, social, and cultural rights could be to the detriment of future generations and lead to violations of their rights. In that sense, most of the so-called economic, social, and cultural achievements of former communist countries should be discounted, as they were unsustainable and financed through distortions to be borne by future generations.

51. According to Gwartney, Skipton, and Lawson (2001), individuals have economic freedom when the following conditions exist: (a) their property is acquired without the use of force, fraud, or theft and is protected from physical invasion by others; and (b) they are free to use, exchange, or give their property to another as long as their actions do not violate the identical rights of others.

52. In that sense, the Declaration on the Right to Development belongs to a long history of thinking, which does not accept the normative and utilitarian beneficent effects of acquisitiveness through the competitive market. As Burke (1795) pointed out long ago, "Popular incomprehension of the conditions that led to the improvement of the standard of living in a commercial society could pose a threat to the development of 'universal opulence'" (cited in Muller 2002, p. 118).

Chapter 4

1. Marks (2003b, p. 19) notes that the right to development is "too often a slogan to make politicians, diplomats, and bureaucrats feel good."

2. Alston (2004, p. 4) observes that a rights-based approach "tend[s] to gloss over the complexities, idealize[s] the characteristics of the human rights mechanisms, [is] overly demanding, and [is] poorly attuned to the need for operational priorities." He then concludes that "human rights advocates need to prioritize, stop expecting a paradigm shift, and tailor their prescriptions more carefully."

3. For Sengupta (1999), the Vienna Declaration settled the controversial debate as to whether the right to development could be regarded as a human right.

4. The numerous resolutions tabled throughout the years since the adoption of the Declaration on the Right to Development have been rejected by some key members, including the United States and, at times, have been subject to many abstentions. For a detailed discussion, see Marks (2003b, 2004).

5. The human rights treaty bodies publish their interpretation of the content of human rights provisions in the form of General Comments on thematic issues. Because the Committee on Economic, Social, and Cultural Rights does not have authority to create new obligations for the state parties to the International Covenant on Economic, Social and Cultural Rights, General Comments are not legally binding, although some have emphasized their quasi-judicial nature and their significant legal weight.

6. A Right to Development Project was launched in 2001 to provide research support to the Independent Expert to study how to realize the right to development in practice, beginning with the rights to food, education, and health.

7. In a series of landmark judgments, the jurisprudence of the South African Constitutional Court upheld claims regarding the violation of socioeconomic rights as established in the South African Constitution. It reasoned that where resource constraints are binding, the responsibilities of the state under these articles can be discharged.

8. For instance, a number of Organisation for Economic Co-operation and Development countries continue to record persistently large unemployment rates despite the fact that the right to work is enshrined in their constitutions (e.g., Italy). As with other positive rights, it is unrealistic to believe that a duty bearer can be held judiciable of someone's right to work.

9. The NEPAD strategic framework document arises from a mandate given to the five initiating heads of state (Algeria, Egypt, Nigeria, Senegal, South Africa) by the Organization of African Unity to develop an integrated socioeconomic development framework for Africa. It was officially adopted in July 2001.

10. For instance, NEPAD aims at halting the marginalization of Africa in the globalization process, placing African countries on a path of sustainable growth and development, eradicating poverty, and accelerating the empowerment of women through good governance, ownership, leadership, and partnership.

11. The EU-ACP partnership agreements emphasize that the "respect for human rights, democratic principles and the rule of law are essential elements of the partnership."

12. UNICEF has adopted the Convention on the Rights of the Child as its normative framework.

13. The eight MDGs aim at (1) eradicating extreme poverty and hunger; (2) achieving universal primary education; (3) promoting gender equality and empowering women; (4) reducing child mortality; (5) improving maternal health; (6) combating HIV/AIDS, malaria, and other diseases; (7) ensuring environmental sustainability; and (8) developing a global partnership for development. The MDGs derive from the UN Millennium Declaration (United Nations 2000) and form a blueprint agreed to by all the world's countries and all the world's leading development institutions.

14. The declaration recalls that "states have the primary responsibility for the creation of national and international conditions favourable to the realization of the right to development," and "states have the duty to take steps, individually and

collectively, to formulate international development policies with a view to facilitating the full realization of the right to development."

15. The UN Development Programme (2003, p. 27) notes that "the basic values of freedom, equality, solidarity, tolerance, respect for nature and shared responsibility" that underpin the MDGs also "mirror the fundamental motivation for human rights."

16. PRSPs describe a country's macroeconomic, structural, and social policies and programs to promote growth and reduce poverty, as well as associated external financing needs. Their five core principles are to be (a) country-driven (promoting national ownership of strategies through broad-based participation of civil society); (b) result-oriented and focused on outcomes that will benefit the poor; (c) comprehensive in recognizing the multidimensional nature of poverty; (d) partnership-oriented, involving coordinated participation of development partners (government, domestic stakeholders, and external donors); and (e) based on a long-term perspective for poverty reduction.

17. Countries where the PRSP deals with human rights include Bolivia, Burkina Faso, Cambodia, Cameroon, Nicaragua, Rwanda, Tanzania, Uganda, and Vietnam. For instance, Nicaragua's PRSP proposes measures to assist the poor to meet housing needs, protect children in high-risk conditions, implement programs for the elderly, prevent domestic violence, strengthen the Office for Human Rights, and protect the rights of indigenous peoples (Leite 2001).

18. In short, the perception is that there is a big gap between policies that are perceived to be in the interests of the poor (e.g., land and agrarian reform, progressive taxation, protection of domestic markets, food sovereignty, social rights and entitlements, and other forms of government protection vis-à-vis the operation of free markets) and those that the IFIs consider sound. For an argued response to these criticisms, see Plant (2005).

19. In that connection, the High-Level Task Force on the Implementation of the Right to Development established in 2004 was mandated to examine the "obstacles and challenges to the implementation of the MDGs in relation to the right to development."

20. Goal 8 calls, inter alia, for "enhanced debt relief for heavily indebted poor countries; cancellation of official bilateral debt; and more generous official development assistance for countries committed to poverty reduction."

21. Expressed as a percentage of developed countries' gross national income, global ODA continues to fall short of the long-standing target of 0.7 percent that was reaffirmed in the Monterrey Consensus (United Nations 2002). According to the Organisation for Economic Co-operation and Development, although global ODA increased to 0.33 percent of gross national income in 2005 (up from 0.26 percent in 2004) to top more than US$100 billion, the increase was mainly due to large debt-relief operations for Iraq and Nigeria and the assistance related to the December 2004 Indian Ocean tsunami. In 2006, total ODA fell back to US$104 billion as debt relief declined (OECD 2008).

22. Put more bluntly, the aid industry has gone on for 60 years with hardly anything to show for the $2 trillion it has spent (Dichter 2005).

23. These programs include, most notably, the various humanitarian and emergency aid programs targeted to helping people in times of disaster, to improve education, or to prolong human life (e.g., food assistance, school vouchers, and immunization programs).

24. Easterly (2005, p. 61) observes that "after 43 years and US$568 billion (in 2003 dollars) in foreign aid to Africa . . . donor officials apparently still have not gotten around to furnishing the 12-cent medicines to children to prevent half of all malaria deaths."

25. As early as 1957, Popper delved into the reasons why utopian plans to help the poor were often doomed.

26. For Dichter (2005), ODA has grown into an industry and, like other industries, is increasingly concerned with maintaining itself and increasing its market share. There are a lot of jobs, money, and institutional interests at stake in the aid industry, which includes not only the aid programs of official bilateral donors and multilateral agencies, but also the activities of thousands of nongovernmental organizations working in the area of development aid.

27. Easterly (2005) cites examples of successful aid programs that passed rigorous evaluation: subsidies to families for education and health costs for their children, remedial teaching, uniforms and textbooks, school vouchers, deworming drugs and nutritional supplements, vaccinations, HIV prevention, indoor spraying for malaria, bed nets, fertilizer, and clean water. There is not much doubt that there is scope for considerable improvement in the methodology for rigorously evaluating development aid programs (Duflo and Kremer 2003).

28. George Edward Moore (1873–1958) brought the following paradoxical sentence to the attention of philosophers: "I know that such-and-such is true, but I don't believe it."

29. Under this logic, poor countries would somehow be too poor to achieve sustained economic growth on their own and escape a "poverty trap" (Sachs 2001).

30. For Sally (2005), "the Sachs Report, with its big-spending hubris and breathtaking political naivety, should get the Nobel Prize for pottiness and recklessness."

31. The joint IMF–World Bank 2006 *Global Monitoring Report* also calls for at least a doubling of ODA within the next five years to accelerate progress toward the MDGs.

32. Notwithstanding the fact we have seen the failure of what was already a "big push" of foreign aid to Africa. According to Norberg (2003, p. 184), "since the beginning of the 1960s, Africa has received development assistance equaling six times the aid sent by the United States under the Marshall Plan following WWII. If the money had gone to investments, African countries would have had a Western standard of living by now."

33. For decades, the aid industry has tried one thing after another to make aid work better and the underlying belief that the right formula is within reach is one of the things that has kept it going (Dichter 2005). In the 1950s and 1960s, ODA aimed at supporting import substitution, industrialization, infrastructure projects, agriculture marketing boards and cooperatives, and other inward-oriented strategies. In the 1970s, ODA rediscovered poverty itself and swung in favor of supporting programs dealing directly with the urban and rural poor (education, health, housing, and so forth). In the 1980s and 1990s, ODA realized the importance of outward-oriented strategies, the need for upstream structural policy reforms and for promotion of sound institutions and good governance. Today, ODA seems to have rediscovered the key role of infrastructure to address poor countries' supply-side constraints.

34. As noted by Dichter (2005, p. 4), "That such a self-evident notion comes along in the seventh decade of the industry tells us something about its capacity for deep self-examination."

35. See www.aidharmonization.org/ah-overview/secondary-pages/editable?key=205.

36. At the extreme, a rigorously applied selective strategy would result in aid being extended only to Finland, Iceland, and New Zealand, given their unequaled record on policy performance and corruption perception (according to Transparency International [2005]). Meanwhile, Chad, which received the 158th and lowest score in the 2005 Corruption Perception Index, is one of the low-income countries to have reached the decision point under the heavily indebted poor countries initiative for debt relief.

37. Sarcastically put, "Aid is like champagne: in success you deserve it, in failure you need it" (Bauer 1981, p. 91).

38. Rajan and Subramanian (2005b) find evidence that aid inflows are associated with declines in the share of labor-intensive and tradable industries in the manufacturing sector and that these effects stem from the real exchange rate overvaluation caused by aid inflows. This effect could easily be compounded by large inflows of foreign direct investment and other private capital flows, as "good policies" would not only attract aid flows but private flows (Alesina and Dollar 1998). However, for Stern, Dethier, and Rogers (2005, p. 376), these "rigid presumptions against extra aid on macroeconomic grounds (which have occasionally emerged from the IMF) are generally unsound and unacceptable."

39. Opinion and Analysis, "Aid Is Not Best Way to Help Africa Progress," *Irish Times*, March 26, 2008.

40. Of course, not all forms of trade are conducive to development. Trade in oil and mineral resources tends to skew a country's politics; encourage rent-seeking behaviors; and dampen incentives to innovate, produce, and compete (Auty 1993). For Thomas Friedman (2006), the first law of petropolitics is that the price of oil and the pace of freedom always move in opposite directions in oil-rich petrolist states.

41. The financing gap refers to the difference between a country's savings and its investment needs to attain a target growth rate. According to this theory (Domar 1946), foreign aid is expected to help fill the gap and achieve a higher growth rate than would otherwise be possible under the prevailing private financing capacities. In the last decades, the notion of financing gap has evolved to refer to the budgetary needs of countries.

42. The 2005 Human Development Report (UNDP 2005, p. 7) is an example of such an approach in the sense that international aid is seen as "one of the most effective weapons in the war against poverty." While the report (rightly) calls for breaking with "business-as-usual" to meet the MDGs, the proposed action plan reads very much as "more of the same" (more external assistance, more trade compensation, more policy "space," and so forth).

43. The last half century has witnessed half a dozen authoritative studies of foreign aid, each of which has suggested ways to reform the implementation of aid programs.

44. In her survey of existing bilateral programs, Piron (2004) notes that since the 1993 Vienna Declaration—and the recognition that democracy, development, and respect for human rights and fundamental freedoms are interdependent and mutually reinforcing—a number of bilateral development agencies have developed policies and guidance on human rights.

Part II

1. Broadly speaking, three theories of economic growth are usually discussed in the literature: the neoclassical growth theory, which emphasizes the accumulation

of factors (labor and capital) and technological progress (exogenous or endogenous) as the primary determinants of growth (e.g., Solow 1956; Romer 1990); the geographic growth theory, which emphasizes climatic conditions, access to major markets, and other locational factors as key to explaining long-term economic development (e.g., Diamond 1997; Sachs 2001); and the institutional growth theory, which stresses the importance of a society's institutional framework, in particular the existence of a market-friendly environment for entrepreneurial activities, in the long-term perfor-mance of economies (e.g., Acemoglu and Robinson 2004; North 1990).

2. The authors find that economic institutions encouraging economic growth emerge when political institutions allocate power to groups with interest in broad-based property rights enforcement, when they create effective constraints on power holders, and when there are relatively few rents to be captured by power holders.

Chapter 5

1. As underlined in Chapter 3, the paradigm presented in this book differs from that discussed by Sen in *Development as Freedom* (1999) in the sense that Sen's capability approach lumps together—and somewhat problematically—elements of negative or liberty human rights with a certain measure of coercion in the form of positive and welfare rights. In particular, the "capability approach" provides direct support for the characterization of poverty, hunger, and starvation as "freedom-restricting" con-ditions. For a discussion of Sen's contributions in the field of human rights, see Vizard (2005). For a discussion of the underlying tension in Sen's approach, see Machan (2006a).

2. Immigration policies, especially in developed countries, tend to be far more protectionist and/or discriminatory than policies regulating foreign trade and capital flows, which in turn explains today's relatively low migration flows, especially when compared with the second half of the 19th century. According to Bertocchi and Strozzi (2005), while citizenship laws did not contribute to the economic forces that determined the early, mass migration waves of the 19th century, these laws have, since World War II, been responding endogenously and systematically to international migration as well as to other factors, such as border stability, the welfare burden, and colonial history.

3. As noted in *Economic Freedom of the World* (Gwartney and Lawson 2004, p. 29): "We do not know where the next ingenious idea will come from. More than any other form of economic organization, a free market makes it possible for a wide range of people to try out their innovative ideas and see if they can pass the market test. If they do, they will improve living standards. On the other hand, if they fail, they will soon be brought to a halt. This process of experimentation and discovery is a powerful force for economic progress."

4. That economic growth is a necessary condition for economic development is by now an almost universally accepted principle. As Krueger (2005b) puts it: "The evidence is clear: the only way to bring about a lasting reduction in poverty is through rapid and sustained economic growth. That sounds straightforward enough. Unfortunately, we cannot legislate for rapid growth any more than we can for poverty reduction. What matters are the policies that will deliver more rapid growth."

5. It has been estimated that an increase in the number of migrants equal to 3 percent of the labor force of the Organisation for Economic Co-operation and Development countries would result in global welfare gains that would surpass those

obtained from the removal of all trade barriers, with significant gains for all parties involved (Walmsley and Winters 2005).

6. Whether it is the destination country ("brain drain") or the country of origin ("brain gain") that benefits the most from migration is largely irrelevant, as all that matters from the perspective of this book is the fate of the individual migrant and the minimization of his "brain waste."

7. Many crucial elements of economic freedom are not observable or readily quantifiable, requiring the use of various "proxies" for these elements. For instance, the freedom to trade internationally could be measured by a number of variables, more or less relevant but always difficult to rank, from tariff and nontariff barriers to various behind-the-border restrictions.

8. See the Fraser Institute's *Economic Freedom of the World* Index, Freedom House's Economic Freedom Indicators, and the Heritage Foundation's Indexes of Economic Freedom.

9. According to their estimates, the various measures of economic freedom explain from 54 percent to 74 percent of the cross-country variation in income, with each coefficient carrying the correct sign and being highly significant. A 10 percent increase in economic freedom can be expected to produce an increase in gross national product per capita of 7.4 percent to 13.6 percent in a representative country.

10. The correlation coefficients among the three indexes are higher than 0.8 in absolute value. The Freedom House index appears to have the least in common, reflecting Freedom House's historic emphasis on civil and political rights, including democratic institutions, as crucial elements of economic freedom, and its relatively light emphasis on the size of government in determining the ranking.

11. They also find some interesting correlations among their four categories of human rights and a number of other parameters, such as the extent of press freedom, the nature of the democratic regime (presidential vs. parliamentary), or the nature of the democratic representation (majority rule vs. proportional representation).

12. The Economic Freedom of the World index is perhaps the most ambitious attempt to quantify economic freedom and its effect on investment and economic growth. Currently available for 141 countries, the index measures the consistency of a nation's policies and institutions with economic freedom, in particular the extent to which various countries rely on open markets to allocate goods and resources.

13. They adjusted for differences in initial income level, tropical location, share of population near an ocean, and human capital.

14. According to the 2007 Economic Freedom of the World index, Hong Kong retains the highest rating for economic freedom. The other top scorers are Singapore, New Zealand, Switzerland, Canada, the United Kingdom, the United States, Estonia, Australia, and Ireland. The majority of nations ranked in the bottom fifth are African, and all the nations in the bottom 10 are African with the exceptions of Venezuela and Myanmar.

15. Interestingly, the share of the income earned by the poorest 10 percent of the population was found to be unrelated to the degree of economic freedom in a nation.

16. Short-term fluctuations in growth rates are influenced by a number of factors that may dominate and conceal the strength of the relationship between economic freedom and growth.

17. The average economic freedom score rose from 5.4 (out of 10) in 1980 to 6.6 in 2005. Five nations increased their scores by more than three points since 1980: Hungary, Peru, Uganda, Ghana, and Israel. Only three nations decreased their score

by more than one point: Zimbabwe, Venezuela, and Myanmar. Other nations that saw reductions are Nepal, Bahrain, Hong Kong, Malaysia, the Republic of Congo, and Haiti.

18. Key structural reforms have been articulated around dismantling the planned-economy apparatus (controlled prices and quantitative plans); fostering an increased role for the private sector in the economy; opening the economy to foreign trade and investment; enhancing the autonomy of state-owned banks and enterprises; and establishing the basic building blocks of a modern tax system and indirect monetary policy (Tseng and Rodlauer 2003).

19. In contrast to the coerced collectivization of agriculture in the 1950s and even more the so-called great leap forward that abolished private property and self-ownership of peasants, which resulted in a decline of Chinese weight in the global economy under Mao Zedong (Lin, Cai, and Li 2003; Maddison 1998).

20. An extreme example is the comparative performance of market-oriented West Germany and highly regulated East Germany, or the current relative performance of South Korea and North Korea. Less dramatic differences on the effect of economic freedom can be found on all continents among both developed and developing countries.

21. This is not to say that all components of economic freedom are necessarily associated with economic growth. While some components of economic freedom are usually found to cause economic growth (e.g., the use of markets and property rights), other components may be caused by growth, and still others jointly determined with growth. Berggren (2003) provides a survey of the empirical findings in this area.

22. To determine what causal relationships exist among economic freedom, political freedom, and economic growth, the authors use a dynamic model and define causality along the lines established by Granger (1969).

23. Within these five broad categories, the EFW index of economic freedom incorporates 23 components themselves made of several subcomponents. Counting the various subcomponents, the EFW index is based on 42 distinct data. For instance, the regulation of credit, labor, and business incorporates a quantification of credit market regulations. This component is itself divided into five subcomponents: the ownership of banks (i.e., the percentage of deposits held in privately owned banks); the degree of competition (i.e., the extent to which domestic banks face competition from foreign banks); the extension of credit (i.e., the percentage of credit extended to the private sector); the extent of credit controls and regulations; and the extent of interest rate controls that lead to negative real interest rates.

24. According to Freedom House's definition (Karatnycky 2002, p. 722), freedom is "the opportunity to act spontaneously in a variety of fields outside the control of the government and other centers of potential domination."

25. A number of observers have pointed to the economic miracle of East Asia in the 1980s or that of China today to emphasize the crucial role of economic freedom in kick-starting economic growth, notwithstanding the absence of civil and political rights.

26. While Jagdish Bhagwati (2006) has questioned the sustainability of the development process when civil and political rights are not respected, pointing to the possible long run comparative advantage of India over China in this regard, Benjamin Friedman (2005) offers a more sanguine view and conjectures that, because material progress leads to moral progress (borrowing from the Enlightenment tradition), China would also eventually move toward liberalization and democratization.

27. More anecdotal evidence would point out that famines rarely occur in democratic societies with a free press or that democracies rarely go to war against each other, or that countries with McDonald's rarely declare war on each other.

28. Huntington (1968), Rao (1984), de Schweinitz (1959), and Vega-Gordillo and Alvarez-Arce 2003.

29. Just to mention one element, reported human rights abuses cannot be equated with actual abuses, as governments with outrageous human rights records will try to conceal such records as much as possible.

30. According to Freedom House's definition (2005), political rights enable people to "participate freely in the political process, including through the right to vote, compete for public office, and elect representatives who have a decisive impact on public policies and are accountable to the electorate." Civil liberties allow for "the freedoms of expression and belief, associational and organizational rights, rule of law, and personal autonomy without interference from the state." The methodology of the survey established basic standards (through a checklist of 10 political rights questions and 15 civil liberties questions) that are derived in large measure from the Universal Declaration of Human Rights.

31. In their survey of 18 studies, Przeworski and Limongi (1993) conclude that social scientists know surprisingly little about the relationship between political regimes and economic growth and that, while political institutions do matter for growth, thinking in terms of regimes does not seem to capture the relevant differences.

32. Smith (1776, p. 788) lists three core functions for the state: (a) "protecting the society from the violence and invasion of other independent societies," (b) "protecting, as far as possible, every member of the society from the injustice or oppression of every other member," and (c) "erecting and maintaining those public institutions and public works, which, though they be in the highest degree advantageous to a great society, are however of such a nature that the profit could never repay the expense to any individual or small group of individuals."

33. Krueger (2005a, p. 77) observes that it would be foolhardy for many private-sector entrepreneurs to enter a given line of economic activity if there were, or might be, public enterprises entering it, if only because of the uncertainty surrounding the extent to which government regulations would favor the public enterprise (e.g., de jure or de facto tax exemption; controlled prices and preferential treatment in the allocation of scarce goods, such as foreign exchange, imports, infrastructure; and so on).

34. In a liberal society, the state should not be seen as a "moral" entity. To quote Hayek (1944, p. 77), it is only "a piece of utilitarian machinery intended to help individuals in the fullest development of their individual personality."

35. This refers to the two conceptions of the nature of man underlying the philosophical debate between Rawls (1971) and Nozick (1974).

36. The theory of public choice brought to the fore long ago the recognition that "government officials were not benevolent disinterested social guardians in the spirit of Mill and Pigou, but were rather often self-interested, much the same as the private economic agents whose maximizing behavior had always been assumed to be selfish" (Krueger 2005a).

37. As noted by Milton Friedman (1962), the necessity of drawing a line between responsible individuals and others (e.g., madmen, children) is inescapable, and there is no avoiding the need for some measure of paternalism and arranging for their care by the government.

38. Uncompromising libertarians such as Rothbard (1978) would consider that state power is immoral in all circumstances and, therefore, the fight for liberty is not just about cutting coercive government but eliminating it altogether, not just about assigning property rights but deferring to the market even on questions of contract enforcement, and not just about cutting welfare but banishing all coercive redistribution.

Chapter 6

1. For North (1990, p. 3), "institutions are the rules of the game in a society or, more formally, are the humanely devised constraints that shape human interaction."

2. "The list of those who can validly claim to have contributed to the rediscovery of the link between free economic institutions and economic growth is long, but it is probably fair to say that the first attempt to systematically measure economic freedom was produced by Gastil and Wright for Freedom House in 1983" (Hanke and Walters 1997, p. 123).

3. The rule of law has also to do with unwritten rules, such as the level of trust and reputation in a society that allows economic agents to trust one another.

4. As noted by Posner (1998, p. 1), while "markets are more robust than some market-failure specialists believe, their vigor may depend on the establishment of an environment in which legal rights, especially property and contractual rights, are enforced and protected."

5. The rule of law is only one, generic aspect of a country's institutional setting. Countries are typically equipped with a wide range of institutions that seek to guarantee the proper functioning of markets, including regulatory institutions, institutions for macroeconomic management, institutions for social insurance, and institutions for conflict management.

6. In an influential article, La Porta and others (1988) argue that countries adhering to common law, which is of English origin, generally have the strongest legal protection for investors, followed by countries adhering to civil law adopted from the German and Scandinavian legal traditions, then by countries rooted in French civil law. See also Mahoney (2000).

7. An informal market activity is one that the government has taxed heavily, regulated in a burdensome manner, or simply outlawed in the past.

8. For many developing countries, strengthening the enforcement of contracts (in number of procedures, time, and cost) is key to strengthening the rule of law. For instance, in Burkina Faso, contract enforcement would typically require 41 procedures and 446 days and would cost about 95 percent of the debt to be collected (World Bank 2005). As noted by Krueger (2005a), "One wonders why any rational person would even attempt to collect, but that in turn raises questions as to whether contracts would even be used in these circumstances."

9. In the "law and development model," the law is central to the development process. It is an instrument that could be used to reform society, and lawyers and judges could serve as social engineers. As noted by Messik (1999), perhaps the most significant reason for the failure of this model was the naive belief that the American legal system (and the legal culture generally) could be easily transplanted to developing countries.

10. From a historical perspective, several authors have presented evidence that the rise of the Western world was based on gradual but fundamental changes in

property rights (e.g., North 1981; North and Thomas 1973; Rosenberg and Birdzell 1986).

11. "Once stated, the intellectual argument for the importance of property rights is compelling. Why does an individual invest unless to gain something for himself and his family? How can he ensure that gains flowing from his activity be appropriated and secured other than through a system of well-defined property rights? To suppose otherwise, is to suppose that human nature will change. That road is a dead end" (O'Driscoll and Hoskins 2003, p. 7).

12. One could argue that economic competition—when undistorted—is the main engine for just and sustainable social redistribution.

13. In de Soto's words (2000, p. 63), "The genius of the West was to have created a system that allowed people to grasp with the mind values that human eyes could never see and to manipulate things that hands could never touch."

14. In his book on the history of property rights, Bethell (1998, p. 99) notes that "the phrase 'private property' barely entered the language before the 19th century." The existence of private property was simply a natural presumption that underlay the work of classical economists, and its absence was simply unthinkable. Private property came under intellectual assault only in the aftermath of the French Revolution and with the Marxist revolution.

15. Demsetz (1967, p. 350) suggests that "the role of property rights is to internalize externalities when the gains of internalization become larger than the cost of internalization."

16. The role of property rights was rediscovered with the institutional school of economic development and was included in the original version of the Washington consensus as the last policy recommendation and only institutional reform (Williamson 1990).

17. Not to mention the abolition of private property in communist regimes, an experiment which turned out to be very costly in lives, human rights violations, and economic prosperity. More recently, the collapse of Zimbabwe is a dramatic natural experiment in the economic consequences of damaging property rights (Richardson 2005).

18. For de Soto, capital is the force that raises the productivity of labor and creates the wealth of nations. It is the lifeblood of the capitalist system, the foundation of progress, and the one thing that the poor countries of the world cannot seem to produce for themselves, no matter how eagerly their people engage in all the other activities that characterize a capitalist economy.

19. Even in the poorest countries, the poor save. According to de Soto (2000, p. 5): "The value of savings among the poor is, in fact, immense—forty times all the foreign aid received throughout the world since 1945. The total value of the real estate held but not legally owned by the poor of the third world and former communist nations is at least US$9.3 trillion, that is, more than 20 times the total direct foreign investment into all third world and former communist countries in the ten years after 1989."

20. In particular, the costs of registering property are high. For instance, registering property in Nicaragua requires 8 procedures, an average of 124 days, and costs about 3.5 percent of the value of the property. In Mali, it takes fewer procedures (5) and fewer days (29), but costs more than 20 percent of the value of the property. In contrast, New Zealand has 2 procedures, it takes 2 days, and it costs 0.1 percent of the value of the property (World Bank 2008a).

21. According to de Soto (2000, p. 7): "The poor do have things, but they lack the process to represent their property and create capital. It is the unavailability of these essential representations that explain why people who have adapted every other Western invention, from the paper clip to the nuclear reactor, have not been able to produce sufficient capital to make their domestic capitalism work."

22. De Soto (2000, p. 168) takes the example of a law enacted in Peru in 1924 to protect natives from further legal ploys by packing thousands of them into rural farming communities where the transfer of rights to any land was expressly prohibited. "In thus protecting the natives from the scheming and swindling elites, they also deprived them, albeit unintentionally, of the basic tools for creating capital."

23. "Exporting a country's system of private property rights ultimately entails exporting its history and political culture" (O'Driscoll and Hoskins 2003, p. 13). It is thus fraught with difficulties.

24. Intellectual property has turned out to be among the more significant elements of international cooperation and treaty making in the past decade. It is divided into two broad categories: (a) industrial property, which includes inventions (patents), trademarks, industrial designs, and geographic indications of source; and (b) copyright, which includes literary and artistic works, such as novels, poems, plays, films, and musical works; artistic works such as drawings, paintings, photographs, and sculptures; and architectural designs. Rights related to copyright include those of performing artists in their performances, producers of phonograms in their recordings, and those of broadcasters in their radio and television programs.

25. In the International Covenant on Economic, Social and Cultural Rights, states recognize the right of everyone "to benefit from the protection of the moral and material interests resulting from any scientific, literary or artistic production of which he is the author."

26. Kinsella (2001a, p. 22) cites Thomas Jefferson (himself an inventor and the United States' first patent examiner) as saying that "he who receives an idea from me, receives instruction himself without lessening mine; as he who lights his taper at mine, receives light without darkening me."

27. As more and more rights win the label "property," property risks losing all significance (Bell and DeLong 2002).

28. Helfer (2003) provides a mapping of the human rights and intellectual property interface.

29. Kinsella (2001b) wonders why, if patents and copyrights are essential to innovation, philosophers persist in writing their tomes, physicists in probing the universe, and mathematicians in toiling away at solving age-old riddles without the reward of a monopolistic ownership in the resulting ideas.

30. Bell and DeLong cite the example of the old doctrine that if you own property on a waterfront you can build a pier. However, if technological changes make it possible to build a square mile's worth of structures on pilings, suddenly your rights change: "You can't fill up San Francisco Bay." In the same vein, the reduction of transaction costs brought about by the digital revolution has nullified the doctrine that one can make limited copies of a copyright-protected creation without paying or seeking permission.

31. Intellectual property critics would point out that utilitarianism is an ends-justifies-the-means philosophy, which is itself problematic. Horrible violations of individual rights can be perpetrated in the name of this philosophy (Kinsella 2001b).

32. However, the extent of monopoly power is often misrepresented. For instance, while a patent gives the holder the right to exclude others from using the new idea commercially, it does not allow the holder to exclude other firms from entering the industry as in the traditional sense of a monopoly.

33. Abraham Lincoln (1859, p. 528) wrote that "the patent system secured to the inventor, for a limited time, the exclusive use of his invention; and thereby added the fuel of interest to the fire of genius in the discovery and production of new and useful things." This idea was formalized by Arrow (1962, p. 15) who, in the absence of property rights, expected a free enterprise economy "to underinvest in invention and research because it is risky, because the product can be appropriated only to a limited extent, and because of increasing returns in use."

34. For the World Intellectual Property Organization, the international protection of the rights of intellectual property owners (i.e., creators, inventors, and authors) acts as a spur to human creativity, advancing the boundaries of science and technology and enriching the world of literature and the arts. By providing a stable environment for the marketing of intellectual property products, it also oils the wheels of international trade.

35. The cornerstones of the WIPO's treaty system are the 1886 Berne Convention for the Protection of Literary and Artistic Works; the 1893 Paris Convention for the Protection of Industrial Property; and the 1961 Rome Convention for the Protection of Performers, Producers of Phonograms and Broadcasting Organizations. These conventions were updated to the Internet age in the 1994 Trademark Law Treaty, the 2000 Patent Law Treaty, and the WIPO Copyright Treaty and WIPO Performances and Phonograms Treaty of 2002. Other relevant international instruments include the 1952 Universal Copyright Convention of the United Nations Educational, Scientific, and Cultural Organization; the 1992 Convention on Biological Diversity; and the World Trade Organization 1995 Agreement on the Trade-related Aspects of Intellectual Property Rights (the TRIPS Agreement).

36. In her seminal paper on the ladder of citizen participation, Arnstein (1969) discusses eight types of participation and "nonparticipation," which she grades from Manipulation (least citizen participation) to Citizen Control (most citizen participation). The bottom rungs of the ladder (Manipulation and Therapy) are contrived to substitute for genuine participation. Their real objective is not to enable people to participate in planning or conducting programs, but to enable policymakers to "educate" or "cure" the participants. The middle rungs (Informing, Consulting, and Placation) progress to levels of "tokenism" that allow citizens to hear and to have a voice, without ensuring that their views will be heeded by policymakers. In the upper rungs (Partnership, Delegated Power, and Citizen Control), participation represents increasing degrees of decisionmaking clout.

37. In that sense, the PRSP approach has been portrayed by many critics as little more than a thinly disguised repackaging of old wine (i.e., structural adjustment loans) in new bottles.

38. In his view: "The prime reason why development agencies adopt such language with its deliberate obfuscations is, of course, to benefit from the moral authority and political appeal of the human rights discourse. The development community is in constant need of regaining the high moral ground in order to fend off criticism and mobilize resources. As the development community faces a deep crisis of legitimacy among both insiders and outsiders, the act of cloaking itself in the human rights mantle

may make sense, especially if it does not force anyone to think or act differently'' (Uvin 2002, p. 4).

39. Indeed, many scholars would argue that discourse changes have real-world effects: they slowly reshape the margins of acceptable action, create opportunities for redefining reputations and naming and shaming, change incentive structures and the way interests and preferences are defined, and influence expectations.

40. In contrast, participatory processes at the microeconomic or project level are easier to formulate and have become increasingly innovative as methods become more established and sophisticated (Isham, Narayan and Pritchett 1995).

41. As observed by Plant (2005, pp. 498–508): ''Can villagers be informed about and have some meaningful input into tradeoffs that might have to be made between service delivery and a more expansive fiscal or monetary policy? Here I am not calling into question the intellectual capacity of a village elder, but only his or her perspective and information base. Are either sufficiently broad to make a meaningful choice? Is it effective to broaden both so he or she can give an opinion? Probably not.''

42. For instance, Kant (1795) opposed the concept of majority rule over the individual and advocated instead a constitutional republic, whereby the elected representatives of the people govern according to existing constitutional law that limits the government's power over citizens.

43. Limiting the liberty and political role of citizens to periodic voting may in turn explain why many contemporary democracies are faced with declining political party membership, decreasing voter turnouts, widespread cynicism, and lack of trust in the institutions of representative government (Dalton, Burklin, and Drummond 2001). Such a democratic deficit is characterized by a structural tendency toward elitism and the disempowerment of the general public, and is rooted in a belief that those who make and implement policy do not adequately represent the interests of the general public (Habermas 1976).

44. According to which, groups and other political participants will use the regulatory and coercive powers of government to shape laws and regulations in a way that is beneficial to themselves but not in the greater public interest.

45. Arrow's impossibility theorem demonstrates that no voting system meets all of a certain set of criteria when there are three or more choices.

46. ''The price we have to pay for a democratic system is the restriction of state action to those fields where agreement can be obtained'' (Hayek 1944, p. 184).

47. A discussion of corporate governance, that is, the conditions under which managers of firms act in the interests of, and are accountable to, their corporations, shareholders, and employees for the use of assets, would be beyond the scope of this book.

48. Even among rich countries, profound differences exist in the way public institutions are accountable or transparent to citizens, and how the public sector is managed. Uvin (2002, p. 5) observes: ''The access to public information that U.S. citizens enjoy under the Freedom of Information Act is absolutely unthinkable in most of Europe. Then again, the degree of financial clout exerted by Wall Street on the U.S. Department of Treasury, or by large corporations on the U.S. Department of Commerce, if not on the entire political system in the United States, would be unacceptable to most European citizens. Yet the extent to which French foreign policy, especially towards Africa, is a private presidential matter beyond democratic scrutiny is unimaginable in most other countries.''

49. Corruption is a narrower concept than governance and is commonly defined as the "misuse of public power for private profit." Acts involving corruption fall broadly into two categories. Conventional bribery, or "petty corruption," occurs when a public official demands, or expects, "speed money" or "grease payments" for performing an act which he or she is ordinarily required by law to do, or when a bribe is paid to obtain services that the official is prohibited from providing. "Grand corruption" occurs when a person in a high position who formulates government policy or is able to influence government decisionmaking, seeks payment, usually offshore and in foreign currency, as a quid pro quo for exercising the extensive arbitrary powers vested in him or her (Jayawickrama 1998).

50. Kaufmann (2004) notes the paucity of the coverage of notions such as the rule of law, independence of the judiciary, and corruption in the UN Human Rights Covenants and in the Declaration on the Right to Development and conversely, the lack of mention of human rights in the UN Anti-Corruption Convention.

51. For Uvin (2002, p. 5), the good governance agenda has fulfilled a rhetorical-political function as "it has allowed the World Bank [and the International Monetary Fund] to discuss the reforms that it proposed as economic and not political matters. In short, it constituted an attempt to de-politicize the concepts of democracy (and *a fortiori* human rights) in order to avoid allegations of undermining state sovereignty."

52. When a government fails or neglects to curb corruption, it also fails to fulfill its human rights obligations in at least three important respects: (a) it breaches the principles of nondiscrimination and equality before the law, including equality of treatment from public officials in the exercise of their powers, duties, and functions; (b) it leads to the infringement of several civil and political rights; and (c) it runs counter to the state obligation of conduct and obligation of result vis-à-vis the progressive realization of economic, social, and cultural rights (Jayawickrama 1998).

53. For Chafuen and Guzmán (2000), the economic cost of corruption is the cost of obtaining privileges that only the states can "legally" grant, such as favoritism in taxation, tariffs, subsidies, loans, government contracting, and other government regulation.

54. Empirical evidence based on cross-country comparisons does indeed suggest that corruption has large, adverse effects on private investment and growth, including through its effect on small and medium-sized enterprises (Mauro 1995; Kaufmann, Kraay, and Zoido-Lobaton 1999; Tanzi and Davoodi 2000).

55. Empirical evidence suggests that the rule of law, effective anti-corruption legislation, the availability of natural resources, the economy's degree of competition and trade openness, and the country's industrial policy all affect the breadth and scope of corruption (Leite and Weidmann 1999).

56. Kaufmann (2004) finds evidence that the extent of cronyism and state capture by oligarchs is related to the degree of civil liberties in a country. In particular, in countries exhibiting quasi-authoritarian tendencies, or "managed" democracies, the extent of state capture by the few elite is significantly higher than in countries where political and civil liberties are very high. In turn, when state capture is high, the author finds that socioeconomic development, including income growth and private-sector development, is impaired.

57. The governance indicators developed by Kaufmann, Kraay, and Mastruzzi (2005) measure governance by means of six indicators: (a) voice and external accountability (including a government's preparedness to be externally accountable through feedback from its own citizens, democratic institutions, and a competitive press);

(b) political stability and lack of violence, crime, and terrorism; (c) government effectiveness (including quality of policymaking, bureaucracy, and public service delivery); (d) regulatory quality; (e) rule of law (including protection of property rights, judiciary independence); and (f) control of corruption.

58. The human right is to express and exchange opinions, beliefs, and information with others. The Universal Declaration of Human Rights (1948) proclaimed that "everyone has the right to freedom of opinion and expression; this right includes freedom to hold opinions without interference and to seek, receive and impart information and ideas through any media and regardless of frontiers."

59. The human right is to secure access to publicly held information and the corresponding duty upon a public body to make information available. In its very first session in 1946, the UN General Assembly adopted Resolution 59(I), stating, "Freedom of information is a fundamental human right and . . . the touch-stone of all the freedoms to which the United Nations is consecrated."

60. Although right-to-information laws have existed since 1776, when Sweden passed its Freedom of the Press Act, Finland was the first country to adopt modern legislation on freedom of information in 1951, followed in 1966 by the United States. Today, more than 50 countries have related legislation, and a number of countries (e.g., Austria, Hungary, the Netherlands, and Poland) have enshrined the right of citizens to access information in their constitutions. According to the United Nations Development Program (2004), the circumstances that have triggered right-to-information legislation vary from country to country and include political transition (e.g., South Africa, Thailand), corruption concerns (e.g., Argentina, Peru, the Philippines), environmental concerns (e.g., Bulgaria), and external pressures for economic reform (e.g., Pakistan).

61. "Public bodies" relates to the type of service provided rather than the legal nature of the body itself. A public body can be assumed to include all branches and levels of government, including local government and state-owned enterprises, as well as the private bodies that carry out public functions (such as those providing utilities, maintaining roads, or operating railway lines).

62. Along with Transparency International and the Organisation for Economic Co-operation and Development anti-bribery instruments, the World Bank has begun constructing an index to help make "transparency more transparent" (Kaufmann 2005).

Chapter 7

1. It is not only the tax side that matters for the alleviation of poverty and pursuit of fairness but also public spending policies: a regressive tax might conceivably be the best way to finance pro-poor expenditures, with the net effect being to relieve poverty (Ebrill and others 2001).

2. The literature abounds in examples of the unfairness and perverse effects of taxation. To give one example, taxing food more lightly than other commodities, and even subsidizing it to achieve a more equitable distribution of the tax burden, could easily benefit the rich more than the poor. While the proportion of income that the rich spend on food may be relatively low, the amount of food they consume may be very large. In one country, Ebrill and others (2001) report that 45 percent of the revenue forgone as a result of zero-rating value-added tax on food benefited the

richest 30 percent of the population, whereas only 15 percent accrued to the poorest 30 percent.

3. As noted earlier, while the Universal Declaration states that (a) everyone has the right to own property alone as well as in association with others and (b) no one shall be arbitrarily deprived of his property (Article 17); the other instruments of the International Bill of Human Rights, including the International Covenant on Economic, Social and Cultural Rights and the Declaration on the Right to Development, are essentially silent on this issue.

4. To the extent that there is broad unanimity on the scope and core functions of the state (and no doubt this is the case in most instances), taxation could be interpreted as the free will of individuals to associate themselves voluntarily around a limited set of common objectives. However, the larger the scope of the state, the lower the probability of finding unanimity on its scope, and the greater the need for coercive taxation to finance it. Taxation is more likely to become a threat to human rights when it finances state activities outside its core functions. Wicksell (1896) was the first to suggest ways to reduce coercion by proposing unanimity, or qualified unanimity, as a criterion for budgetary decision. Lindahl (1919) further formalized the analysis by providing a theoretical process whereby taxes and the output of public goods were jointly decided by a bargaining process among the affected decisionmakers.

5. What is the definition of "equals" (e.g., equality of income or wealth, endowment or consumption, at a given point in time or over the life cycle)? What exactly is "equal tax treatment" (e.g., equality in absolute tax payments or in tax payment relative to a particular determinant)? To decide how unequal "unequals" should be treated, should one use a utilitarian notion of distributive justice (i.e., social welfare is the sum of individual welfare) or a Rawlsian notion (i.e., social welfare is the welfare of the least well-off)? And so on.

6. According to the Universal Declaration of Human Rights, all human beings are born free and equal (Article 1); they are entitled to all the rights and freedoms set forth in the declaration, without distinction of any kind, such as social origin, property, birth, or other status (Article 2); no one shall be subjected to punishment (Article 5); all human beings are equal before the law and are entitled without any discrimination to equal protection of the law (Article 7); and no one shall be arbitrarily deprived of his property (Article 17).

7. Human beings differ in all sorts of characteristics (biological, cultural, emotional, spiritual, and so on), with financial characteristics only a narrow subset of the potential source of inequalities. Equal treatment means that some individuals should not be negatively or positively discriminated against based on their relative endowment of certain characteristics.

8. According to the Universal Declaration of Human Rights, everyone shall be subject only to such limitations as are determined by law solely for the purpose of securing due recognition and respect for the rights and freedoms of others and of meeting the just requirements of morality, public order, and the general welfare in a democratic society (Article 29).

9. For instance, Boadway, Cuff, and Marchand (2000) identify special cases in which the marginal tax rate either optimally increases or optimally decreases with incomes, and conclude that in plausible cases the pattern of marginal tax rates has an inverted U shape, being highest in the middle part of the income distribution.

10. The seminal contribution of Mirrlees (1971) was to demonstrate that the solution to the general problem of designing an optimal nonlinear income tax schedule was

indeed close to a linear tax schedule. In other words, weighed against the practical difficulties that nonlinear schedules imply—in administration, compliance, and the potential for tax arbitrage—the implication appeared to be that a flat tax would be a close proxy for the best possible income tax (Keen, Kim, and Varsano 2006).

11. The flat tax concept has gained enormous momentum since the pioneering work of Hall and Rabushka (1983). Flat tax systems were introduced in the Baltic states in the mid-1990s followed by a number of other East European and former Soviet countries in the early 2000s. For a review of experience with the flat tax, see Keen, Kim, and Varsano (2006).

12. One problem with hidden taxes (e.g., some indirect taxes, corporate tax, payroll tax) is that people perceive the "price" of government to be artificially low, which in turn causes the "demand" for government to be too high. Thus, a flat tax system should aim for taxes that are not only simple, but visible (C. Edwards 2006).

13. In practice, Keen, Kim, and Varsano (2006) observe in their review of experience with the flat tax that the distributional effects of the flat taxes are not unambiguously regressive, and in some cases they may have increased progressivity, including through the effect on compliance. They also conclude that movement to a flat tax system may plausibly strengthen the automatic stabilizers, not weaken them.

14. The poll tax and its disconnection from income, assets, purchases, or any other variables over which individuals have any control, may be the only—albeit drastic—way to avoid the problem of inefficiency of taxation.

15. Higher tax rates interfere with the ability of individuals to pursue their goals in the marketplace. The marginal tax rate confronting an individual is in effect a "price" paid for supplying the next economic effort or engagement in an entrepreneurial venture. What remain after the tax is subtracted are the "rewards" of the effort. The higher the price of effort or entrepreneurship, the fewer the rewards and the less likely that people will go in for it.

16. Paradoxically, in such complex tax systems, the richer you are, the more likely you are to benefit from the various loopholes and shelters.

17. In the case of the United States, Chris Edwards (2006) reports that 61 percent of U.S. taxpayers use paid tax preparers to navigate the 66,498 pages of federal tax rules (code, regulations, and Internal Revenue Service rulings). Overall, Americans spend around 3.5 billion hours doing their taxes (an average of about 26 hours per household) for an annual compliance cost of about US$265 billion.

18. Another undesirable effect of corporate income tax is that, in conjunction with the personal income tax, it causes double-taxation. The same shareholders pay corporate tax on profits and income tax on their after-tax profits (dividends).

19. Milton Friedman (1962) reports that the potency of the control over money is dramatized in Lenin's famous dictum, "The most effective way to destroy a society is to destroy its money."

20. Misconceptions about the role of monetary policy can be illustrated in this quote from the UNAIDS report recounted by ActionAid USA (2006, p. 21): "The short-term inflationary effects of increased and additional resources applied towards tackling the HIV epidemic pale in comparison with what will be the long-term effects of half-hearted responses on the economies of hard hit countries."

21. To deal with recurring abuses of monetary power by the state, Hayek (1978a) and White (1984), among others, have advocated the repeal of the state monopoly in the supply of base money.

22. Barro (1991); Bruno and Easterly (1998); Fischer (1983, 1993); Khan and Senhadji (2000).

23. Even when inflation has no significant effect on growth, it is worth emphasizing that seigniorage remains a discriminatory and nontransparent tax instrument.

24. Sarel (1996) estimates the threshold of inflation above which inflation slows growth to be an annual inflation rate of 8 percent. Ghosh and Phillips (1998) found a substantially lower threshold effect at 2.5 percent annual inflation rate. Khan and Senhadji (2000) estimate the threshold at 1–3 percent for industrial countries and 7–11 percent for developing countries. Christoffersen and Doyle (1998) estimate the threshold at 13 percent for transition countries. Somewhat outside the single digits range, Bruno and Easterly (1998) detect a negative effect of inflation on growth only for inflation rates higher than 40 percent.

25. In their review of monetary frameworks in the post–Bretton Woods era, Cottarelli and Giannini (1997) found that the world had gradually moved toward monetary frameworks in which, through appropriate institutional devices, a better tradeoff between credibility of goals and flexibility of instruments could be achieved, with country performances reflecting prevailing perceptions and preferences, the structural features of the economy, and the nature and performance of a whole set of other institutions.

26. Cottarelli and Giannini (1997) show that many developing, and, in some cases, nondemocratic, countries have been able to precommit themselves by submitting their economic policies to the conditionality implicit in IMF-supported programs.

27. The authors found that strengthening supervision had a neutral or negative effect on banking development, reduced bank efficiency, and increased the likelihood of a crisis. One explanation would be that corruption in bank lending tends to be higher in countries with strong supervisory powers of bank regulators, except in places with strong legal systems and political institutions.

28. It should be noted that, in practice, there is also a broad democratic legitimacy for independent central banks with popular majorities in many countries that could, but typically do not, infringe on them. This reflects the desire of the population (principal) to constrain the ability of its representatives (agents) to undertake adventures that may benefit the agents but not the principal.

29. To Hayek (1948, p. 95): "The extent of the control over all life that economic control confers is nowhere better illustrated than in the field of foreign exchange. Nothing would at first seem to affect private life less than a state control of dealings in foreign exchange, and most people will regard its introduction with complete indifference. Yet the experience of most continental countries has taught thoughtful people to regard this step as the decisive advance on the path to totalitarianism and the suppression of individual liberty. It is in fact the complete delivery of the individual to the tyranny of the state, the final suppression of all means of escape—not merely for the rich, but for everybody."

30. Estimating the macroeconomic causal relationship between capital account liberalization and economic growth in developing countries is fraught with difficulties. Recent work using microeconomic evidence on the substantial and pervasive costs of capital controls may be more conclusive and compelling (Forbes 2005). A general observation is that most developing countries to have initiated financial integration have continued along this path despite temporary setbacks, while the most advanced economies all have open capital accounts.

31. Article VIII, Section 2(a) of the IMF's Articles of Agreement prohibit members, without IMF approval, from imposing restrictions on the making of payments or transfers for current international transactions.

32. Studies generally find a positive correlation between capital controls and the occurrence of currency crises (Eichengreen 2003; Glick and Hutchinson 2000).

33. In the IMF classification, exchange rate arrangements range from "hard pegs" (i.e., currency boards or no separate domestic currency [dollarization]) to "floating" (i.e., managed float with no specified central rate or independent float) via an intermediate group of "soft pegs" (i.e., conventional fixed pegs, crawling pegs, horizontal bands, and crawling bands).

34. "Each of the major international capital market-related crises since 1994— Mexico in 1994, Thailand, Indonesia and Korea in 1997, Russia and Brazil in 1998, and Argentina and Turkey in 2000—has in some way involved a fixed or pegged exchange rate regime. At the same time, countries that did not have pegged rates— among them South Africa and Israel in 1998, Mexico in 1998, and Turkey in 1998— avoided crises of the type that afflicted emerging market countries with pegged rates" (Fischer 2001).

35. As a result of the gradual removal of capital controls across the world, the proportion of "soft peg" arrangements declined significantly during the 1990s, with a corresponding gain over the same period for the hard pegs on one side and more flexible arrangements on the other.

36. However, because of the pervasiveness of capital controls and their limited involvement with modern global financial markets, developing countries actually exhibit a wide range of regimes, including some form of exchange rate peg or band or highly managed float (Mussa and others 2000).

37. The free operation of open markets should only be restricted in the presence of nonpecuniary externalities, defined as the effects of a particular exchange on third parties that do not pass through the price system (e.g., pollution).

38. While a number of preferential regimes were introduced with the good intention of "positively" discriminating in favor of poor developing countries, they had a number of perverse consequences not only for third countries but for the beneficiaries themselves. Furthermore, preferential regimes have broader systemic implications in the sense that preference-dependent countries do not have any incentive to support multilateral trade liberalization on a nondiscriminatory (i.e., most favored nation [MFN]) basis that would erode their preferences; thus, they can block or delay efforts toward a freer multilateral trading system.

39. Open trade is often accused of being unfair, of exacerbating inequality, both within countries and at the international level, and of inciting a race to the bottom over matters such as social welfare standards, environmental standards, worker protection legislation, and so on.

40. The authors estimate that during 1985–2000, countries captured about 20 percent of their average geographic neighbors' and trading partners' levels of, and changes in, economic freedom. Although these results provide evidence that freedom spreads, they also suggest freedom does not spread as strongly as suggested by the "domino theory" that underpinned American and Soviet foreign relations during the cold war.

41. The increases in input costs caused by tariffs and nontariff barriers are ultimately borne by companies unable to pass the increase on to the output price—the most important being export industries. As is well-known, a tax on imports is a tax

on exports. Duty drawback and other similar schemes, which are designed to eliminate the bias against exports, are usually difficult to administer.

42. Dollar 1992; Sachs and Warner 1995; S. Edwards 1998; Frankel and Romer 1999.

43. Along the same line of thought, the authors find that once they have controlled for institutions, geography—the other school of international trade theory—has at best a weak direct effect on incomes, although it has a strong indirect effect by influencing the quality of institutions.

44. Rent seeking refers to largely unproductive, expropriating activities that bring positive returns to the individual but not to society (Krueger 1974).

45. While developing countries clearly need flexibility in the implementation of a number of "noncore" rules and standards designed for and by developed countries (e.g., some trade-related aspects of intellectual property rights and various sanitary and phytosanitary requirements), an "opt-out" strategy by some developing countries in the Doha Round may just create a self-defeating two-tier multilateral trading system, with one tier of countries subject to new rules, commitments, and benefits, and a second tier left on the sidelines. The seemingly generous concept of a round-for-free for least developed countries may well turn out to be anti-development.

46. It is the government's responsibility to develop policies to temporarily alleviate the burden falling on those individuals and groups adversely affected by the adjustment process.

47. Some would go so far as to consider that a pro-business orientation (defined as favoring the incumbents and producers over the potential competitors and consumers) could be superior to a pro-market orientation at an early stage of development (Rodrik and Subramanian 2004). Such a discriminatory orientation would not be consistent with the approach taken in this book.

48. According to the World Bank (2005), the time it takes to register a new business ranges from 2 days in Australia (at a cost equal to 2 percent of per capita income) to more than 200 days in Haiti (at a cost equal to 153 percent of per capita income).

49. According to World Bank Investment Climate Surveys, policy-related risks are the main concern of firms in developing countries.

50. Narayan (2000) found that poor people identified getting a job as their most promising path out of poverty. Better job opportunities also increase incentives for people to invest in their education and skills, thus complementing efforts to improve human development.

51. By their nature, labor markets are not necessarily perfectly competitive (Debrun 2003). The most common imperfections include information asymmetries (e.g., the difficulty for employers to fully monitor workers' efforts or skills and for workers to evaluate their contribution to the firm's productivity); market power (e.g., if employers or workers dominate labor relations, wages can be pushed too low or too high); and market failures (e.g., to provide sufficient insurance against unemployment risk given the aggregate nature of such risk).

52. Proponents of right-to-work laws in several U.S. states (under provisions of the Taft-Hartley Act) would point to the constitutional right to freedom of association, as well as the common-law principle of private ownership of property, to prohibit collective bargaining from making union membership a condition of employment.

53. The minimum wage is a striking example of misguided compassion as it typically hurts those it is intended to help (i.e., the poor, low-skilled, and young workers, and welfare recipients). Attempts to cast doubt on the negative effect of an increased minimum wage on employment (e.g., Card and Krueger 1994) have usually

not remained unchallenged (e.g., Neumark and Wascher 1995), and a refutation of the law of supply and demand has yet to be discovered.

54. For instance, the Declaration on Fundamental Principles and Rights at Work (ILO 1998) provides a labor framework to uphold basic human values, including the freedom of association and the right to collective bargaining; the elimination of forced and compulsory labor; the abolition of child labor; and the elimination of discrimination in the workplace.

55. The World Bank's index of difficulty on the ease of hiring and firing workers provides a quantitative benchmark of the degree of protection of economic freedom in labor markets (World Bank 2008a). In Mozambique, for example, the difficulty of hiring index is 83 (on a scale of 0 to 100), the difficulty of firing index is "only" 20, but a laid-off worker must be paid 143 weeks of salary!

56. One such experience is Denmark's flexicurity policy: a mix of easy hiring and firing with both efficient reemployment services and decent out-of-work incomes.

Conclusion

1. Cultural relativists such as Boas, Benedict, and Herskovits sought not simply to demonstrate that standards of morality and normalcy are culture-bound (the Kantian idea that our perception of the world is filtered through our preexisting conceptual categories) but to call into question the ethnocentric assumption of Western superiority (Dundes Renteln 1988).

2. As noted by Martin (2003), Roman Catholic social thought has come to regard development as what Pope Paul VI in his encyclical *Populorum Progressio* called "authentic development" or "integral development," development that concerns the human person in the integrity of his or her existence. Later, Pope John Paul II in his encyclical *Centesimus Anus* brought home the fact that integral human development was not just focused on the human person, but placed the human person as the subject of this process.

3. Although for many Muslims today, shari'a is the sole valid interpretation of Islam and as such ought to prevail over any human law or policy, An-Na'im (1990) observes that human rights advocates in the Muslim world need not be confined to this particular historical interpretation of Islam and that a modern version of Islamic law could be entirely consistent with current standards of human rights.

4. These individualist values and cultures have undeniably served Western nations well in their quest for economic development in the modern age.

5. Rorty (1993) would go as far as to argue that human rights are based not on the exercise of reason, but on a sentimental vision of humanity and are therefore not rationally defensible.

184

Appendix: Declaration on the Right to Development

Adopted by United Nations General Assembly Resolution 41/128
of December 4, 1986

The General Assembly,

Bearing in mind the purposes and principles of the Charter of
the United Nations relating to the achievement of international co-
operation in solving international problems of an economic, social,
cultural or humanitarian nature, and in promoting and encouraging
respect for human rights and fundamental freedoms for all without
distinction as to race, sex, language or religion,

Recognizing that development is a comprehensive economic,
social, cultural and political process, which aims at the constant
improvement of the well-being of the entire population and of all
individuals on the basis of their active, free and meaningful participation in development and in the fair distribution of benefits resulting therefrom,

Considering that under the provisions of the Universal Declaration
of Human Rights everyone is entitled to a social and international
order in which the rights and freedoms set forth in that Declaration
can be fully realized,

Recalling the provisions of the International Covenant on Economic, Social and Cultural Rights and of the International Covenant
on Civil and Political Rights,

Recalling further the relevant agreements, conventions, resolutions, recommendations and other instruments of the United Nations
and its specialized agencies concerning the integral development of
the human being, economic and social progress and development
of all peoples, including those instruments concerning decolonization, the prevention of discrimination, respect for and observance
of, human rights and fundamental freedoms, the maintenance of
international peace and security and the further promotion of

friendly relations and co-operation among States in accordance with the Charter,

Recalling the right of peoples to self-determination, by virtue of which they have the right freely to determine their political status and to pursue their economic, social and cultural development,

Recalling also the right of peoples to exercise, subject to the relevant provisions of both International Covenants on Human Rights, full and complete sovereignty over all their natural wealth and resources,

Mindful of the obligation of States under the Charter to promote universal respect for and observance of human rights and fundamental freedoms for all without distinction of any kind such as race, colour, sex, language, religion, political or other opinion, national or social origin, property, birth or other status,

Considering that the elimination of the massive and flagrant violations of the human rights of the peoples and individuals affected by situations such as those resulting from colonialism, neo-colonialism, apartheid, all forms of racism and racial discrimination, foreign domination and occupation, aggression and threats against national sovereignty, national unity and territorial integrity and threats of war would contribute to the establishment of circumstances propitious to the development of a great part of mankind,

Concerned at the existence of serious obstacles to development, as well as to the complete fulfillment of human beings and of peoples, constituted, inter alia, by the denial of civil, political, economic, social and cultural rights, and considering that all human rights and fundamental freedoms are indivisible and interdependent and that, in order to promote development, equal attention and urgent consideration should be given to the implementation, promotion and protection of civil, political, economic, social and cultural rights and that, accordingly, the promotion of, respect for and enjoyment of certain human rights and fundamental freedoms cannot justify the denial of other human rights and fundamental freedoms,

Considering that international peace and security are essential elements for the realization of the right to development,

Reaffirming that there is a close relationship between disarmament and development and that progress in the field of disarmament would considerably promote progress in the field of development and that resources released through disarmament measures should be devoted to the economic and social development and well-being of all peoples and, in particular, those of the developing countries,

Recognizing that the human person is the central subject of the development process and that development policy should therefore make the human being the main participant and beneficiary of development,

Recognizing that the creation of conditions favourable to the development of peoples and individuals is the primary responsibility of their States,

Aware that efforts at the international level to promote and protect human rights should be accompanied by efforts to establish a new international economic order,

Confirming that the right to development is an inalienable human right and that equality of opportunity for development is a prerogative both of nations and of individuals who make up nations,

Proclaims the following Declaration on the Right to Development:

Article 1

1. The right to development is an inalienable human right by virtue of which every human person and all peoples are entitled to participate in, contribute to, and enjoy economic, social, cultural and political development, in which all human rights and fundamental freedoms can be fully realized.

2. The human right to development also implies the full realization of the right of peoples to self-determination, which includes, subject to the relevant provisions of both International Covenants on Human Rights, the exercise of their inalienable right to full sovereignty over all their natural wealth and resources.

Article 2

1. The human person is the central subject of development and should be the active participant and beneficiary of the right to development.

2. All human beings have a responsibility for development, individually and collectively, taking into account the need for full respect for their human rights and fundamental freedoms as well as their duties to the community, which alone can ensure the free and complete fulfillment of the human being, and they should therefore

promote and protect an appropriate political, social and economic order for development.

3. States have the right and the duty to formulate appropriate national development policies that aim at the constant improvement of the well-being of the entire population and of all individuals, on the basis of their active, free and meaningful participation in development and in the fair distribution of the benefits resulting therefrom.

Article 3

1. States have the primary responsibility for the creation of national and international conditions favourable to the realization of the right to development.

2. The realization of the right to development requires full respect for the principles of international law concerning friendly relations and co-operation among States in accordance with the Charter of the United Nations.

3. States have the duty to co-operate with each other in ensuring development and eliminating obstacles to development. States should realize their rights and fulfill their duties in such a manner as to promote a new international economic order based on sovereign equality, interdependence, mutual interest and co-operation among all States, as well as to encourage the observance and realization of human rights.

Article 4

1. States have the duty to take steps, individually and collectively, to formulate international development policies with a view to facilitating the full realization of the right to development.

2. Sustained action is required to promote more rapid development of developing countries. As a complement to the efforts of developing countries, effective international co-operation is essential in providing these countries with appropriate means and facilities to foster their comprehensive development.

Article 5

States shall take resolute steps to eliminate the massive and flagrant violations of the human rights of peoples and human beings affected by situations such as those resulting from apartheid, all forms of racism and racial discrimination, colonialism, foreign domination and occupation, aggression, foreign interference and threats against national sovereignty, national unity and territorial integrity, threats of war and refusal to recognize the fundamental right of peoples to self-determination.

Article 6

1. All States should co-operate with a view to promoting, encouraging and strengthening universal respect for and observance of all human rights and fundamental freedoms for all without any distinction as to race, sex, language or religion.

2. All human rights and fundamental freedoms are indivisible and interdependent; equal attention and urgent consideration should be given to the implementation, promotion and protection of civil, political, economic, social and cultural rights.

3. States should take steps to eliminate obstacles to development resulting from failure to observe civil and political rights, as well as economic, social and cultural rights.

Article 7

All States should promote the establishment, maintenance and strengthening of international peace and security and, to that end, should do their utmost to achieve general and complete disarmament under effective international control, as well as to ensure that the resources released by effective disarmament measures are used for comprehensive development, in particular that of the developing countries.

Article 8

1. States should undertake, at the national level, all necessary measures for the realization of the right to development and shall ensure, inter alia, equality of opportunity for all in their access to basic resources, education, health services, food, housing, employment and the fair distribution of income. Effective measures should be undertaken to ensure that women have an active role in the development process. Appropriate economic and social reforms should be carried out with a view to eradicating all social injustices.

2. States should encourage popular participation in all spheres as an important factor in development and in the full realization of all human rights.

Article 9

1. All the aspects of the right to development set forth in the present Declaration are indivisible and interdependent and each of them should be considered in the context of the whole.

2. Nothing in the present Declaration shall be construed as being contrary to the purposes and principles of the United Nations, or as implying that any State, group or person has a right to engage in any activity or to perform any act aimed at the violation of the rights set forth in the Universal Declaration of Human Rights and in the International Covenants on Human Rights.

Article 10

Steps should be taken to ensure the full exercise and progressive enhancement of the right to development, including the formulation, adoption and implementation of policy, legislative and other measures at the national and international levels.

Index

About the Author

Educated at the Panthéon-Sorbonne University in Paris, Jean-Pierre Chauffour has extensive policy experience with international institutions in Brussels, Geneva, and Washington. He spent 15 years at the International Monetary Fund, where he held various positions, including representative to the World Trade Organization and United Nations in Geneva. He has worked in many areas of the developing world, most extensively in Africa, the Middle East, and Eastern Europe. He is currently economic adviser in the World Bank's International Trade Department. He lives in Washington, DC.

Cato Institute

Founded in 1977, the Cato Institute is a public policy research foundation dedicated to broadening the parameters of policy debate to allow consideration of more options that are consistent with the traditional American principles of limited government, individual liberty, and peace. To that end, the Institute strives to achieve greater involvement of the intelligent, concerned lay public in questions of policy and the proper role of government.

The Institute is named for *Cato's Letters,* libertarian pamphlets that were widely read in the American Colonies in the early 18th century and played a major role in laying the philosophical foundation for the American Revolution.

Despite the achievement of the nation's Founders, today virtually no aspect of life is free from government encroachment. A pervasive intolerance for individual rights is shown by government's arbitrary intrusions into private economic transactions and its disregard for civil liberties.

To counter that trend, the Cato Institute undertakes an extensive publications program that addresses the complete spectrum of policy issues. Books, monographs, and shorter studies are commissioned to examine federal budget, Social Security, regulation, military spending, international trade, and myriad other issues. Major policy conferences are held throughout the year, from which papers are published thrice yearly in the *Cato Journal.* The Institute also publishes the quarterly magazine *Regulation.*

In order to maintain its independence, the Cato Institute accepts no government funding. Contributions are received from foundations, corporations, and individuals, and other revenue is generated from the sale of publications. The Institute is a nonprofit, tax-exempt, educational foundation under Section 501(c)3 of the Internal Revenue Code.

CATO INSTITUTE
1000 Massachusetts Ave., N.W.
Washington, D.C. 20001
www.cato.org